SACRED GROVES IN INDIA

AN OVERVIEW

SACRED GROVES IN INDIA

AN OVERVIEW

Kailash C. Malhotra, Yogesh Gokhale,
Sudipto Chatterjee & Sanjiv Srivastava

INDIRA GANDHI RASHTRIYA MANAV SANGRAHALAYA
Bhopal

ARYAN BOOKS INTERNATIONAL
New Delhi

SACRED GROVES IN INDIA: AN OVERVIEW

ISBN-81-7305-323-5

Published in **2007** by:
INDIRA GANDHI RASHTRIYA MANAV SANGRAHALAYA
(National Museum of Mankind)
Shamla Hills, Bhopal - 462 013 (M.P.)
and
ARYAN BOOKS INTERNATIONAL
Pooja Apartments, 4B, Ansari Road, Darya Ganj, New Delhi - 110 002 (India)
Tel.: 23287589, 23255799; Fax: 91-11-23270385; E-mail: aryanbooks@vsnl.com

Computer Typeset and Printed in India at
ABI Prints & Publishing Co., New Delhi

FOREWORD

We have great pleasure in publishing the monograph *Sacred Groves in India: An Overview* written by a team of experts – Kailash C. Malhotra, Yogesh Gokhale, Sudipto Chatterjee and Sanjiv Srivastava. Sacred Groves are a form of nature worship and are dedicated to deities or ancestral spirits. These provide a good example of traditional mode of conserving biodiversity. In an age when our ecology is believed to be 'fragile' and our planet earth is said to be 'fractured', the ongoing conservation strategy by traditional means is an effective way to fight the onslaughts of environmental degradation on the one hand and to ensure sustainable development on the other. Sacred Groves, an integral part of our traditional knowledge system, nourish diverse species of trees and associate species, and also act as a nursery and storehouse of tribal and folk medicines. Our Museum has been in the forefront in not only documenting intangible cultural heritage of India, but also in emphasizing that culture is an important input in sustainable development. A very good example of this is the case of Sacred Groves. It was in 1999 when Dr. Kalyan K. Chakravarty was the Director, the Museum had organised the First Festival of Sacred Groves alongwith an indoor exhibition. During that time an effort was also made to recreate Sacred Groves from different ecological zones of India by installing them in various sections of the open air exhibitions within our 200 acre campus at Bhopal. In continuance of such attempts to propagate the tradition, a travelling exhibition on the theme developed earlier has been further modified to strengthen the variety of Sacred Groves related to local management practices and knowledge system. This exhibition has travelled to different parts of the country eliciting good response. I congratulate the authors for completing the monograph for publication coinciding with the celebration of the Second Festival of Sacred Groves in our campus in March, 2007. Our sincere thanks are also due to our co-publisher Aryan Books International for publishing it within a short time span. We sincerely hope that this publication will be received well by one and all.

February, 2007

Kishor K. Basa
Director
IGRMS, Bhopal

PREFACE

In India, as elsewhere in many parts of the World, a number of communities practise different forms of nature worship. One such significant tradition is that of providing protection to patches of forests dedicated to deities and or ancestral spirits.

These patches of forests are known as sacred groves (SGs). The institution of SGs is very ancient and once was widespread in most parts of the world. Over 50,000 SGs have so far been reported from different parts of India. SGs are the rich heritage of India and play an important role in the religious and socio-cultural life of the local people. SGs are ecosystems by themselves and perform all the ecological functions.

Many threatened, endangered and rare species find safe refuge in the SGs. The groves are repositories of biological wealth of the nation. This institution in many parts of the country, however, now shows signs of weakening in both cultural and biological integrity.

The overview presented here has been prepared on belhalf of the Indira Gandhi Rashtriya Manav Sanghralaya, Bhopal. The overview covers various cultural and ecological dimensions of SGs in India, and describes the recent initiatives undertaken by various stakeholders in the country to revive and strengthen this institution.

We are extremely grateful to Sri A.R.K. Sastry and Archana Chatterjee of WWF-India, New Delhi, Dr. Debal Deb and Himanshu Mishra of IGRMS for their help in developing chapter on biological and ecological value of sacred groves. We express our sincere thank to Dr. B.V. Bhanu for his over-all inputs. Help rendered by Rajendra Rajoriya of IGRMS and Sidhartha Kumar Das of Orissa Development Action Forum in editing this book is gratefully acknowledged. We are grateful to all our colleagues who kindly permitted us to use their unpublished works and photographs.

We express our profound gratitude to Dr. K.K. Chakravarty, former Director, Indira Gandhi Rashtriya Manav Sangrahalaya, Bhopal for his constant encouragement and guidance in preparation of the book.

On behalf of the authors of this book, I express my deep appreciations and gratitude to Professor Kishor K. Basa, Director, Indira Gandhi Rashtriya Manav Sanghralaya, Bhopal for providing intellectual and logistic inputs in preparation of this book.

We are grateful to the Indira Gandhi Rashtriya Manav Sanghralaya, Bhopal for publishing the book.

While the manuscript of this book was in press, we lost our co-author Shri Sanjiv Srivastava who left for heavenly abode on 18th December, 2006. Sanjiv was the moving spirit behind this book. We **dedicate** this book on Sacred Groves to the loving memory of our dear friend Sanjiv.

December, 2006

Kailash C. Malhotra
Ph.D., FASc, FNA

CONTENTS

LIST OF ILLUSTRATIONS

FIGURES

PLATES

1

SACRED GROVES IN INDIA: AN OVERVIEW

In the present day Indian society, as elsewhere in many parts of the world, there are a number of communities that practise many forms of nature worship. Thus, it may be highlighted that the nature worship related practices depict a vast range of variation: these could be individual, family/lineage specific, clan specific and community (endogamous group) specific, region specific or pan Indian (Fig. 1). One such significant tradition of nature worship is that of dedicating and according protection of patches of forests to ancestral spirits/deities. These vegetation patches have been designated as Sacred Groves (SGs). Groves may consist of a multi-species, multi-tier, primary forest or a clump of trees, depending on the history of the vegetation. Although there is a variation in the way these groves have been described/ defined, most of the scholars emphasize the near natural nature of the vegetation and the preservation of vegetation through local taboos and sanctions that entail spiritual and ecological values. Thus, SGs are segments of landscape, containing vegetation and other forms of life and geographical features that are delimited and protected by human societies under the belief that to keep them in a relatively undisturbed state is an expression of important relationship to the divine or to nature (Hughes and Chandran, 1998). Diverse cultures perceive this relationship in different ways, and institutionalize various rules of behaviour (taboos) in regard to the sacred space and its elements. But wherever SGs occur, they are of an immense cultural and ecological interest.

Deb and Malhotra (2001) developed a framework for the study of different forms of nature worship. The framework they have proposed has essentially three elements—ethos, institutions and conservation implications. These have been shown in Fig. 2. The SGs fall under the category of habitat protection.

The institution of SGs has been fairly well studied in India from anthropological as well as biological conservation points of view. For an overview on anthropological studies, see Roy Burman, 1995; Gupta, 1998; Malhotra, 1998; Das and Malhotra, 1998; and for biological conservation related studies, see Chandrashekara & Sankar, 1998; Deb *et al.*, 1997; Deshmukh *et al.*, 1998; Pushpangadan *et al.*, 1998; Gokhale *et al.*, 1998; Ramakrishnan, 1998; and also see Ramakrishnan *et al.* (eds.), 1998 and Kunhikannan and Singh, 2005. These publications contain several articles on the subject. Summaries of 146 publications on SGs in India could be found in Malhotra, Gokhale and Das (2001a).

In this revised second edition an attempt has been made to provide an overview of various dimensions of SGs in India. The materials have been described under four chapters: (1) Anthropological Dimensions, (2) Biological and Ecological Dimensions, (3) Threats and (4) Opportunities.

SPECIES / HABITAT PROTECTION

PAN INDIAN

REGION SPECIFIC

ENDOGAMOUS GROUP SPECIFIC

CLAN SPECIFIC

FAMILY/ LINEAGE SPECIFIC

Fig. 1. Different levels of conservation ethos (After Malhotra, 2003).

1. ANTHROPOLOGICAL DIMENSIONS OF SGs

The material in this part has been described under the following heads and draws substantially on an earlier review article of Malhotra (1998) and Gokhale (2002):

- Distribution of SGs in Space and Time
- Geographical Distribution of SGs in India
- Number and Size Distribution of SGs
- Ownership Pattern and Management of SGs
- Ethnicity and SGs
- Gender and SGs
- Interfaces between People and SGs
    - Religious
    - Socio-cultural
    - Economic
- Political Dimensions of SGs
- SGs as Common Property Resourses.

1.1 Distribution of SGs in Space and Time

Several scholars have noted that SGs are a very ancient and widespread institution in the Old World cultures. There is evidence of sacred groves in past and present in many parts of the world, and among people with many different religions and forms of social and economic organization.

In this section we briefly describe the distribution of SGs in space and time in different parts of the world (except India which is dealt with details in section 2). The account given below is primarily based on a review article by Hughes and Chandran (1998). Fig. 3 gives the past and present distribution of SGs in different regions of the world.

1.1.1 Africa

SGs still exist widely in almost every sub-Saharan section of the continent. In East Africa among the Kikuyu, Frazer (1935) reports, "Groves of this tree [the mugumu] are sacred. In them no axe may be laid to any tree, no branch broken, no firewood gathered, no grass burnt; and wild animals which have taken refuge there may not be molested. In these sacred groves sheep and goats are sacrificed and prayers are offered for rain or fine weather or in behalf of sick children." In West Africa as well, the aura of holiness has kept botanically rich groves from

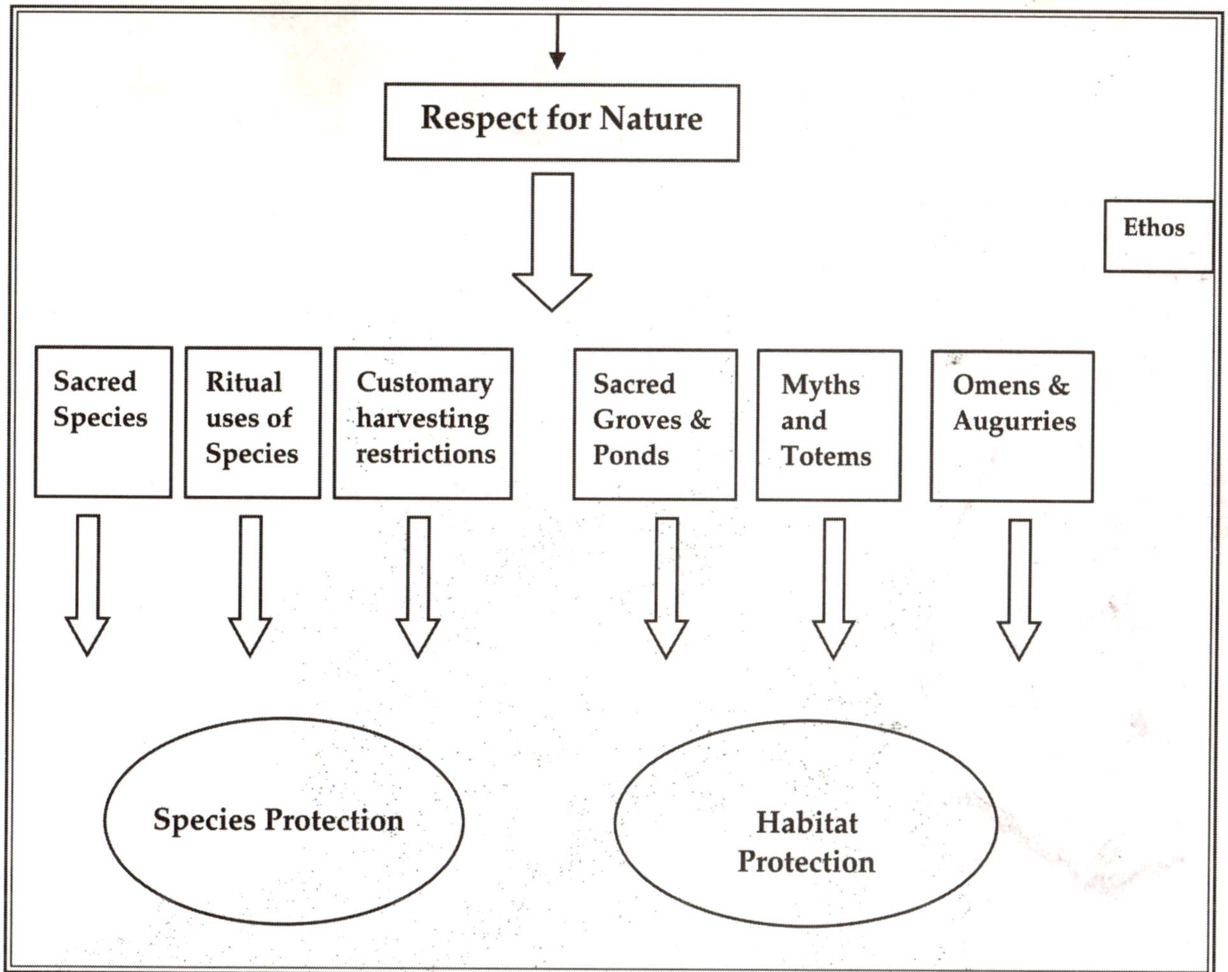

Fig. 2. Conservation consequences of the semiotics of biophilia in indigenous cultures (After Deb and Malhotra, 2001).

falling prey to lumber companies (Bachmann, 1992). Sacred groves of Sierra Leone are repositories of medicinal plants of value to traditional medical practitioners (Lebbie and Guries, 1995). The government of Ghana has recognized the sociocultural and religious importance of sacred groves. The religion of the Senufo, inhabitants of the Ivory Coast, is "centered inside a sacred grove, where ritual initiations are held and objects of power are stored" (Spindel, 1989). Among the many groves in Nigeria is one in Oshogoo dedicated to the goddess Oshun (Molyneaux, 1995). In Old Calabar, the village folk worshipped a grove of trees in a ravine with a clear stream (Frazer, 1935). There are many sacred groves associated with villages in the southern nations of Africa, such as Zimbabwe and South Africa (Farieda Khan, personal communication). In rural Africa one often finds a "King's Grove," where permission for use is entirely the responsibility of the local tribal leader. In Egypt, a North African country, it was the practice in ancient times to have a sacred grove, along with a sacred lake, in the precincts of every sizable temple (Erman, 1894). These groves were planted with many species of trees including sacred species such as palm and persea (Mimusops laurifolius or schimperi; called ished in Egyptian) (Manniche, 1989). Egyptian gods and goddesses were believed often to reside in trees (Budge, 1911).

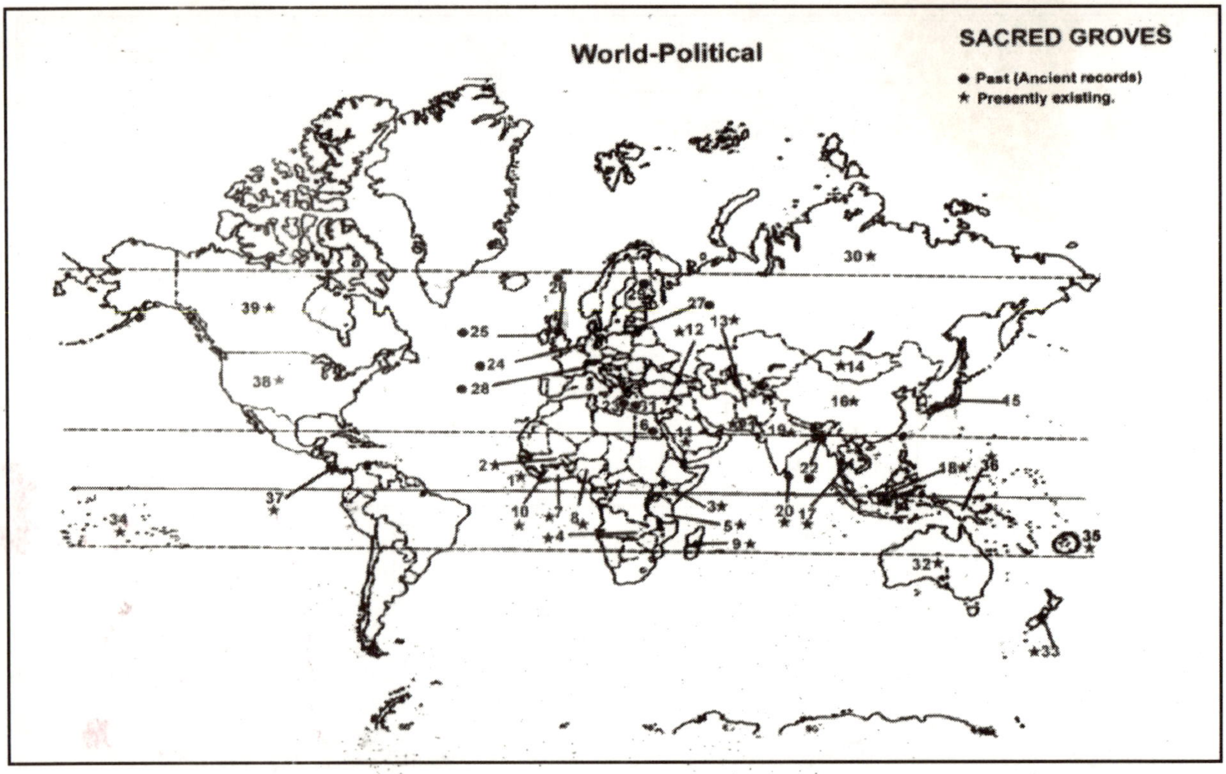

Fig. 3. Past and present distribution of sacred groves in different part of the World (IGRMS, 2000).

The Sacred Kaya Forests in Kenya

The account given below regarding SGs in Kenya and Ghana is based on the article by Michaloud and Dury (1998). The Kayas are small relict patches of forests in Kwale and Kilifi Districts of coastal Kenya which once sheltered the fortified villages of the Mjikanda people. Here, *Kaya* means the forested area surrounding and including the original village clearing.

Today, one only sees fragmented relicts which still retain the sacred significance, whereas the Kayas were probably far more extensive when the Kaya culture was at its height.

The Digo tribe (belonging to the Mjikanda culture) split into many small groups and set up secondary and tertiary Kayas, which explains the number of small Kaya forests in Kwale district. Through population dynamic, quite few of secondary Kayas were established.

As the threat from hostile people of other tribes receded, and as the population of each Kaya grew, the Mjikenda groups (which include the Digo tribe) moved out of the forests and established villages in the more open countryside. In so doing they cleared areas of forest and woodland but their original Kaya forest patches survived and were protected by customs and used for ceremonies. The most respected and senior Elders lived on in the Kaya clearing, or returned there for the periods of ceremony and celebrations. The Kaya remained the spiritual centre of each tribe of Mjikenda, sheltering the graves of important Elders, and the traditional carved memorial posts (*Vigango*).

However, over the past few decades, increased formal education, and government policy aimed at reducing dependance on witchcraft, has led to an increasing disregard for traditional values and a decline in respect for the Elders. This has led to some Elders being unable to prevent, or even cashing in on, exploitation of these small forests (with for instance the Vigango being nearly all now stolen or sold for tourist curios), and associated sacred groves, and some have almost disappeared. As a consequence, there has been concern about the disappearance of the indigenous plants used in traditional medicines, as well as awareness of environmental degradation resulting from forest clearance. Some of these patches also protected many small but important watersheds of the coastal foothills, particularly on the narrow rivers cutting through the Jurassic limestone, and ameliorating the effect of the erratic rainfall of the coast by ensuring constantly flowing streams. Destruction of the forest on coral rag for the cultivation of the fragile calcium-rich soils, as at Waa, was also observed leading to barren rocky platforms, useful only for coral block diggings and then very difficult to rehabilitate. Also, developers often burnt or slashed all the indigenous vegetation and were then laced with landscaping for tourist and residential buildings with imported materials at vast expense (for instance, extra soil in which to plant the ubiquitous bougainvillea and frangipani).

In respect to conservation, the idea of gazettement as National Monuments was put forward to give the Kayas protection at a national level, as it appeared to be the only suitable category in Kenyan law for such small areas of natural importance.

In November 1990, a private member's motion in Parliamant advocated that all Kayas in the Kwale district should be registered under the Kenya National Museums as prohibited areas. This motion was approved by the House.

Sacred Groves in Ghana

Sacred groves still exist in Ghana. For nearly three centuries, the community of Malshegu in Northern Ghana has preserved a small forest (0.8 ha) that they believe houses a local spirit. Although threatened by various nearby activities such as mining and the building of roads and power lines, this grove is being protected by the strong traditional religious beliefs of the community. The fact that local people guard it against fires; farming, grazing, gathering of forest resources, and hunting have allowed this grove to grow from a once open forest into a partially closed forest (Dorm-Adzobu *et al.*, 1991).

Although environmental degradation is widespread in Ghana, small pockets of residual closed canopy forests remain near human settlements and are scattered throughout the country. Many of these forest pockets are, in fact, "sacred" or "fetish" groves which have survived environmental degradation because of religious belief. The groves cover small areas, sometimes less than five hectares each, but they constitute areas where the Guinea savanna climax and proclimax vegetation may be approximated in an otherwise extensively degraded environment. Fortunately, the rehabilitation of degraded areas ranges high in the policy of the Government of Ghana and the national Environmental Protection Agency (EPA) takes a positive stand in using sacred groves as indicator sites for potential natural vegetation and the rehabilitation of degraded areas.

The role played by the sacred groves in the socio-economic and cultural lives of many rural folks in Ghana has been possible because of the collective efforts of people to protect them. It is estimated that over 80 per cent of the sacred groves in Ghana serve as watershed or catchment areas that protect drinking sources and provide readily available essential herbs of medicinal value.

Almost all existing sacred groves in Ghana have been, and continue to be protected by taboos, traditional beliefs and some local customs. Because of the reverence people attach to the sacred groves, people's general perception of the groves has resisted encroachment or unwarranted exploitation of resources within the groves.

However, the beliefs and reverence hitherto so absolute and binding on the people seem to be eroding in the minds of the youth in particular, and rural folks in general, due to trial breaking of taboos with no immediate consequence or retributions. The belief in <modernization> seems to be eroding traditional values and virtues which consequently are demotivating the local people's drive to consolidate their long-standing beliefs which have environmental conservation values.

The UNESCO-Ghananian "Integrated Project on Savanna Ecosystems in Ghana (CIPSEG)" addressed the problem of environmental degradation by basing intervention measures (rehabilitation) on sacred groves and using an integrated and people-participatory approach. Three sacred groves and their adjoining village communities in northern Ghana were at the heart of the project. Multi-disciplinary research teams (biologists, geographers, soil scientists, agronomists, foresters, anthropologists, education experts, etc.) carried out studies with a view to assessing whether sacred groves can indeed play an important role in environmental conservation.

Environmental education on the importance of conservation and involving local people in all project stages was considered essential for the success of the project. One project result for educating young people was a project video film entitled "Going back in time". The central focus of the film is the Dagbon Sacred Grove (in the western Dagomba district) and environmental conservation. The documentary is about the village Katariga which in the past years has suffered from drought. It is through this grave situation that the senior citizens of the village remember the better past and they are now telling the younger generation how good life was in the past: very good harvests without fertilizers, consistent water supply from the wells throughout the year and reliable fish supply from the village pond all year round. This, in no small measure, raised the social status of the village in the eyes of its neighbours.

Today, people of the Katariga village spend about 80 per cent of their time in gathering fuel wood and water. The grove, which was the symbol of their unity and the source of their strength and protection, is now being tampered with impunity. The trees in the grove have all been harvested and the gods have been stripped naked. And very soon the flora and fauna around Katariga may face a similar fate. Even medicinal plants for the treatment of common colds and malaria are gradually disappearing, and the people have to trudge to Tamale (the nearest town) for expensive medical care. At the peak of this calamity, the women finally speak out and with the support of their husbands challenge the chief and his elders to do something about their situation. They set up a committee for the protection of the environment and with the assistance and support of UNESCO-CIPSEG they succeed.

At the field level, the CIPSEG Project promoted well adapted techniques for savanna rehabilitation: village men and women were trained in micro catchment techniques; seminars were held on controlling bush fires and the establishment of fire belts around the sacred groves; fodder banks were set up to provide feed during the lean seasons in order to reduce the pressure of livestock on the sacred groves; and agro-forestry techniques coupled with cash-crop production (e.g., cashew nuts) were introduced to provide an economic income to the local people, especially women.

The taboos and obligations, i.e. the "do's" and "don'ts", vary from one sacred grove to the other, but there are also several common features. For instance, creating shelter belts around the groves through communal labour is an obligation to everybody in the village community. The strict observance or adherence of the rules associated with the sacred groves is considered important and cannot be compromised.

1.1.2 Western Asia

In Western Asia, one of the earliest literary traditions deriving from ancient Sumeria (fourth millennium BC) reveals their existence. Gilgamesh, King of Uruk, and his companion Enkidu, a formerly wild man, are said to have made a journey to distant mountains where a cedar grove stood surrounded by a palisade and guarded by a semidivine giant named Humbaba (Sandars, 1960). The defeat of Humbaba and the logging of the grove represent a historical process of deforestation on the margins of Mesopotamia. Later Babylonians and Assyrians planted groves; the "Hanging Gardens," one of the Seven Wonders of the World, was possibly a grove high on a ziggurat; archaeologists have found provisions for water drainage in these temple mounds. The Roman writer Diodorus of Sicily (Oldfather, 1933) reported a palm forest in Arabia, with "an altar very old in years, bearing an inscription in ancient letters of unknown tongue," adding that the inhabitants are long-lived. A sacred oak grove was venerated in Asia Minor by the Galatians. Hebrew tradition honours groves associated with the patriarchs: Abraham built an altar among the holy oaks of Mamre, and planted a grove in Beersheba (Genesis 13: 18, 21:13). Similarly Christians, who often zealously cut down groves where others worshipped, sanctified the Garden of Gethsemane, an olive grove where Jesus prayed, building a church beside it, and preserved groves of Lebanon cedars in monastery precincts (Mikesell, 1969). Christian cemeteries in the Holy Land, planted with cypresses and other trees, often resemble ancient sanctuaries. To the north, in Armenia, Christians to this day make offerings by tying cloths to sacred trees, and sacrificing sheep in groves. In pre-Christian times, their neighbours in the Caucasus, the Tzanoi, according to the Byzantine historian Procopius (Dewing, 1961), lived independently, "regarding as gods the groves and birds and various creatures besides, and worshipping them". Among the Ingushes of the Caucasus, each community had its own SG.

1.1.3 North, East and Southeast Asia

In north Asia, many Siberian people honoured SGs, and used them for the rites of shamanism. The Ostyaks and Voguls, nomadic people of the Ob River basin, had SGs in which nothing could be touched, "no grass or wood might be cut, no game hunted, no fish caught, nor even a drop of water drunk" (Frazer, 1935). Eagles which alighted in a grove were also sacred. Among the Buryats, each tribe has a grove of firs where its esteemed shamans are buried. When in open country, these are visible from afar. There are also village groves in Korea (Kim, 1994). In Japan, Shinto shrines are as a rule surrounded by trees, and often by extensive thick forests including sacred trees. Indeed, the grove itself is one of the reasons for originally locating the shrine there (Ono, 1962). Deer are often kept in these precincts, and one of the ritual acts of worship is to release captive birds and animals. Many Buddhist temples both in Japan and China have carefully tended gardens, including trees that have the aspect of groves. Traditional Chinese religion honoured sacred mountains which were tree-covered, and Taoism is well-known for its respect for nature; its shrines and hermitages were often located in forests. Monastery groves preserved species such as the Ginkgo (*Ginkgo biloba*), a curious archaic gymnosperm (Bachmann, 1992). In Yunnan province, China, members of hill-farming' communities designated sacred woodlands where the gods were believed to dwell, and strictly forbade anyone from entering, except to make annual sacrifices to the mountain and earth gods. Since villagers felt that trespassing for tree felling, cultivation, hunting or gathering would bring disaster, these forests generally remained pristine. Remnants of them exist as patches of primary forest among villages in Lancang County and the Xishuangbanna Region. The idea of sacred forests was not limited to swidden cultivators such as the Dai minority, but the wet rice cultivators in the lowland basins also venerated sacred hills, preserving the local fauna and flora, including medicinal plants, from destruction (Yin, 1991, 1994; Wachtel, 1993). Southeast Asia, Thailand in particular, has many sacred groves associated with Buddhist monasteries and temples. The Balinese, in Indonesia, have "monkey forests," fragments of the ancient rainforest where animals sacred to the monkey-god Hanuman are protected.

1.1.4 Europe

Europe had thousands of sacred groves in ancient times, although most of them have disappeared. There, as elsewhere, groves were the original temples. Ancient Greece was as full of them as Bacchus' leopard skin was full of spots, according to mythology, and were dedicated to gods, major and minor (Hughes, 1984). Their management and protection was in the hands of the poleis, or cities. The situation was similar in Italy, the homeland of the Romans. Frazer (1935) based his monumental work, *The Golden Bough*, on the practices of succession to the priesthood of Diana in the grove of Aricia, near the lake and village of Nemi (Nemus is a Latin word for grove). The Celts, Slavs, and Germans, the Romans' northern barbarian neighbours, customarily worshipped in groves, and regarded the oak as the most divine tree. The Celtic word for sacred grove is nemeton, a wilderness sanctuary where nature worship occurred and earth-festivals were celebrated (Vest, 1985). There the Druids, the Celtic shamans, learned their lore and practiced their spirit-journeys. Many SGs existed in the British Isles; Frazer (1935) gives numerous examples such as that of a sacred lake and grove on the Isle of Skye in Scotland where not a twig could be broken, and Belly parish in Ireland, where in the grove around the chapel of St. Ninian, it was considered a sacrilege to take branches or fruit. Often the sacred precincts were demarcated by banks or ditches. Holy Island, off Wales, has a place name, Llwyn-y-Berth, meaning "the beautiful grove," only one among many Welsh names including Ilwyn (grove). The Dumnonii had a grove of their tribal god by the Tamar River between Cornwall and Devon. Boudicca, the Briton queen, fought a battle against the Romans at Vernemeton, a sacred grove in the centre of Britain.

On the continent, there were manifold groves in Gaul (France), and Tacitus says that the Semnones, a Germanic tribe, considered their SG to be the "cradle of the race and the dwelling-place of the supreme god to whom all things are subject and obedient". There were groves in the Scandinavian countries; the Swedish sacred centre at Uppsala had one in which every tree was divine. The Baltic-Slavic people honoured powers called siela that guarded the groves and would not allow anyone to whistle or shout there (Vest, 1985). They also protected animals, particularly the bear (*Ursus arctos*). The Lithuanians maintained oracles in holy groves about their villages and houses, and believed anyone who injured a grove would die within a year (Frazer, 1935). The Finno-Ugric people of Finland and arctic Russia commonly fenced their SGs, permitted no wood to be hewn, and excluded women from certain ones, a common rule in many parts of the world, although in other cases it was men who were banned. A fir grove survived to 1650 in Kuopio, Finland. The artist-ethnographer Wassily Kandinsky found active SGs among the Zyrians (Komi) in 1889 (Weiss, 1995). Relics of SGs exist to this day for the Nenets of the Arctic. The holy grove at Kozmin Copse in the Kanin tundra is a notable survival in which offerings are still made including modern industrial products such as a thermos and an alarm clock. The trees in this grove, mostly birch and fir, are sacred

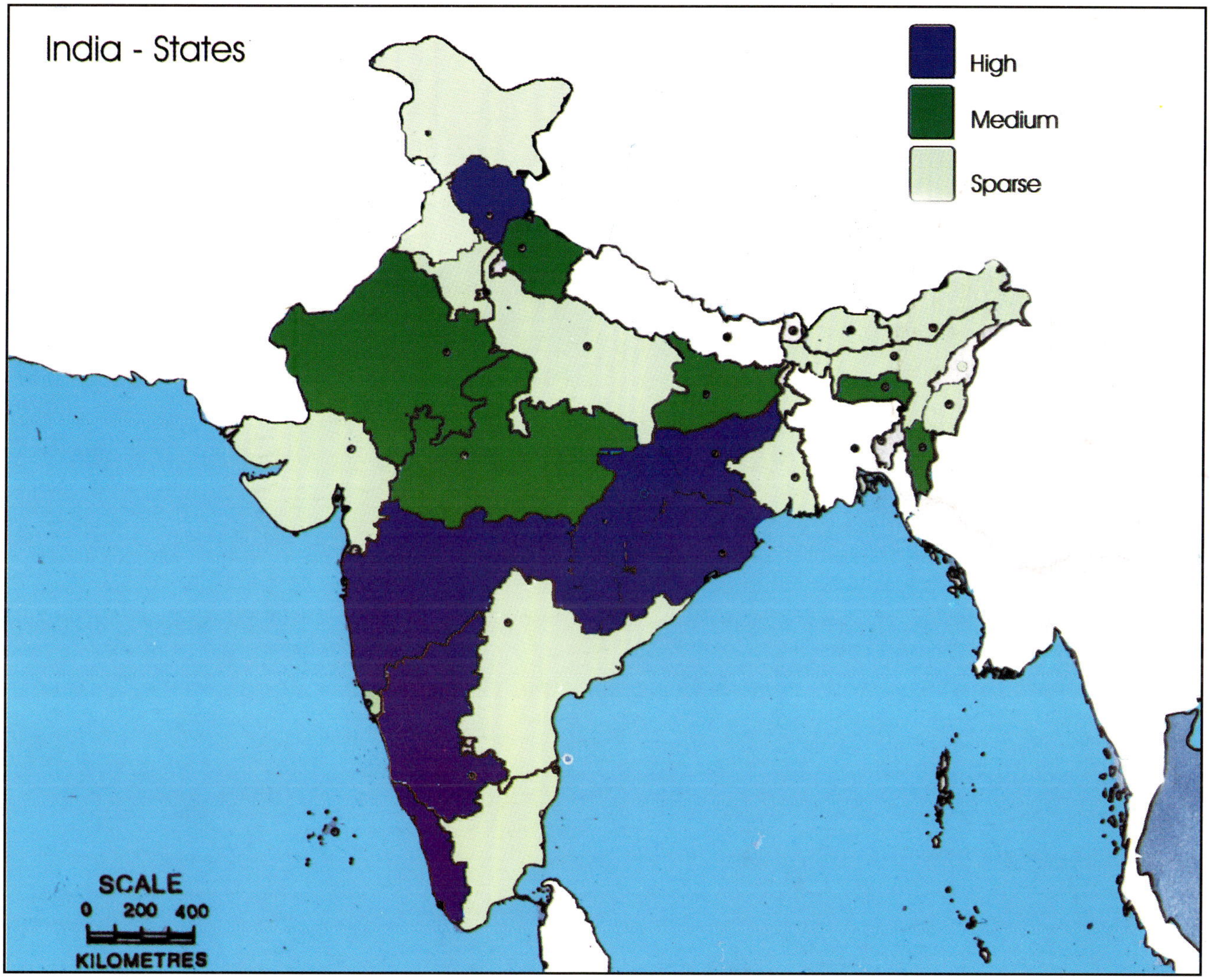

Fig. 4. Distribution and qualitative abundance of sacred groves in India (IGRMS, 2005).

Pl. 1. A sacred grove from Anantapur, Andhra Pradesh.

Pl. 2. Ritual objects made of bamboo in a Assam grove.

Pl. 3. A sacred grove without any man made object in Chhattisgarh.

Pl. 4. A sacred grove from Goa.

Pl. 5. A sacred grove from Gujarat.

Pl. 6. A sacred grove from Himachal Pradesh.

Pl. 7. A sacred grove from Coorg, Karnataka.

Pl. 9. A sacred grove from Pune district, Maharashtra.

Pl. 10. *Yangoi Ningthou* sacred grove from Manipur.

Pl. 12. A memorial monolith in Nongtluh SG.

Pl. 8. A temple in a grove from Kerala.

Pl. 13. The Daloi Stone of *U Ryngkew* (protector) of peace (26.6 feet in height) in Nongtluh SG.

Pl. 11. Megaliths in *Mawphalong* sacred grove, Meghalaya.

Pl. 14. A bamboo sacred grove from S. Orissa.

Pl. 15. A sacred grove in Thar desert, Rajasthan.

Pl. 16. A Gumpa sacred grove from Sikkim.

Pl. 17. A sacred grove in Chengalpeth, Tamil Nadu.

(Ovsyannikov and Terebikhin, 1994). The Wotyaks, who live toward the Urals, believed that the violator of a grove would die the very next day.

1.1.5 *Austro-Pacific Region*

SGs are widely known in the Austro-Pacific region. Australian aborigines find groves among the many natural spots made sacred by the experiences of ancestral spirits in the ancient "Dreamtime" when the landscape was shaped. They also have countless groves of different trees for different uses, including ritual and worship. The Yarralin people of the Northern Territory have a "Dreaming" grove for uninitiated males (*karu*); each tree represents one *karu*, and there is a huge tree called *boss karu* (Molyneaux, 1995). The Dieri tribe of Central Australia regards certain trees, believed to be their fathers transformed, as very sacred, and they take care to see they are not cut or burnt (Roy Burman, 1992). For the Maoris of New Zealand, humans form an intimate part of the environment Maori sacred sites, Waahi Tapu, include trees and forests among many other natural features (Matunga, 1994). In Polynesia, the coconut, breadfruit, etc., play important parts in myths and some groves of them were sacred places.

1.1.6 *Americas*

In the Americas, a widespread view in pre-Columbian times was that Earth and all her creatures are sacred. Trees were seen as having spirits and the power to help or hurt; their permission would have to be sought before any part of them was taken or used, and if harmed unwillingly, they could cry out and seek revenge (Hughes, 1996). In light of this universal sacredness, the marking out of specific groves is problematic. Still, the native people believed that although the whole Earth is sacred, still in certain places the spirit power manifests itself more clearly and readily, "like a fawnskin" with its many white spots (Hughes and Swan, 1986). Many of these power places were groves of trees. Pedro Simen, an early Spanish explorer of Costa Rica, described "copses" of many species of trees decorated with small golden bells (National Museum, San Jose). Bishop Diego de Landa wrote in the Yucatan in 1566, "They have sacred groves where they [the Maya people] cultivate certain trees, like cacao" (Tozzer, 1941). Cacao (*Theobroma cacao*) produced a valuable drink for Mayan priests and royalty, and its seeds were widely used as currency in Mesoamerica. Its existence in arid Yucatan was unknown to botanists until 1977, when surviving specimens were found in sacred natural limestone sinkholes called cenotes (Gomez-Pompa *et al.*, 1990). Tribes such as the Ojibwas and Utes reserved certain sections of forest where they would not hunt any animals except in case of great need. Americans of European descent also have sometimes hallowed groves of trees. Certain ones have been dedicated to early settlers, or to the war dead, or to noted leaders. Muir Woods National Monument, north of San Francisco, has a redwood grove (*Sequoia sempervirens*) named for the great conservationist, John Muir. Muir wrote that the "clusters" of Sequoia trees (*Sequoia gigantea*) were places where he could worship "King Sequoia... Lord Sequoia" and take the sacrament with "Sequoia wine" (Cohen, 1984). There are also Sequoia groves in California dedicated to the memory of General-President Ulysses S. Grant and President William McKinley, of the Humboldt Pioneers, of Jedediah Smith, Julia Pfeiffer Burns, Harris Whittemore, Henry Cowell, Franklin K. L'ane, and many others. It might also be claimed that some of the national parks are sacred groves of a "civic religion". In Golden Gate Park in San Francisco itself, a quiet, wooded grove of six hectares was designated as the AIDS National Memorial Grove in 1996. It is dedicated to those lost to AIDS, and in support of those living with HIV. It is funded through private donations, is cared for by volunteers and a city gardener, and local people visit it to plant, to "pour water into bowls carved into rocks for small flower bouquets... and each week, one man gently places eggs in rock crevicesa Hindu offering" (Associated Press, 6th October 1996). Other such groves are planned in San Luis Obispo and other cities.

2. GEOGRAPHICAL DISTRIBUTION OF SGs IN INDIA

According to Kosambi (1962) the institution in India is very ancient and dates back to the pre-agrarian hunting-gathering stage, before humans had settled down to raise livestock or till the land. In the present day India the tradition of SGs is reported from most parts of the country (Fig. 4). The intensity of abundance of SGs in different States has been shown as high, medium or low. It may be noted that the intensity of abundance in any given state is based on the data available for that State. Therefore, it must not be inferred from the figure that a given abundance as shown in the map is true for all parts of that State. In fact, the abundance in most States is likely to show vast inter-district variation. We describe below the salient features of the distribution of SGs in different parts of the country.

2.1 Andhra Pradesh (Pl. 1)

The report of WWF-A.P. (1996) has listed more than 750 SGs from 23 districts of the State as follows (figures in parenthesis are number of groves in the respective district) - Adilabad (2), Anantapur (73), Chittoor (133), Cuddapah (76), East Godavari (10), Guntur (17), Hyderabad (13), Karimnagar (4), Khammam (4), Krishna (12), Kurnool (115), Mahabubnagar (9), Medak (4), Nalgonda (9), Nellore (87), Nizamabad (7), Prakasam (59), Ranga Reddy (10), Srikakulam (30), Visakhapatnam (30), Vizianagar (32), Warangal (3), West Godavari (17).

A study by Prakash (personal communication, 2004) in the Eastern Ghats of Andhra Pradesh indicates the following species are commonly found in the SGs such as neredu (*Syzygium jambolana*), chintha (*Tamarindus indica*), mamidi (*Mangifera indica*), panasa (*Artocarpus integrifolia*), vepa (*Azhadiracta indica*), gummidi (*Gmelina arboria*), ganuga (*Pongamia glabra*), sampange (*Michelia champaca*), teku (*Tectona grandis*), juvvi (*Ficus retusa*), medi (*Ficus glomerata*), ravi (*Ficus religiosa*) and marri (*Ficus benghalensis*). Several groves usually measuring from a few square feet to an acre of land can be found in the habitation area or economic zone and the common land such as a valley, a stream, a pond or foothills of the eastern ghat villages.

2.2 Arunachal Pradesh

Arunachal Pradesh has SGs attached to Buddhist monasteries called as Gumpa Forest Areas (GFAs), which are managed by Lamas. The monasteries are mainly found in the western districts, namely, Tawang and West Kameng. 58 GFAs are reported from the State. Other districts, namely, Lower Subansiri, Siang are also having SGs (Chatterjee *et al.*, 2000).

2.3 Assam (Pl. 2)

In plains and foothills of western Assam, the forest dwelling tribes like Bodo and Rabha have tradition of SGs locally called *than*. Karbi Anglong district also has about 40 SGs (Deb, 1995). In Haflong district in the foothills of Assam, SGs of the Dimasa tribe are called *madaico*. The size of *madaico* is generally not more than an acre. SGs are also found in the plains of Brahmaputra in Assam. The Vaishnav monasteries like Shankaradeva maths distributed all over the State also have SGs. Gupta (2003) reports SGs from Barak valley of Assam (Box.1).

Box 1. Sacred Groves in Barak Valley of Assam

Unlike the sacred groves of Meghalaya, which usually enclose a large area of climax virgin forest, the sacred groves of Barak Valley are small, commonly having 5-10 trees. These groves, locally called 'thans', are mostly maintained by the tea tribals, tribes, as well as by the Bengali Hindu community. One or more deities are associated with these thans where total conservation is enforced. Lopping off of branches or twigs, removal of leaf litter and dead wood are usually prohibited and violation is believed to incur the wrath of the presiding deity. Visitors are required to remove footwear and advised not to harbour any evil thoughts in their minds when inside the grove. Animals inside the grove are also accorded protection. We have observed relatively higher animal diversity in the form of spiders and insects, mammals like squirrel, civet, mongoose, monkey, etc., several species of birds and snakes inside these groves, as compared to the barren areas surrounding them. Besides the *thans*, several Muslim graveyards also have a dense vegetative growth inside, which are not disturbed. People often plant trees inside the graveyards, as it is considered of religious merit (Guha, K. *et al.*, 1999; Gupta and Guha, 2002).

Of the nine *thans* recorded by us in Cachar and Karimganj districts, four are maintained by the Bengali Hindu community, in association with temples of goddess Kali, four by the tea tribe community, and one graveyard by the Muslim Khadims. The major tree species found inside these small groves include *Ficus benghalensis*, *F. religiosa*, *Flacourtia cataphracta*, *Dillenia pentagyna*, *Carallia integerrima*, *Artocarpus lakoocha*, *A. heterophyllus*, *Bombax ceiba*, *Aegle marmelos*, *Cynomefra polyandra*, *Michaelia* sp., *Vitex altissima*, *Xanthoxylum budrunga*, *Mangifera indica*, *Alstomia scholaris*, *Aquileria agallocha*, *Amoora wallichii*, various species of bamboos, canes like *Calamus tenuis* and *C. mastersianus*, and a rich ground flora including many medicinal plants. The wildlife commonly found include squirrel, mongoose, civet, fruit bat, Rhesus Monkey, Phayre's Leaf Monkey, Chinese Pangolin, occasional visitors like the Muntjac or Barking Deer, and wild boar among the mammals, Green Pigeon, Roseringed Parakeet, Black-headed Oriole, Racket-tailed Drongo, Common Myna, Hill Myna, Red-vented Bulbul, Woodpecker, Blue Rock Pigeon. Ring Dove, and Tree Pie among the birds, and different types of snakes, lizards, butterflies, other insects and spiders. These groves are small, ranging in area from around 0.05 – 0.80 ha. (Gupta, 2003).

2.4 Bihar

No information is available about SGs in the State. However, there are several tribes among whom this tradition is present inhabit the State. Therefore, there is a strong possibility of the existence of a substantial number of SGs in Bihar.

2.5 Chhattisgarh (Pl. 3)

Many anthropological studies on tribals give account of the tradition of SGs in Chhattisgarh, the new State carved out from the Madhya Pradesh.

Villages in Bastar have three kinds of SGs, namely, *matagudi*, *devgudi* and *gaondevi*. Different tribes have their own *mata* or *gaondevi* or goddess in *devgudi*. The Chhotanagpur part of the State shows the predominance of *sarana* or *jahera* kind of SGs plotted all over the State (Patnaik and Pandey, 1998; Pandey, 2000). The *saranas* are of different types such as *sarhul sarana*, *mahadani sarana*, etc. Generally, area occupied by the *sarana* is less than an acre.

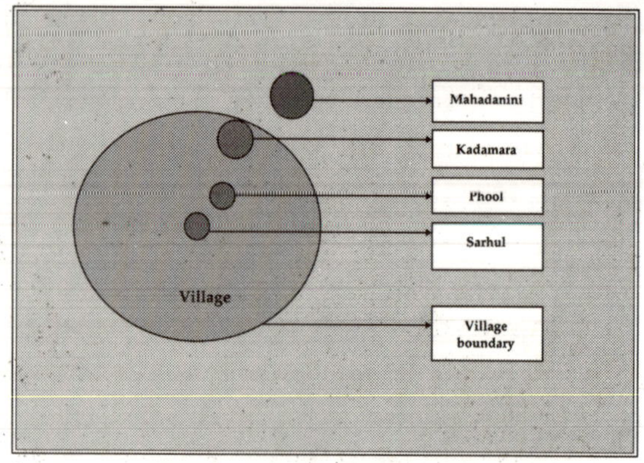

Fig. 5. Location and size of four types of *saranas* in a village in Chhattisgarh (Adopted from Patnaik and Pandey, 1998).

2.6 Goa (Pl. 4)

Fifty five SGs have been reported from Pernem (02), Bicholim (02), Sattari (29), Canacona (03), Sanguem (08), and Quepem (11) Talukas of Goa (Rajendra Kerkar, personnel communication, 2004). SGs are known by name such as *devrai*, *devgal*, *devran*, or devavan. All forms of vegetation within the groves are considered sacred. Even during *ganu bhoomi* (traditional hunting by villagers) hunting in the groves is strictly prohibited.

2.7 Gujarat (Pl. 5)

Twenty nine SGs have been reported from Banaskantha district of Gujarat. The sizes of the groves range between one acre to two square kms (Gupta *et al.*, 2000).

2.8 Haryana

In Haryana unlike in many States there is no generic name for SGs although the sites are protected for similar reasons. There are in all 248 SGs enumerated in Kurukshetra district where Kurukshetra tahsil has 190, Pehowa tahsil 30 and Shahabad tahsil 28. Out of the 248 groves studied, temple groves account for 30 per cent, Tirath groves 20 per cent, Gurudwara groves 18 per cent, Samadhi groves 8 per cent and others (under Ashram, Dharamshala, Vidyapeeth, Church, etc.) 16 per cent (NAEB, 1995).

2.9 Himachal Pradesh (Pl. 6)

In Himachal Pradesh, the tradition of sacred groves is generally known as *dev van*. The tradition is reported from Shimla, Mandi, Kullu districts and Lahul and Spiti. All these districts have dense forest cover according to maps of Forest Survey of India except Lahaul and Spiti where the groves are useful in maintaining the perennial source of water in harsh environmental conditions (Chhatre *et al.*, 1998). Groves of various sizes are found. However, larger groves spread over few hectares are used for controlled use of resources by the local people. There are about 10,000 temples in the State with well defined management committees and *biradari panchayats* (caste councils). Almost all the major deities in the State have their own groves and hence the State can be called as Land of Deities and Sacred Groves (Sharma, 2000).

2.10 JHARKHAND

The newly formed State is extensively dotted with sacred groves. The townships like Ranchi which were earlier tribal settlements, even today harbour SGs. Various anthropological studies report the tradition from Jharkhand. The tradition is popularly known as *sarana* or *jaherthan*.

Table 1. Typology of *saranas*

Type	*Sarhul*	*Phool*	*Kadamara*	*Mahadani*
Location	Near Village	In Village	Away from Village	Village Boundary
Size (in ha.)	0.5-2.0	0.2-1.5	0.5-14.0	2.0-21.0
Diety	*sarana* Mata Beru Bhagvan	*sarana* Mata	Budha Dev Khuts Spirits	Mahadev Bhuria Spirits
Function	*sarhul* Pooja Recreation Marriage	Recreation	Buffalo sacrifice in every twelve years	Human sacrifice
Biomass harvesting	—	—	NTFP	NTFP

These groves are usually small forest patches not more than an acre. In the Chhotanagpur area there are various types of *sarana* for different purposes like *sarhul, phool, kadamara, mahadani,* etc. The relative location, size and function of these groves are given in table 1 and Fig. 5. In Mundari language *sarhul* means nature's festival. Tribals also describe it as a beautification of Mother Earth. The *sarhul* festival is celebrated in *sarhul sarana*. The festival is celebrated when *sal* (*Shorea robusta*) trees start flowering.

2.11 KARNATAKA (Pl. 7)

The links of the forests with the deities of their respective villages of the Western Ghats of Karnataka were referred to by Buchanan (1870), who travelled through Uttara Kannada in 1801:

> The forests are the property of the gods of the villages in which they are situated, and the trees ought not to be cut without having leave from the *Gauda* or headman of the village, who here also is the priest to the temple of the village god.

The SGs are referred to by different names in various parts of Karnataka such as - *devarabana, devarakadu, hulidevarakadu, nagabana, bhutappanbana, jataka-ppanbana, chowdibana, kans,* etc. The groves in the Western Ghats broadly fall under two categories. The smaller groves are entirely protected; no tree felling or other biomass extraction may be allowed. On the other hand, larger groves function as resource forests, offering both livelihood sustenance and ecological security. The people of the village may gather fallen deadwood, non-wood produce such as pepper, mango, jackfruit, etc., and tap toddy from a palm (*Caryota urens*) (Chandran and Gadgil, 1993). The forested districts in the Western Ghats, namely, Uttara Kannada,

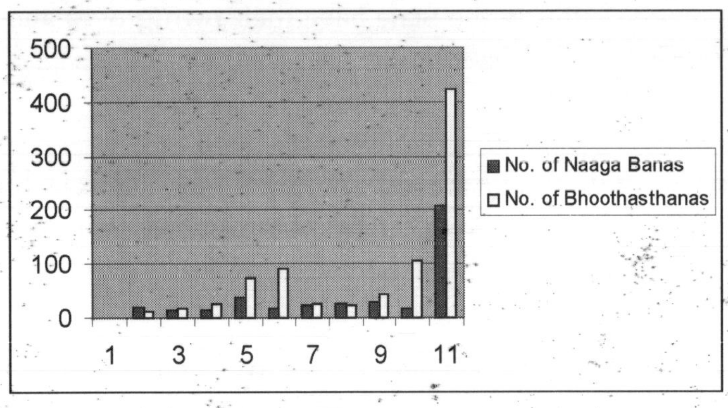

Fig. 6. Sacred groves of Dakshina Kannada district, Karnataka (Sources: Achar and Naik, 2006). Numbers on the X axis correspond with the numbers given in column 1 of table 3: number 11 represents total.

Shimoga, Udupi, Mangalore, Dakshina Kannada and Kodagu harbour 1424 SGs (Kalam, 1996; Gokhale, 2000). In Kodagu about 873 *devarakadus* spread over 10,865 acres were counted, registered and their boundaries were marked in 1873 by the forest department (Kalam, 1996). According to the records of the forest department about 1214 *devarakadus* spread over an area about 6299.61 acres exist; where 352.28 acres are encroached resulting to 5947.23 acres under the *devarakadus* in Kodagu district (Kalam, 1996).

Kans - The Sacred Groves of Western Ghats of Karnataka

Kans are the sacred groves constituting of patches of evergreen forests in the Western Ghats of Karnataka. These forests are reported from Uttara Kannada district and Old Mysore State districts like Shimoga and Chikmagalur.

It is estimated that historically about 6% of the landuse was under *kan* forests. Uttara Kannada in a 25 kms area enabled to reconstruct the traditional landuse system. Percentages of land under different landuses in the focal area are given below in table 2.

The treatment of *kans* by British Government was different in the erstwhile Bombay Presidency and the Old Mysore State. The Bombay Presidency curtailed the rights of local people on the *kans* and treated these forests for timber exploitation. In the Old Mysore State local landlords enjoyed the rights over the *kans* till 1970s. Thus, the area under Old Mysore State had formulated elaborate rules and regulations regarding the management of *kans*. The rights of people over the produce were also identified.

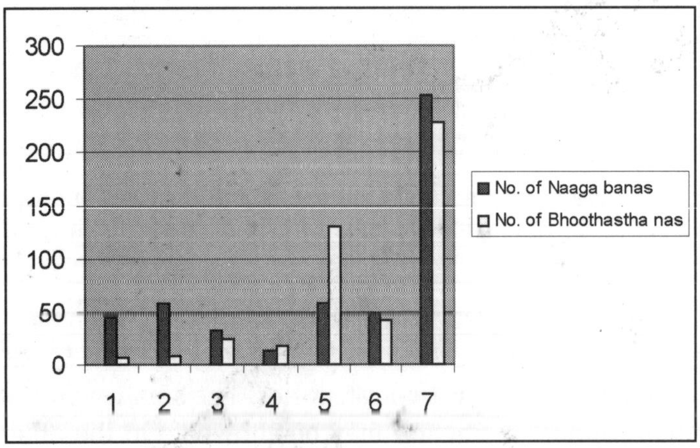

Fig. 7. Sacred groves of Udupi district, Karnataka (Sources: Achar and Naik, 2006). Numbers on the X axis correspond with the numbers given in column 1 of table 4: number 7 represents total.

As regards the kan holder, the kan shall be deemed to be a district forest and as regards strangers, it shall be deemed to be as state forests within the meaning of the Forest Rule of 1878 and all breaches of these rules will be liable to be punished under the Forest Rule of 1878 or under the Indian Penal Code.

The status of *kans* in mainly two ranges of Sirsi forest division - Siddapur and Kyadagi administratively falling into Siddapur taluk is given below.

Siddapur taluk shows large number of *kans* - about 113 *kans* - (84 in Siddapur range and 29 in Kyadagi range) according to the records of Village Forest Registers (VFRs). Most of the *kans* form a contiguous forest patch by merging with the *kans* of neighbouring village.

In contrast to *kans* in Siddapur taluk, Sorab taluk *kans* are still retaining better potential. There were 116 *kans* in the taluk but according to the forest department the present number of *kans* is 65. The total number of *kans* in Sorab taluk could be more than 65 as many earlier *kans* are now under the status of Minor Forest or District Forest (Gokhale, 2002).

Table 2. Proportionate reconstructed land use pattern in the Western Ghats of Karnataka.

Sl.No.	Land Use	% area
1.	Kans	5.85
2.	Supply forest	24.14
3.	Shifting cultivation lands	23.40
4.	Grazing lands	6.46
5.	Fields and other cultivated lands	28.19
6.	Area under miscellaneous uses	6.12
7.	Ponds and rivers	2.00
8.	Hamlets	3.84
	Total	**100.00**

Source: Chandran and Gadgil (1993).

Two recent studies undertaken by Nagarika Seva Trust (NST 2003 and Achar and Naik, 2006) in 96 villages of Dakshina Kannada and Udupi districts reported altogether 2626 SGs. Tables 3 and 4 & Figs. 6 & 7 give the number of SGs and their geographical areas in the 15 villages of Dakshina Kannada and Udupi districts.

Table 3. Sacred groves of Dakshina Kannada district, Karnataka.

Sl. No.	Name of the Village	Name of the Taluk	No. of Naaga Banas	No. of Bhoothasthanas	Total Area (in Acres)
1.	Sorneshwar	Mangalore (urban)	22	12	2.11
2.	Kemral	Mangalore (urban)	15	18	1.23
3.	Mantradi	Mangalorc (Rural)	15	27	0.49
4.	Vii	Bantwal	37	73	4.09
5.	Amtoor	Bantwal	19	92	5.68
6.	Bellippadi	Puttur	23	26	2.82
7.	Ramakunia	Puttur	27	24	2.48
8.	Peruvaie	Sullia	31	44	2.19
9.	Thodikana	Sullia	17	107	8.87
		Total	**206**	**423**	**29.96**

Sources: Achar and Naik (2006).

Table 4. Sacred groves of Udupi district, Karnataka.

Sl. No.	Name of the Village	Name of the Taluk	No. of Naaga Banas	No. of Bhoothasthanas	Total Area (in Acres)
1.	Vandse	Kundapur	45	07	2.18
2.	Haladi	Kundapur	57	08	1.69
3.	Nadsal	Udupi	32	24	4.90
4.	Baikadi	Udupi	13	17	0.82
5.	Bola	Karkala	58	130	9.81
6.	Padukudur	Karkala	48	42	3.92
		Total	**254**	**228**	**23.32**

Sources: Achar and Naik (2006).

2.12 Kerala (Pl. 8)

The first authentic report on the SGs appeared in the Census report of Travancore published in 1891 in which Lt. Ward and Lt. Corner reported the presence of 15,000 sacred groves in Travancore (1827). A serpent *kavu* or abode of snakes was an indispensable adjunct to each well-to-do Nair and Nambudiri family of Kerala (Chandran and Gadgil, 1993). The serpent worship is an important feature of SGs in the State. The SG tradition in Kerala can be broadly classified as follows:

The SGs owned collectively by the villagers are mostly dedicated to Lord Ayyappa and called as *Ayyappan kavu* or *Sastham kavu* and those dedicated to goddess *Bhagavathi* are called *Bhagavathi kavu* or *Amman kavu*. Sacred groves owned by the tribal communities are dedicated to *vanadevatha*, the goddess of the forest or to spirits, demons or to ancestors. These groves are known as *Madan kavu* or *Yekshi kavu*.

The other castes like Nair, Namboodiri, Ezhava and coastal fisher folk Dheevara also maintain the groves called *cheema* or *cheerumba* (Pushpangadan *et al.*, 1998).

In most of the groves the presiding deity is the local goddess. The presiding deity may be one in most cases while in a few cases more than one. In many groves there are sub-deities the number of which varies and goes up to even 16 sub-deities, all of which are worshipped as seen in Thirur Palliyara Bhagavathy *kavu* in Kollam district. The subdeities are called by different names and there are as many as 133 sub-deities as could be seen from a detailed study of 63 sacred groves in Kerala. The number can increase, if detailed studies are conducted in all the groves (Basha, 1998).

The most common god worshipped is the snake god which is a presiding deity in only about 30% of the groves, but they are largely worshipped as subdeity in the majority of the groves (60%). There are also groves without any deity as in Oachira *kavu* in Kollam district. Here "Parabrahmam" (the universal creator or lord and father of all creatures) is worshipped. In the Kanayi Bhagavathy *kavu* dedicated to Kanayi Bhagavathy in Kanathodam and the Muthappan *kavu* of Kanjangad dedicated to Sastha, there are no idols or deities in the worship place. In the Bhayankavu of Malappuram district, people worship *Bhadrakali* but before a mirror which represents God. There are many such varied phenomena which remain to be investigated. The festivals in these groves are varied and highly interesting from the cultural and religious points of view. It is suffice to state that cultural diversity of groves is fantastic and unique to Kerala (Basha, 1998).

In Kerala distribution of sacred groves does not overlap with the forested areas. SGs are mainly found in the plains of Kerala. It is estimated that about 500 ha of forest area is under SGs (Prasad and Mohanan, 1995) contributing 0.05% of the total forest area of the state (Chandrashekara and Sankar, 1998).

However, Basha (1998) provides a somewhat different scenario in terms of SGs in Kerala. During the survey of the Travancore region alone Ward and Conner (1894) came across the existence of thousands of groves. During the beginning of the 19th century there were more than 30,000 groves in Kerala (Velupillai, 1940; Logan, 1951). A recent survey conducted by Induchoodan (1996) revealed presence of only 761 sacred groves of which 399 (52.17%) were of less than 0.02 ha in extent. Only 362 groves were larger than 0.02 ha. Of the 362 groves having an area of more than 0.02ha, 286 (79%) are below 0.5 ha, 24 (6.6%) between 0.5-1.0 ha, 41 (11.4%) between 1.0 and 5ha and 11 (3.02%) above 5 ha. The total extent of the sacred groves in Kerala is about 440 ha. The district-wise extent and number of sacred groves are given in table 5.

Table 5. District-wise distribution and extent of sacred groves in Kerala.

Sl. No.	**District**	**Number**	**Total area (ha)**	**Av. area (ha)**	**% of Total**
1.	Thiruvananthapuram	43	1.78	0.04	0.40
2.	Kallam	44	6.67	0.15	1.52
3.	Pathanamthitta	33	115.27	3.49	26.20
4.	Alappuzha	49	18.56	4.38	4.22
5.	Idukky	3	6.54	2.18	1.49
6.	Kottayam	10	2.18	0.22	0.59
7.	Ernakulam	7	12.22	1.75	2.77
8.	Thrissur	17	3.48	0.20	0.79
9.	Palakkad	3	5.16	1.72	1.17
10.	Malappuram	11	7.35	0.67	1.67
11.	Kozhikode	23	27.88	1.21	6.34
12.	Wyanad	5	109.25	21.85	24.83
13.	Kannur	54	100.21	1.86	22.27
14.	Kasargode	60	23.44	0.39	5.33
	Total	**362**	**440.00**	**1.22**	**100.00**

Source: Basha (1998).

Poonkavanam of Pathanamthitta District and Pakshipathalam of Wyanad District are the two bigger groves having an extent of more than 100 ha and are parts of the Reserved forests lying contiguous to forest areas. These two are well protected by the forest laws. Though Kasargode District contains more number (60) of groves, Kannur district with 54 groves excels in extent with 100.21 ha. In many districts the groves are small with poor floral diversity. Side by side with the decline of biological diversity an increase in cultural diversity (totems and rites) is observed in a large number of groves.

2.13 Madhya Pradesh

The anthropological accounts of the tribes in the State suggest the existence of the institution in regions like Bundelkhand, Aravalli ranges in the northern part, Panchamahal as well as central Madhya Pradesh.

2.14 Maharashtra (Pl. 9)

In Maharashtra SGs are found in tribal as well as non-tribal areas. The SGs in western part are called *devrai* or *devrahati* whereas in the eastern part Madiya tribals call them *devgudi.* Gadgil and Vartak (1981) documented 233 SGs from Thane, Raigad, Jalgaon, Pune, Satara, Kolhapur, Yewatmal, Bhandara and Chandrapur districts. A recent study by Bombay Natural History Society shows existence of about 2799 SGs in Maharashtra (Deshmukh, 1999). Mahadev Koli tribe in the Western Ghats of Maharashtra also has the tradition of sacred groves (Roy Burman, 1992).

The distribution of SGs overlaps with the distribution of forests in the State. No reports are available for the central semi-arid region regarding presence of the groves. The average size of the groves is a few acres. Large groves are found occasionally. Smaller groves in the western and eastern parts rarely allow extraction of resource from the groves. Sacred groves form an important landscape feature in the deforested hill ranges of the Western Ghats of Maharashtra.

2.15 Manipur (Pl. 10)

Among the Gangte tribe in Churachandpur district of Manipur, extensive tracts of land were traditionally not subjected to shifting cultivation, since these were considered to be SGs, and believed to be abodes of spirits.

There were also forest belts protected as sacred around the habitations called as *gamkhap*. Gangte tribals also have small reserves of bamboo called *mauhak*. Extraction of bamboo shoots from *mauhak* is totally prohibited (Gadgil, Hemam and Reddy, 1998).

Meitei in Manipur practice nature worship and ancestor worship. The lofty hills, which surround the valley, are named after the deities. Their deity *umanglai* (jungle deity) is also derived from nature worship. There are 365 *umanglai* groves in Manipur (Devi, 2000).

The cultural practices such as maintenance of *Umang Lai Laikon* (areas of the *Umang lai*) and celebration of *Umang Lai Haraoba* (annual festival of the *Umang lai*) and village and clan level observance of *Jinu* (taboo) among the hill tribe had been a cultural tendency to control the society in maintaining harmonious relation with nature. Since time immemorial such kind of cultural practices have been a powerful source in maintaining ecological balance of the region (IGRMS, 2002).

The interpretation of *Umang Lais* as the veneration of forest deity by the colonial writers has been discarded by the people of this region. The Meiteis believe in the existence of their ancestral souls who possesses the divine power to regulate the society under his good or evil desires. The maintaince of *Apokpa shrine* (representing the progeny of a particular clan) on clan level; *Khungi Lai* – village deity on village level are looked upon by the scientists as a functional means to control the society. This tradition on the other hand has a very profound concept of preserving the plant and animal species under the totemic cult of sanctity and sacredness.

According to the local belief *Umang Lais* are those ancestral or guardian deities who indicate and reserve his permanent abode by divine actions. *Umang lais* are not the forest deity but they are the spirit of ancestors whose presence is indicated to the people at one sight and vanished suddenly. This may be literally translated as *U* or *00* or *Uba* to see and *Mang/ maangkhiba* = to vanish; i.e. the divine spirit who can give you an instant sight and suddenly vanish (IGRMS, 2002).

2.16 Meghalaya (Pl. 11)

Tiwari *et al.* (1998) report 79 SGs from the State. The distribution of these groves in different regions of Meghalaya given in table 8 & Fig. 8. All together these groves covers an area of 8580 ha.: East and West Khasi hills contribute substanially.

Table 6. Distribution of sacred groves in different parts of Meghalaya.

Sl.No.	Region	No. of SGs	Area (ha.)
1.	Jaintia Hills	15	866
2.	Ri Bhoi	3	1080
3.	East Khasi Hills	32	4528
4.	West Khasi Hills	13	1800
5.	East Garo Hills	8	125
6.	West Garo Hills	8	181
	Total	**79**	**8580**

Source: Tiwari *et al.* (1999).

Rodgers (1994) mentions categorization of protected groves in Meghalaya, which was formulated by Durbar of Khasis in 1925 as follows:

Ki Law Lyngdoh: forests under the control of the traditional religious leader (or now village councils): no public use permitted.

Ki Law Kyntang: forests of great sacred value for sacrificial and religious ceremonies.

Ki Law Niam: religious forest (may not be distinct from above).

Ki Law Adong: forest protected for non-commercial use, e.g. water.

Ki Law Shnong: forest resources for village use.

Brandis (1897) mentioned the existence of SGs in Garo hills. Bamboo reserves dedicated to deities are also reported from the Garo hills. The ancestral worship is traditionally performed in forest patches by the Garo people. In forested areas the focus of worship is more on the ancient monoliths.

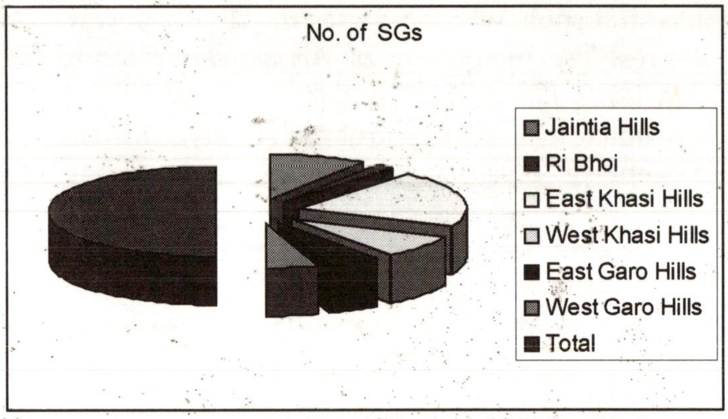

Fig. 8. Distribution of sacred groves in different parts of Meghalaya (Source: Tiwari *et al.*, 1999).

Nongtluh Sacred Grove and Its Associated Monoliths (Pl. 12)

There is a strong tradition in Meghalaya to erect monoliths in the memory of departed souls in the SGs. We give here description of one of the SGs Nongtluh in Rai Bhoi region of Meghalaya. This grove is unique in having hundreds of monoliths of varying sizes. It is well known that SGs perform multiferous function. This grove illustrate extremely well this aspect. As will be seen from the account given below that t' is grove performs a variety of functions that includes ancestral worship, religious, political, socio-economic, etc. The account given below is based on a note prepared by Shri Dolai Malai (2006) of Nongtluh village.

It is believed that the Nongtluh sacred grove was established by U Buda Syiem (Raja) in the fourteenth century, that is, after the destruction of the Umlaram village by the soldiers of Synteng (Taintia) Raja. It is better for us to know little about the coming of the Synteng to destroy the Umlaram village which is only three to four kilometers away from the Sacred Grove that exists today.

During the years of great rivalry between the Ahom King and the Kachari King on one hand and the Synteng on the other hand, the land south eastward of the river Brahmaputra belonged to the Khasi Syiem (Raja) and it was divided into two Kingdoms - the Domuria and the Gubha. These were looked after by the hill tribes of that region. The Ahom King got the Domuria region but the Synteng (Jaintia) were not happy with it and they wanted it back. They asked for it from the Ahom King and planned ways to get it back but the Ahom King who was in no mood to give it back. Thus, soldiers were kept at Sunapar to look for a chance to declare war on the Ahoms to get back the Domuria Kingdom. It was during this time, a youth from the side of the Ahom King established a kingdom in Umlaram village and thus the soldiers of the Synteng King attacked the village. The attack of the Synteng soldiers during the time of least preparedness and in the absence of the said Ahom King and that also during night time resulted in escape of only few who were able to flee to nearby forests and caves. The news of destruction of the Umlaram village reached the Gubha Kings and one of them by the name of Buda left for the village by following the course of the river Umtrew (Dikaru) till it met the river Umiam and then followed the course of river Umiam till it met the river Umsiang and followed the river Umsiang till it met the river Umta. He then followed the river Umta to Rongeln, a part of the river Umta is near the Sacred Grove. It was from here that they climbed up a small hill having an area of eighty sq. km. It is said that those who followed him were the ones who ran away to escape from being killed by the synteng soldiers at Umlaram. These included the Lamorai, the Lamalieh, the Syrliang, the Mathiang and with them together he formed the Syrmi, the Mawpi, the Mawlu, the Mawbai, the Kumblu and the Mawbludans which do not exist now. Till that time no uniform religion of the clans was there; each had their own religion.

Though Buda was a hill tribal, but since he was living adjacent to the plains of Assam his religion was mixed with the culture of the Assamese and he was well aware that his subjects were unhappy about it and they may leave him. Thus he first of all asked them to find a person who could bring uniformity in religion amongst his subjects. But no one dared to come forth as it was only the one from lyngdoh clan who could do it. It is said that one of the maternal relatives of the Lamalieh clan gave an idea to approach and request the Lyngdoh clan who ruled in Mawsam that was not for away. This village is near the Mawlong village in the eastern side, the marks of the drain, bund and house foundations and Jhum land proved the presence of the said village. After a long period, it was possible to bring the Lyngdoh of Mawsam and he is the one who established the religion of the Nongtluh. The name of this person was U Mok lyngdoh who was very religious and honourable. It is said that he got his wisdom from his walking stick which he never kept in his home but he used to keep it in a cave called the Diengdang Cave (this cave was very beautiful, it had an open space which can accommodate about hundred people to shield them from rain) and was about 100 to 200 yards away from his dwelling. It is said that he used to go to the cave to take the stick in the morning whenever there was any Dorbar or any religious function but he used to take it back to the cave at night. It was he who established the religion and the marriage practices. After establishing his religion the ruler started to think about expanding his kingdom. All around the village, there were small *elakas* whose rulers lived and ruled freely and had the power to address any dispute in their domain. With hard work intelligence and courage, he was able to bring along other Lyngdohs like the NongshapHang Lyngdoh of the Tado clan, the Lamorei Lyngdoh of the Matong clan, the Lyngdoh from Lumjrong of the Manih clan, the Mawsam Lyngdoh from the Lyngdoh clan and lastly the Majaw Lyngdoh of the Malai clan. These Lyngdohs were appointed in high posts in his kingdom and those from their clans were appointed as his ministers. Those who were unwilling to be associated peacefully were driven from their *elakas* and the *elakas* were annexed to his kingdom. He gave the rulers of these annexed *elakas* the freedom to rule freely but their *elakas* were to be under his Kingdom.

After he was convinced that the Kingdom he established at the end of the 14th century was firm enough in his hand and that he could put the ones he appointed under his control, he started to think about beautifying the Kingdom he established. Firstly, because performing of the religious rituals in worshipping the Ki Ryngkew Ki Basa (Protectors) of his kingdom was a difficult task and since it fell under the shoulders of his youngest sister, he divided the duty amongst his trusted ones to complete all the requisite rituals. To make them willing to take the responsibility, he gave them special honour in the Raid (Kingdom) and shared the revenue. These included - the donation once a year from each household. They were honoured by allowing them to dance around the dancing ground five times, to be cheered five times when the dancers of their dan come to the ground and to be entitled to the gun salute. He knew that the main power of the village lay in the youths so he appointed a Deputy King from amongst the youths and built the Khynraw (youth) stone platform so that they can administer justice for the youths there from. He built a lawn in the dwelling place of the King's sister to be a place for performing traditional dances fencing the western side by stone wall and then raising the mud wall from the eastern side. He gave all those well to do clans, who were well versed in the requisite rituals to be considered eligible for permanent settlement in the village, and the right to erect monoliths for their revered ones.

Thus, monoliths came into being on both sides of the ditch which served as a path to the village. He ordered the ditch to be dug deep and plant trees with tall and pointed spikes. He ordered to make fenced drainage and to plant the same trees all around the village as the means of protection. He also ordered to make a strong gate made of only bamboo and wood to be tied together with the strips made out of cane. The gate was very strong and it was to be closed every night after all the villagers return from their work and to open it in the morning so that people could go to their work and the cattle can go out for grazing. He prohibited cutting of timbers and bamboos outside the village boundaries so that these would serve as a protection and hiding place from enemy attack. The gates are to be on eastern and western sides of the village.

At this time when they were busy improving their village there came the news about the advance of the Synteng soldiers and there was a great threat to their village and a chance that they may be overwhelmed by the Synteng soldiers. Thus, the King sent spies to the region from where the news came and he got confirmed information that the Synteng soldiers under the leadership of a youth named U Bai Shulai were advancing towards the village. It is said that this youth was the son of the Captain of the Synteng soldiers who earlier destroyed the Umlaram village of U Trait Syiem (Chief) and while returning back this leader married Jrang Malai, whom he converted to Shullai clan. She was also the younger sister of Majaw Lyngdoh who was now on the side of the Nongtluh King.

The son of Bai Shuai's aunt named Skud Malai had grown to be strong and was so adept in swords and shields that the King of Nongtluh appointed them as the leader to take the soldiers to the battle. After every arrangement were made for the battle, as was informed by the spies, the Synteng soldiers advanced towards their village with an intention to destroy the Kingdom. The two sides met by the sides of the Ummyrsiang river, one on either side. It was the eloquence of U Doser who made the Synteng to disclose the name and the tribe of the invading soldiers.

Thus, Bai Shulai, the Captain of the Synteng said "I am Bai Shulai, the eldest son of Jrang Mallai from Majaw village and my eldest maternal uncle is Dorjang Malai." At this instance, Doser and his brother, Darjoh couldn't utter a word and tears began to shed because they were the sons of the sister of Bai Shulai's mother. The Synteng were about to attack but then Doser said "Brother, I am your cousin, son of Skud Malai from Majaw and the eldest maternal uncle is here now" and all the three advanced forward to embrace each other. The soldiers of both sides were astonished and they also couldn't stop their tears from dropping when they witnessed something that never happened before. Thus the battle was stopped and message was sent to Dorjang Lyngdoh and the King to give permission to the Synteng to enter the village. Captain Bai was so happy to meet his eldest uncle and aunt who were suffering from leprosy, but in spite of that he embraced and kissed her. The King arranged a Dorbar and they took the oath that they will never come for invasion but to come and help when need be. After they stayed for the night they left and from that day the Synteng never came to trouble the Nongtluh villagers. This was the special occasion in the history of the Raid Nongtluh. Thus, the King and his Dorbar decided to build a structure as a remembrance. They decided to erect monolith so that the memory remains for generations and for this the responsibility was given to U Kynduit the Doloi from the Lamalieh clan, who was one of those who was adept in making unique stone. He was also well versed in the art of praying. Thus, before the work started he searched for a stone that could really resist the weather and remain as a memorial. After performing prayer and rituals, a stone of 26 feet and 6 inches was found at one place. All villagers were called upon to drag and erect the stone outside the main gate on the western side of the village ahead of the ditch and it was named Daloi stone.

After erecting the stone, they wanted to associate the stone with religion so that this event will not disappear as long as there is soil in that place. Then the Lyngdoh stood up to ask permission from God by asking signs on the egg shells that he broke on a wooden plate and after permission was granted the stone was cleaned and washed before it was made the "memorial of peace" and the feeling of oneness amongst the clans. The responsibility of performing the rituals was given to Malai clan, so that they will be the caretaker and the ones to perform the rituals. It can be said that it is very rare to come across a tribe having such kind of a "memorial of peace". The following monuments (monoliths and place of performing rituals) are found inside the SGs of the Raid Nongtluh

From the east towards the west we will find:

1. The place of worship of the *Ryngkew* (protector) of Matong clan and the place of worship of their forefathers.
2. The monoliths and the place of sacrifice of *Ka Thu Manih* (clan).
3. The monoliths they call the *Uaibnai* stone.
4. The monoliths and the *Dungkyrnein* stone.
5. The place where the visitors from the east wait for permission from the King and the nobles to enter the village during the important days of the Raid.
6. The Synri stone and the place of worship of *Ryngkew* (protector) of the Manih clan and the memorial stone of *U Her Malai, U Roni Malai and U Kordit Matong* which was erected in the year 2004 by the clans.
7. The crossed ditch and the gate of the village.
8. The memorial stone of U Dorjang Lyngdoh Malai and U Daser Daloi Malai the warrior of the Battle of Peace with the Synteng.
9. The Youth Stone platform erected to administer justice among the youths, looked after and run by the Youth Chief (Deputy Syiem).
10. The garden of the Lyngdoh, cultivated with plants needed during the performance of rituals, and the foundation of the house of *Ka Sad Lyngdoh*.
11. The foundation of the house of Syiem Sad (King's sister), the dancing ground and the Lamarai Stone towards the south which is the place for the Dorbar of the King.
12. In the middle of the ground, there is a place for Duhalia (musician) by the side of the ground where a monolith of U Shak Syiem erected by Bril Malai, his wife and four sons at the total expense of ten ton of rice for feeding when pulling the monolith from *Thang Maw Malai.*
13. The Dwar Sing, said to be the first king who buried half a kilo of gold during the time of construction.
14. The playing field of the watchers of the village.
15. The village gate and the crossed drainage.
16. The Daloi Stone of *U Ryngkew* (protector) of peace (26.6 feet in height) (Pl. 13).
17. The altar for the Ranglein, the altar of the cave of *U Ryngkew* owned by the Khymdeit clan and a number of stones which were destroyed recklessly by the people.
18. There are many stones which now we have no knowledge they belong to whom. We know only about the memorial stone of *U Der Malai,* the great warrior of the Thaiang Battle together with the brother-in-law of U Shak Syiem. It was erected by the first son of Ka Pah Makdoh.
19. This is followed by the place where cairns are found, many of which are in ruins.

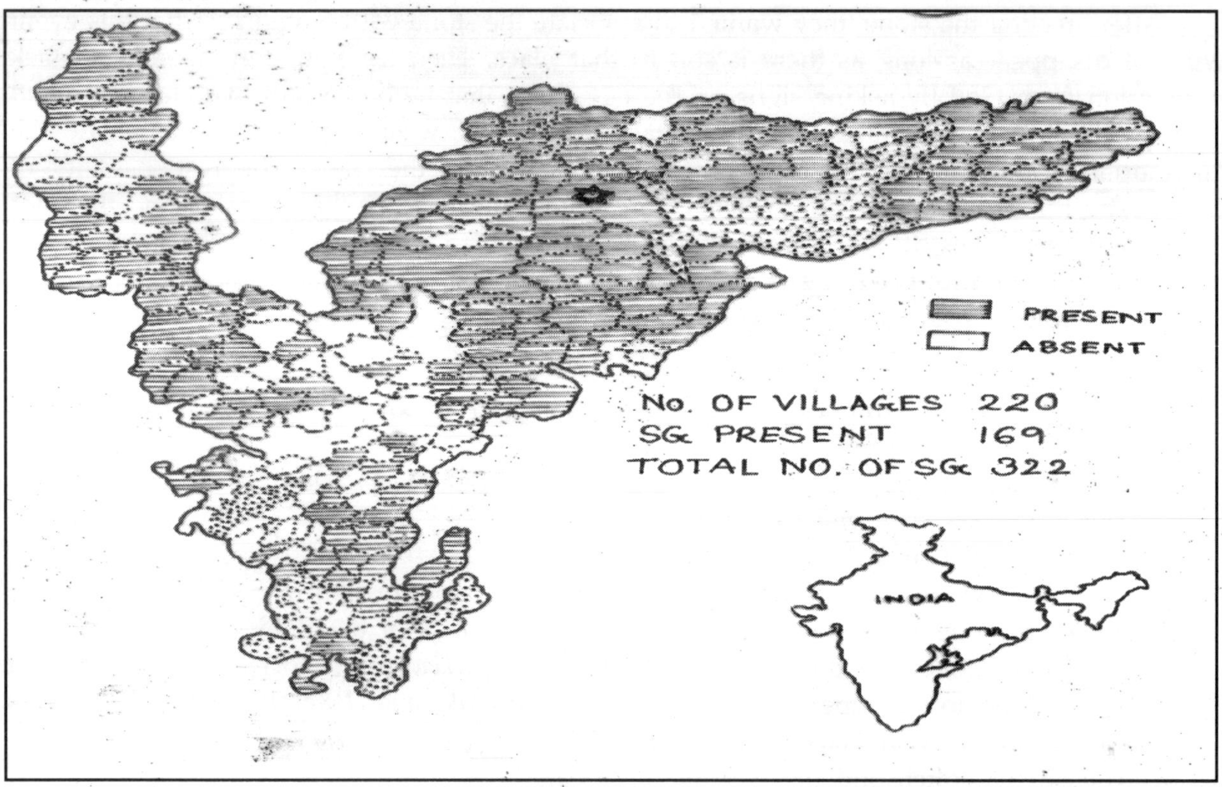

Fig. 9. Presence and absence of sacred groves in Semiliguda block of Koraput district, Orissa (Malhotra *et al.*, 1998).

20. South ward till Maw Kododok there are beautiful monoliths but now we do not know of which clans barring the Maw Sata of the Manih that lies between the cairns of Manih clan that had the privilege to erect the Maw Sota but do not know the meaning of the said Maw Sota.
21. A little away to the north from the place where Ka Thu Manih was killed, there is a stream which comes out from the rock and it is said that it was in this stream that the blood stains were cleaned during the Thaiang and Nongtluh Battle. Till today they call it the *Umsaitwait* (stream for cleaning the swords).

2.17 Mizoram

Mizo tribals have *safety* reserves and *supply* reserves around the villages. These *safety* forests are continuation of the SGs of the pre-Christian period. They also have bamboo reserves called *mawmund* in Sialkal region of northeastern Mizoram (Malhotra, 1990; Gokhale *et al.*, 1998).

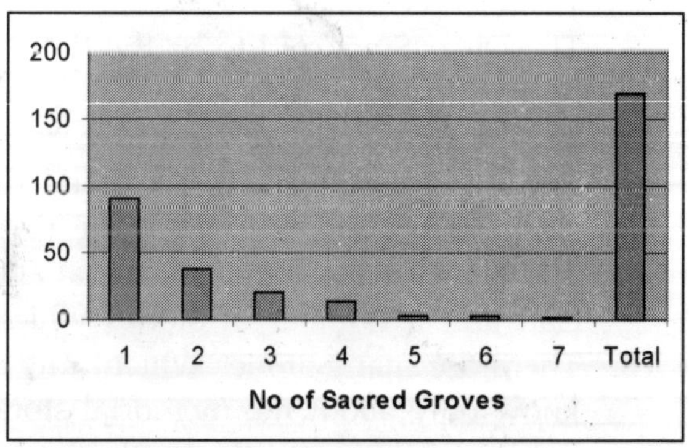

Fig. 10. Distribution of number of sacred groves in villages of Semiliguda block. Source: Malhotra *et al.* (1998).

2.18 Orissa (Pl. 14)

The instituion of SGs in the State is recognized by various names like *jahera, thakuramma*, etc.

Pl. 18. Terracotta votives of Tamil Nadu.

Pl. 19. Image of Shiva in a sacred grove of West Bengal.

Pl. 20. A family owned grove from Chhattisgarh.

Pl. 21. A clan managed sacred grove in Meghalaya.

Pl. 22. A grove managed by temple trust in Himachal Pradesh.

Pl. 23. Rituals in a sacred grove of Chhattisgarh.

Pl. 24. Annual ritual in a sacred grove of Meghalaya.

Pl. 25. Ritual in a sacred grove of Kerala.

Pl. 26. Bhoothakola, a cultural performance in a grove, Karnataka.

Pl. 27. A sacred grove festival in Chhattisgarh.

Pl. 28. Biomass being harvested in a grove from Chhattisgarh.

Pl. 29. Oath ceremony to protect sacred groves in N. Orissa.

Malhotra *et al.* (1997) and Malhotra *et al.* (1998) report 322 SGs from Semiliguda block of Koraput district (Fig. 9). In this study it was observed that in many villages where SGs were present often they occurred in excess of one. There was in fact one village in which 7 separate SGs were found (Table 7 & Fig. 10).

Table 7. Distribution of number of sacred groves in villages of Semiliguda block.

No. of SGs	No. of Villages*	% to Total
1	90	53.25
2	38	22.50
3	20	11.83
4	14	8.27
5	3	1.78
6	3	1.78
7	1	0.59
Total	**169**	

* 51 villages without SGs have not been included in this table.
Source: Malhotra *et al.* (1998).

SGs although not studied and documented have been observed by a team of researchers from IGRMS (2005) in several districts primarily inhabited by various tribal communities such as Angul, Dhenkanal, Kalahandi, Keonjhar, Mayurbhanj, Nabrangpur, Phulbani and Malkangiri districts. Among Bondas of Malkangiri districts the institution of SGs is widley practiced (Box 2).

Box 2. Sacred groves among the Bondas of Orissa

The Bondas of Badapada village of Mudilipada grampanchayat in Koraput district of Orissa have left a whole hill with dense forest as a sacred grove because the villager deity *Thajurari* lives in the forest. Collection of fuel wood, logs and other non-timber forest products from this grove are prohibited. Even shifting cultivation is a taboo.

The Bondas of Andrahal grampanchayat regard Bali dongar (Bali Parbat) as sacred and do not collect any biomass from it, nor is shifting cultivation permitted. The village god, Mahaprabhu resides in this sacred forest (B. Modak and P.K. Das, personal communication 2002).

2.19 Rajasthan (Pl. 15)

SGs are found from the western part of Rajasthan to the east of the Aravalli range. The SGs in Rajasthan are instanced by the *vanis* of Mewar, the *kenkris* of Ajmer, the *orans* of Jodhpur, Jaisalmer, Bikaner and the *shamlat dehs* and *devbanis* of Alwar. It is reported that *orans* account for 8 to 9 per cent of the desert area (Mitra and Paul, 1994).

The tradition in Rajasthan is an ideal example of support of the tradition for ecosystem services. The resources in the groves are used in controlled fashion or only in case of emergency.

Most of these groves are also associated with streams (Pandey, 1998). *Orans* in the western arid tract are a major source of green fodder for the livestock as well as water. The arid districts such as Jodhpur, Jaisalmer, Bikaner support *orans* spread over huge areas often exceeding thousands of acres as in the case of *degrai oran* at village Rasla in Jaisalmer district (Gokhale *et al.*, 1998).

2.20 Sikkim (Pl. 16)

SGs in Sikkim are attached to Buddhist monasteries called Gumpa Forest Areas (GFAs) which are managed by Lamas. Total number of SGs in Sikkim is 56 spread over 4 districts in the State. Most of the GFAs are not fenced, but are in continuation with the surrounding protected areas. They are well protected, and use of resources vary from monastery to monastery (Chatterjee *et al.*, 2000).

2.21 Tamil Nadu (Pl. 17)

Tamil Nadu has two important institutions, namely, *kovilkadu* or SG, and *sthalavriksha* which are the sacred trees protected all over the State. 448 groves have been reported from 28 districts of the State and their distribution in different district together with area covered is given in table 8 (Amrithalingam, 1998a, b). Out of the districts studied, the eastern districts without any forest cover have more number of SGs than forested districts on the western side. More than 250 *sthalavrikshas* are documented. They belong to more than 70 species; most of them are trees, while a few are herbs (Paulraj, 1996). The study of 42 SGs in *Pudukottai* and Tanjore districts give account of 105 species belonging to 95 genera distributed among 44 families of flowering plants (Britto and Balaguru, unpublished).

Table 8. Number and area of sacred groves in the districts of Tamil Nadu.

District	No. of Groves	Total Area (ha)
Coimbatore	10	201.76
Cuddalore	3	7.68
Dhannapuri	31	4421.39
Dindugul	6	1147.79
Erode	21	6248.97
Kanchipuram	4	9.49
Kanyakumari	12	35.14
Karur	8	15.77
Madurai	3	46.13
Nagapattinam- -	II	21.48
Namakkal	20	157.59
Nilgiri	32	2100.93
Perambalur	63	131.11
Pudukottai	28	111.41

contd.

Ramanathapuram	17	22.87
Salam	24	714.47
Sivaganga	5	48.88
Thanjavur	5	5.90
Teni	12	397.58
Thiruchirappalli	34	65.81
Thirunelveli	12	709.63
Thiruvallur	3	1.10
Thiruvannamalai	47	1847.41
Thiruvarur	3	2.23
Tuticorin	5	42.70
Vellore	16	1918.37
Villupuram	7	12.92
Virudhunagar	6	556.58
Total	**448**	**21003.90**

Source: Amrithalingam (1998b).

Terracotta plays a major role, representing the powers of renewal inherent in the earth and all the deities and votive offerings are made of clay. At the shrine of Mother goddess people make offerings of terracotta horses to *Ayyanaar*, the village *kaaval kaaran* (watchman). The horses range from 12 inches to 20 feet or more in height, depending on the district, local practice and economic status of the devotees (Krishna, 1997) (Pl. 18).

2.22 Uttar Pradesh

In Uttar Pradesh, the areas like Gangetic plains due to highly commercialized agriculture have almost lost the tradition of SGs. The tradition has been reduced to worship of single tree species like *Ficus religiosa*.

2.23 Uttaranchal

The villages in the hills of Garhwal and Kumaon of Uttaranchal State have many sacred conservation traditions like *bugyal* (sacred alpine meadows), *dev van*, etc.

2.24 West Bengal (Pl. 19)

Das and Malhotra (1998) and Deb *et al.* (in press) have found many types of SGs such as *garamthan, shitalathan, harithan, sabitrithan, santalburithan* and *jahera* along with sacred burial grounds. Over 670 SGs have been reported from Bankura, Birbhum, Midnapur, Purulia and Jalpaiguri districts of the state (Deb *et al.*, 1997; Deb *et al.*, in press). Debal (unpublished, 2006) has reported 423 SGs from four blocks of Purulia districts. These groves cover an area of 50 ha (Table 9 and Figs. 11 & 12).

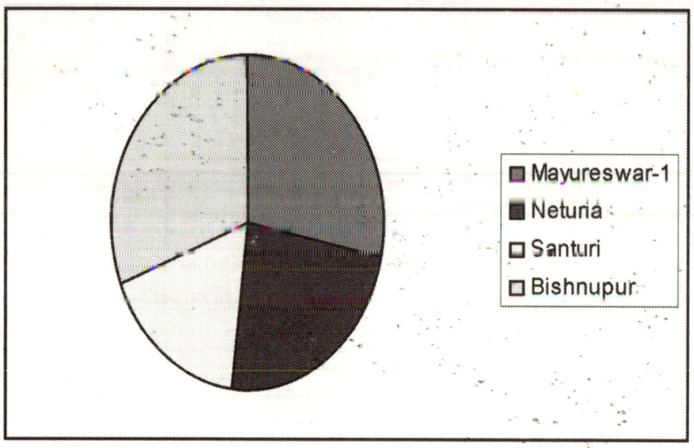

Fig. 11. No of sacred groves in four blocks. Source: Deb (unpublished, 2006).

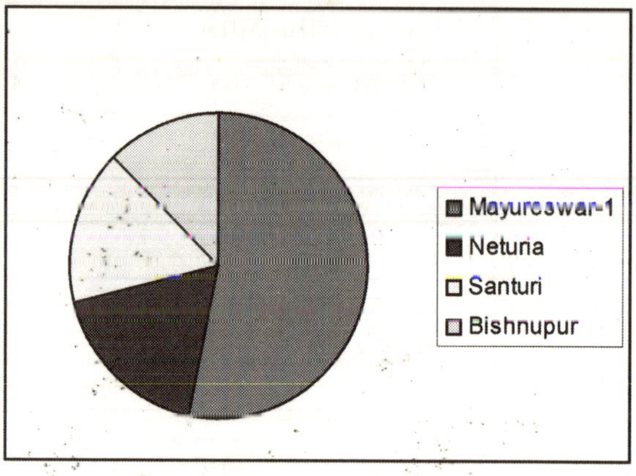

Fig. 12. Distribution of area in sacred groves of four blocks. Source: Deb (unpublished, 2006).

Table 9. Number of sacred groves and their area in four blocks.

Block	No. of SGs	Area
Mayureswar-1	120	26.19
Neturia	99	9.06
Santuri	72	7.99
Bishnupur	132	6.24
Total	**423**	**49.48**

Source: Deb (unpublished, 2006).

These SGs are very small, generally less than an acre and are not used for harvest of any biomass. Bamboo groves are found in Jalpaiguri and Coochbihar districts.

3. SACRED MANGROVES

The coastal people, over the ages, have acquired a vast knowledge on the useful properties of various species of plants and animals. To conserve these species from extinction, these settlers knowingly used religious beliefs. The materials presented in this section have been drawn from Untawale *et al.* (1998).

Shravan - Kavadia, Rann of Kachchh

Shravan-Kavadia is an isolated temple in the Banni region of the great Rann of Kachchh. There is a mangrove patch of about 200 *Avicennia marina* trees near the temple. The trees are around 100 years old, with girth (at breast height) ranging from 50-200 cm and an average height of 12-15 m. Apart from this *Avicennia* patch, the entire area is desertic, devoid of any vegetation except for the *Suaeda maritima* species. The mangrove tress are never cut, either for sustenance or for any religious rites like lighting sacred fires. This mangrove patch has been able to withstand the extreme range in temperature (5°C - 45°C) and tidal flushing with the Gulf of Kachchh waters. During the last 3-4 years, the tidal waters have rarely reached up to the Shravan-Kavadia temple. As a result, the subsoil moisture appears largely below a depth of about 15-20 cm. Though the mangrove trees have survived the extreme environmental conditions for so many years, the lack of tidal flushing, if it continues, might lead to their degradation.

Pirotan Island, Gulf of Kachchh

Pirotan island off Jamnagar is a small uninhabited island within the Gulf of Kachchh Marine National Park. The island is known for its rich biodiversity and has a good growth of Rhizophora mucronata, Bruguiera sp., Ceriopus tagal and Avicennia marina. A "darga" (a religious site for Muslims) in this island is quite popular among the coastal communities who flock to this island for offering the prayers (Urs). The mangrove vegetation around the "darga", which is otherwise exploited extensively by these people for firewood and fodder in other islands, is never touched by the pilgrims, even when they camp here.

Khodiyar Mata, Gulf of Kachchh

Long ago there were crocodiles in the mangrove swamps of the Gulf of Kachchh. Crocodiles palustris, a fresh water species but adapted to sea water was common. Because of large scale poaching, this species is almost extinct. However, there is a temple dedicated for this crocodile which is worshipped as a Khodiyar Mata (goddess). Unfortunately, this is a case where even religious beliefs could not help conserve the biodiversity—the temple remains but not the crocodile.

Achra Mangroves, Maharashtra

Achra is a small coastal village in the Sindhudurg district of Maharashtra. A mangrove forest covering about 273 ha lies between the village and the sea coast. The dominant mangrove species are *Avicennia officinalis, A. marina, Bruguiera cylindrica, B. gymnorhiza, Sonneratia alba* and *S. caseolaris.*

The entire mangrove forest area of Achra belongs to the temple trust of Shri Rameshwar, the deity installed in the local temple. There is no direct religious belief attached to the mangroves but the very fact that they belong to the temple trust is enough to deter people from cutting or otherwise exploiting the mangroves.

Crocodile Conservation in Goa

The crocodile (Crocodilus palustris) is a common inhabitant of the mangrove swamps of the Cumbarjua canal connecting the Mandovi and Zuari estuaries of Goa and upstream region of the two rivers.

A popular belief among Goan fishermen is that the crocodiles prey on the predator fish and thus help keep high the yield of the edible fish and prawns from mangroves. Over the years, this popular belief has assumed a religious cover to the extent that the worship of crocodile has become an annual feature. In the Bhoma and Durbhat villages, in the full moon night of March, a figurine of the crocodile is cast from mangrove mud, decorated with shells and flowers and offered animal sacrifices. Curiously, only males from the local community are present at this function, known as "Mange-Thapani". The religious significance thus attached to the estuarine crocodiles, helps in their conservation, and through it, the conservation of the mangroves on the whole.

Chidambaram, Tamil Nadu

In the magnificent temple of Chidambaram, Tamil Nadu, there is a stone-carving of the mangrove plant *Excoecaria agallocha*, locally known as "Thillai". The stone-carving is worshipped everyday even now. In the earlier times the temple pond was surrounded by these plants and there was a belief that if the lepers take a bath in this pond, they would be cured of leprosy. This belief may be because of the medicinal property of the yellowish milky juice of the plants belonging to the family Euphorbioceae. We do not have documented evidences of the effect of extracts from this plant on leprosy, and it might be a worthwhile case to study. In the recent years, *Euphorbia agallocha* plants have disappeared from the temple pond due to the developmental activities.

Sunderbans, West Bengal

The Sunderbans delta is famous for two species: one is the *Sundri* tree (*Heretiera spp.*) and the other is the Royal Bengal Tiger (*Panthera tigris*). Goddess Durga, the most popular deity in this region, is depicted in the mythology as riding tigers and lions. The associations of tiger with the goddess and its worship serve many purposes.

Until recent times, the support of folk tales, folk songs, mythological stories, etc. was taken to inculcate the spirit of conservation. As a result, the ecological balance was maintained. However, with the rapid urbanization in the last few decades, this concept faded. Because of this, in some areas only traditions have been left behind but not the species. For example, Khodiyar Mata and Chidambaram. On the other hand, in a civilization that has evolved with assorted traditional religious beliefs, practices and mythologies, conservation written in the language of religious pertinence is a more effective tool of spreading the message. Thus, the association of the message with a religious practice is the surest way of encouraging the local populations to accept conservation measures.

4. NUMBER AND SIZE DISTRIBUTION OF SGs

As noted in section 2, although SGs are known to be present in many States of the country, we, however, do not as yet have even an estimate of the number of such groves in India. In Table 10 readily available data in terms of number of SGs in India are presented. Pooling together all the data in Table 10, at least 22,968 SGs have been reported so far.

Table 10. Reported number of the SGs in India.

State	**No. of SGs.**[1]
Andhra Pradesh	750
Arunachal Pradesh	58
Assam	40
Chhattisgarh	600
Gujarat	29
Harayana	248
Himachal Pradesh	10000
Jharkhand	21

contd.

Karnataka	4050
Kerala	2000
Maharashtra	2799
Manipur	365
Meghalaya	79
Orissa	322
Rajasthan	9
Sikkim	56
Tamil Nadu	448
Uttranchal	1
West Bengal	1093
Total	**22968**

1. For references see section 2 and the earlier edition, 2000.

Table 11. Reported area of SGs in India.

State	No. of SGs	Area (ha.)	References
Karnataka			
Kodagu	1214	5947	Kalam,1996
D.Kannada	629	30	NST,2003
Udupi	482	23	Achar and Naik, 2006
Kerala	2000	500	Rajendraprasad, 1995
Maharashtra (1)	483	3570	Gadgil and Vartak,1981
Maharashtra (2)	2799	5248	Deshmukh, 1999
Meghalaya	79	26326	Tiwari *et al.* 1998
Orissa	322	50	Malhotra *et al.* 1998
Rajasthan (1)	1	83	Singh and Saxena, 1998
Rajasthan (2)	8	158	Jha *et al.*, 1998
Tamil Nadu (1)	10	127	Swamy *et al.*, 1998
Tamil Nadu (2)	448	21004	Amrithalingam, 1998 b
Uttaranchal	1	5500	Sinha and Maikhuri, 1998
West Bengal (1)	7	2	Malhotra *et al.*, 1998
West Bengal (2)	290	15	Deb *et al.*, in press
West Bengal (3)	423	50	Deb., 2006
Total	**9196**	**68633**	

Somewhat detailed inventories are only known for certain regions of the country. Gadgil and Vartak (1981) report 483 groves in Maharashtra. Actually, they reported only 233 groves, but the total area of 3,570 ha. included areas from Ratnagiri district also. Godbole *et al.* (1998) report the existence of over 250 groves in Ratnagiri district. Thus, addition of these 250 and 233 yields a total of 483 groves. Deshmukh (1999) on behalf of Bombay Natural History Society carried out extensive survey in Maharashtra and reported 2,799 sacred groves covering an area of 5,248 ha. (Table 12 and Fig. 13).

Table 12. Distribution of sacred grove in Maharashtra.

Sl. No.	District	No. of SGs	Area (ha.)
1.	Ratnagiri	834	1208.78
2.	Sindhudurg	1492	1898.78
3.	Raigad	20	475.35
4.	Thane	32	375.31
5.	Kolhapur	132	302.75
6.	Pune	230	668.47
7.	Satara	22	24.16
8.	Nasik	1	0
9.	Ahmadnagar	7	91.93
10.	Sangli	12	136.7
11.	Jalgoan	4	13
12.	Yeotomal	4	20.8
13.	Bhandara	5	28.7
14.	Chandrapur	4	3
	Total	**2799**	**5247.73**

Source: Deshmukh (1999).

Kalam (1996) reports 1,214 groves in the Kodagu district of Karnataka. In Meghalaya 79 groves have been listed by Tiwari *et al.* (1998). Rajendraprasad (1995) reports the existence of over 2,000 well-preserved sacred groves in Kerala. In one block, Semilguda of Koraput district in Orissa, Malhotra *et al.* (1998) surveyed all the 220 villages and found in 169 villages 322 sacred groves. WWF India, Andhra Pradesh State office (1996) reported over 750 groves in 23 districts of Andhra Pradesh. Amrithalingam (1998 b) carried out a survey in 28 district of Tamil Nadu and reported 448 SGs. Two recent studies undertaken by Nagarika Seva Trust (NST, 2003) and Achar and Naik (2006) in 96 villages of Dakshina Kannada and Udupi Districts reported altogether 2,626 SGs. Deb (unpublished, 2006) reported 423 SGs in four blocks of Bankura district, West Bengal covering an area of 50 ha. There are about 10,000 temples in Himachal Pradesh with well defined management committees and *biradari Panchayats* (Sharma, 2000). Each temple has a SG of its own.

It may be pointed out that this figure of 22,968 is only an indication of the extent and magnitude of the presence of SGs in the country. It is certainly difficult to make a guess

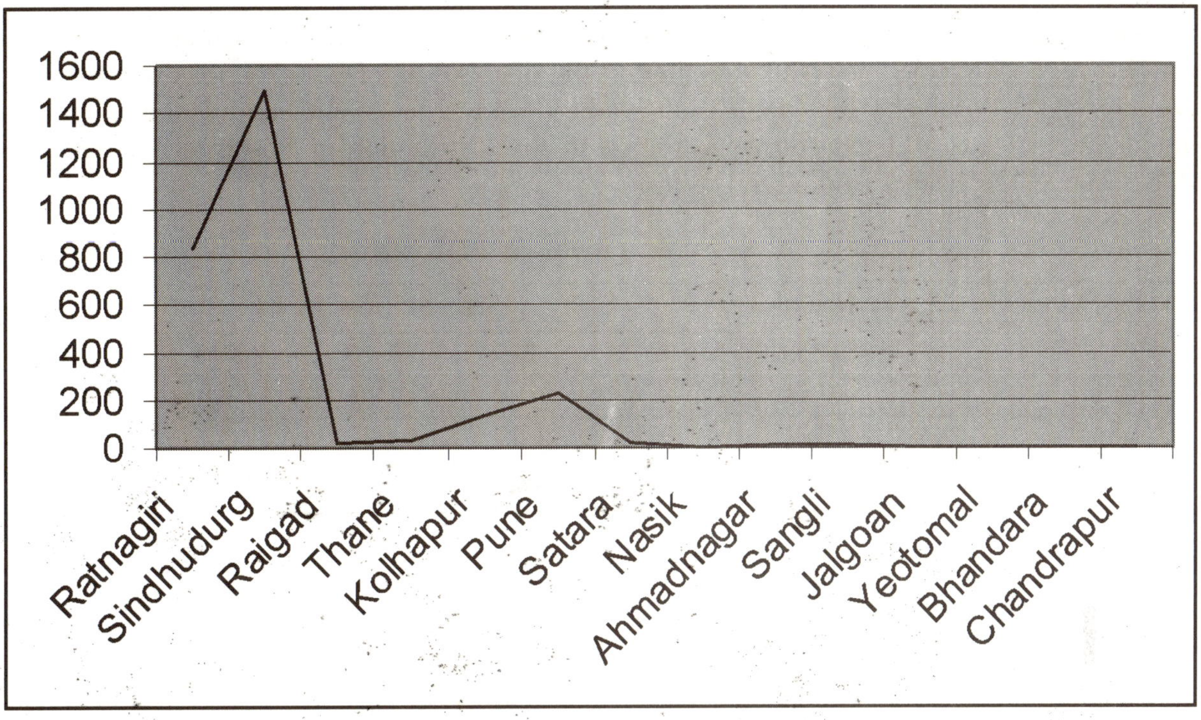

Fig. 13. Distribution of sacred grove in Maharashtra. Source: Deshmukh (1999).

regarding the total number of SGs in the country, but in view of the known presence and pattern of distribution of sacred groves in Chattisgarh, Jharkhand, Karnataka, Orissa, Uttranchal, Madhaya Pradesh and West Bengal for which detailed inventories are not available, and the recent studies by Achar and Naik (2006) in northern coastal districts of Karnataka reporting only in 15 villages 1111 SGs, we strongly feel that the number of SGs in India is likely to be between 100,000 and 150,000 (Malhotra, 1998).

The limited data that are available suggest the existence of inter-district (region) variations in the extent of presence of SGs. Thus, on examination data of Gadgil and Vartak (1981) and Godbole (1998) pertaining to Maharashtra reveal:

(a) that the number of groves in the Western Ghat districts of Maharashtra (Table 13) are much bigger compared to Khandesh (Jalgaon district) and Vidarbha in eastern Maharashtra;

(b) even the six districts of the Western Ghats show considerable variation, the observed range being from a minimum of 15 in Kolaba to a maximum of 250 in Ratnagiri district; and

(c) there seems to be a gradient of increase in the number of groves from north to south, thus, while in Thane and Kolaba districts, the number of groves are 21 and 15 respectively, further south in Pune and Kolhapur districts, the number is 70 and 97 respectively, and the southernmost Ratnagiri district has over 250 groves. We certainly cannot take this inter-district variation at the face value, since we do not know whether the density of groves is a function of the size of geographical area and number of villages, and their ethnic composition in different districts, or it is a function of the intensity of the institution in itself. Only future well-planned studies in the region will clarify the situation.

Data reported by Kushalappa and Kushalappa (1996) in Kodagu district of Karnataka also shows considerable inter-taluk variation in the distribution of SGs. The maximum number are observed in Virajpet taluk (n=508) followed by Somvarpet (n=400) and Madikeri (n=306). Similar inter-district and inter-region variation in the distribution of SGs is also observed in Maharashtra, Meghalaya and Tamil Nadu.

Table 13. The Size distribution of sacred groves in Maharashtra, inter-district variation.[1]

District	No. of Sacred Groves	Size of SGs in ha.				
		Up to 2 (%)	2-5 (%)	5-10 (%)	10-15 (%)	>15 (%)
Thane	21	9.5	33.4	14.3	4.7	38.1
Kolaba	15	6.7	0.0	20.0	20.0	53.3
Pune[2]	66	81.8	9.1	3.0	4.6	1.5
Satara	16	93.7	0.0	6.3	0.0	0.0
Kolhapur	97	82.5	11.3	4.2	1.0	1.0
Jalgaon	4	100.0	0.0	0.0	0.0	0.0
Vidarbha[3]	7	85.7	0.0	0.0	0.0	14.3
Total	**226**	**71.7**	**10.6**	**5.7**	**3.6**	**8.4**

1. Data given by Gadgil and Vartak (1981) in Appendix I has been re-analysed to examine inter-district variation in the number and size distribution of sacred groves in Maharashtra.
2. Out of 70 sacred groves, area for four was not available, thus reducing the total to 66.
3. Sacred groves from Yeotmal (n=3), Bhandara (n=3) and Chandrapur (n=4) have been pooled together; however, area for only 7 groves was available.

Literature review suggests that the size of the groves varies considerably from a cluster of a few trees to several hectares. Unfortunately, not many scholars have given the sizes of individual sacred groves. However, pooled total areas are available for some States/regions/localities. In Table 11 we have documented the available data in terms of the area under SGs in different parts of the country. The data reveal that there exists a vast inter-State variation in the extent of area under SGs. It appears that SGs in Western Ghats, Kodagu, Meghalaya, Tamil Nadu and Rajasthan are relatively larger, compared to the groves in Karnataka, Orissa and West Bengal. Data in terms of area are available for 9,196 sacred groves. These groves cover an area of 68,633 ha.

According to Gokhale *et al.* (1998), the total area of SGs in India as a whole would be about 33,000 ha or 0.01 per cent of the total area of India. There seems to be some error in this estimate as just 9,196 SGs reported so far cover over 68,633 ha (Table 11). Although based on the rather incomplete data, it is not possible to come up with a reasonable estimate. However, it can safely be said that the area under SGs will be many times more than Gokhale *et al.* have estimated.

As noted above, there also exists inter-State-region variation in the number as well as size of SGs. It is likely that there also exists an intra-State variation in the size of the groves. The inventory prepared by Gadgil and Vartak (1981) provides an excellent opportunity to examine this aspect. These authors documented SGs in nine districts of Maharashtra. This data is re-analysed by the authors to capture the inter-district variation. The results are presented in Table 13. It is evident that the size of the groves depicts considerable variation between the districts. Thane and Kolaba districts have much larger groves compared to the adjacent southern districts of Pune, Satara and Kolhapur. Over 80 per cent of the groves in these latter districts are up to only 2 ha, while in the former districts such groves are less than 10 per cent. Likewise there are a significant number of groves measuring above 10 ha in Thane and Kolaba (20 out of 36, i.e. 55.6 per cent) in the southern districts they are only 6 out of 179, i.e. 3.4 per cent.

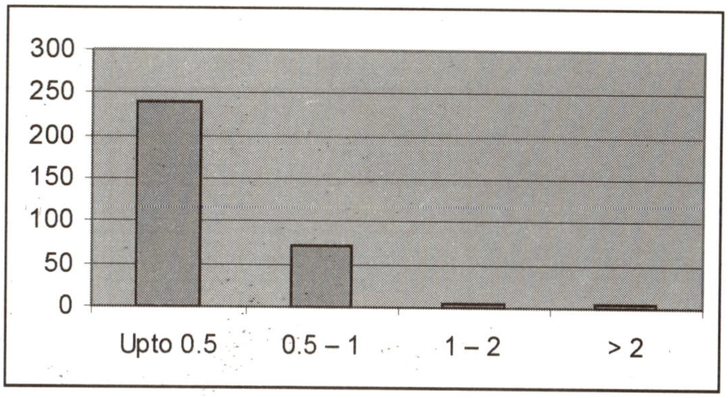

Fig. 14. Size distribution of sacred groves in Semiliguda block. Koraput district, Orissa. Source: Malhotra *et al.* (1998).

Further, there seems to be an inter-regional variation in the size of the groves in Maharashtra; compared to the groves in the Western Ghats, the groves in eastern Maharashtra are much smaller in size. Similar inferences can be drawn from the data reported by Deshmukh *et al.* (1998) for 14 districts in Maharashtra.

A gradient of increasing number of SGs from north to south in the Western Ghats was observed. In terms of the size of the groves, interestingly the reverse pattern is seen, i.e. the number of groves with larger size show an increasing trend from south to north (see also Deshmukh *et al.*, 1998).

A large number of sacred grove in Kodagu are small in size – 45.8% of the groves are less than 0.4 ha and 80.8% less than two ha. There are only 123 groves, i.e. 10.1% of the total, which have recorded area of more than 5 ha. Hence, a very large proportion of sacred groves in Kodagu are "islands" surrounded by other land uses (Kushalappa and Kushalappa, 1996). Similar situation is also witnessed in Karnataka, Kerala, Semiliguda, Tamil Nadu, and West Bengal (Tables 14 to 17 and Figs. 12 to 16). It may be highlighted that unlike this pattern, the groves in Meghalaya are much larger in size (Table 16).

Table 14. Size distribution of sacred groves in Semiliguda block. Koraput district, Orissa.

Size (class (acre)	No.	%
Upto 0.5	240	74.5
0.5 – 1	72	22.5
1 – 2	5	1.5
> 2	5	1.5
Total	**322**	**100**

Source: Malhotra *et al.*, (1998).

Table 15. Size of the sacred groves of Tamil Nadu.

Area in ha.	Number	%
< 1 ha.	87	19.42
1 – 5	189	42.19
5 – 10	29	6.47
10 – 20	19	4.24
20 – 50	44	9.82
50 – 100	22	4.91
100 – 200	14	3.12
200 – 400	28	6.25
400 – 500	11	2.46
> 500 ha.	5	1.12

Source: Amrithalingam (1998 b).

Table 16. Area and size classes of sacred groves in Meghalaya.

Size Classes	Number	Percentage
upto 10	14	17.7
11- 50c	33	41.8
51- 100	16	20.2
101 - 200	7	8.9
201 - 300	1	1.3
301 - 400	5	6.3
>401 - 500	3	3.8
Total	**79**	**100**

Source: Tiwari *et al.* (1999).

Table 17. Area and size classes of sacred groves in Maharashtra.

Size class	Number	Area (ha.)
< 01 ha.	1849	581.28
01 - 05 ha	662	1466.23
05 - 10 ha	103	718.91
10 - 25 ha.	63	1018.09
25 - 50 ha.	17	610.34
50 – 100 ha.	7	489.04
>100 ha	2	235.58
Not Measured	105	0
Total	**2808**	**5119.47**

Source: Deshmukh (1999).

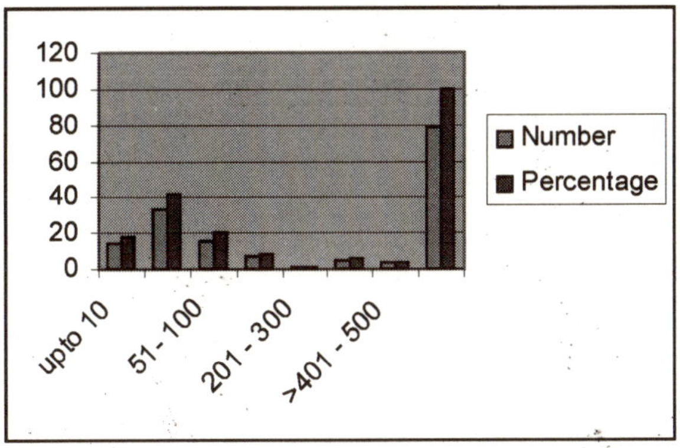

Fig. 15. Area and size classes of sacred groves in Meghalaya. Source: Tiwari *et al.* (1999).

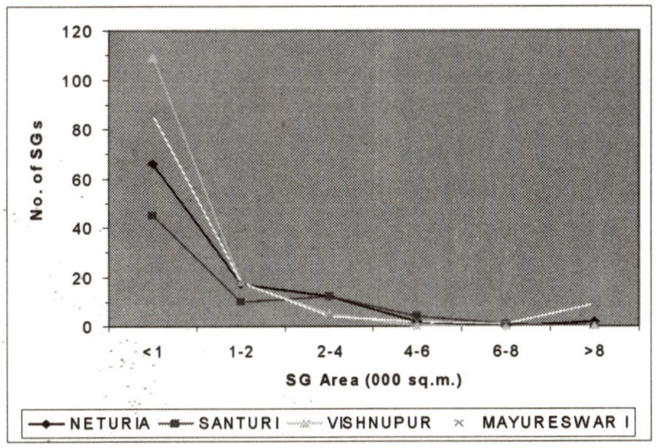

Fig. 16. Size distribution of SGs in four administrative blocks of Southwest Bengal.

5. OWNERSHIP AND MANAGEMENT OF SGs (Pls. 20-22)

The literature on this aspect, though sparse and scanty, suggests the existence of a wide variation in the legal status and management of SGs in the country. It appears that in terms of the legal tenurial rights, SGs fall under three categories:

- SGs under the control of State forest departments;
- SGs under the control of revenue and other government departments; and
- Privately owned SGs.

A large number of SGs in Maharashtra are under the control of the Forest Department. Gadgil and Vartak (1981) have documented 223 such groves. Legally all sacred groves in Meghalaya are under the control of District Councils (Tiwari *et al.*, 1998). Kalam (1996) reports that *devarakadus* in Kodagu district of Karnataka are under the control of the Revenue Department.

Godbole *et al.* (1998) and Roy Burman (1996) reported that many SGs in western Maharashtra are under the control of the Revenue Department. Roy Burman further mentions that a few thousand temples and their groves in western Maharashtra were brought under the scrutiny of the government by forming the *Paschim Maharashtra Deosthan Prabodhan Samiti* in the 1960s.

Several SGs are also privately owned by a family, a group of families, a clan, or a trust body. Chandrashekara and Sankar (1998) give examples of such groves in Kerala: *Ollur kavu* is owned by a single family, the S.N. Puram grove owned and managed by several families, and the *Iringole kavu* owned and managed by a temple trust. The ownership pattern in Maharashtra is shown in table 18 and Fig. 17 and in Semiliguda in table 19.

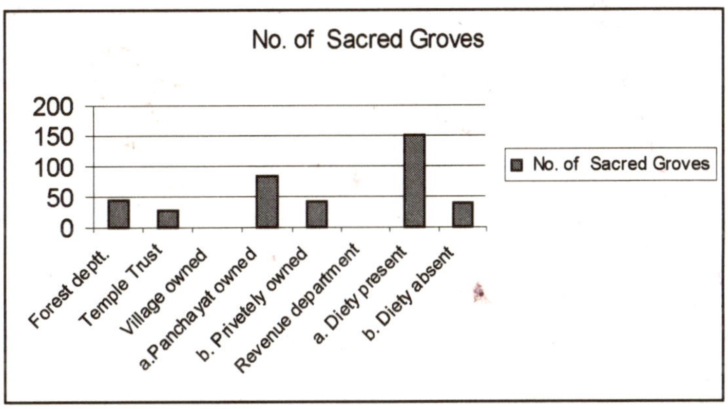

Fig. 17. Ownership Status of SGs in Maharashtra. Source: Deshmukh (1999).

Table 18. Ownership status of SGs in Maharashtra.

Sl. No.	Ownership	No. of SGs	%
1.	Forest deptt.	45	11.66
2.	Temple Trust	28	7.25
3.	Village owned		
	a. Panchayat owned	82	21.24
	b. Privately owned	42	10.88
4.	Revenue department		
	a. Diety present	149	38.6
	b. Diety absent	40	10.36

Source: Deshmukh (1999).

Table 19. Ownership pattern of sacred groves in Semiliguda block, Koraput district, Orissa.

Owned by	No. of villages	%
Priest	34	20.12
Clan(s)	24	14.20
Ethnic group	5	2.96
Whole village	106	62.72
Total	**169**	**100.00**

Source: Malhotra *et al.* (1998).

The privately owned groves in Kerala can be grouped into four types (Basha, 1998):

1. *Family owned,* where management will be looked after by a single family as in *Mannarassala* sacred of Alappuzha District dedicated to Snake god or managed by a group of families like the family trust as in *Pambumekattumana* grove of Thrissur District again dedicated to the Snake god.
2. *Establishment owned* where, the management is entirely left to the hands of Dewaswam Boards or Hindu Religious and Charitable Endowment (HR & CE). Here the establishments provide annual maintenance grants to the temples situated inside the groves. Most of the groves located in the southern parts of Kerala are under the Dewaswam Board and many situated in the northern parts of Kerala are supported by HR & CE organizations.
3. *Community owned* where some groves are under the ownership of certain communities as in Cheermakavu dedicated to Sri Kurumba Bhagavathy in Neeleswaram of Kasargode District. Here the "Asari" (carpenter) community is managing the affairs.
4. *Local trust owned,* where many groves are managed by the local, committees or trusts. These committees have come into existence as a result of disintegration of the families which originally owned the groves. *Pramancheri Kavu* in Kannur District is one such grove managed by the *Pramancheri Kavu Samrakshana Samithi.* There are a few more under this type of management.

There are significant variations in terms of management practices of the SGs, i.e. upkeep, protection, performance of rituals and festivals, conflict resolution and harvesting of biomass. To cite a few examples: *orans* in Rajasthan are usually managed by Gram Panchayats (Jha *et al.*, 1998); the Haryali grove in Garhwal is managed by a temple committee consisting of members of three villages (Sinha and Maikhuri, 1998); Roy Burman (1996) mentions that among the Mahadeo Kolis of Pune district, the management is usually vested with the clan elders, whereas among the Kunbis of Kolhapur district the groves are managed by village elders; the *kantabanshini thakurma* SG in Koraput district is managed by two clans of the Proja tribe (Hemam *et al.*, 1997). Clan-based management appears to be a widespread practice among the Santhal, Oraon, Munda, Kharia and other tribes of central, eastern and north-eastern India.

6. ETHNICITY AND SACRED GROVES

In this section we examine if there exists any pattern in terms of association of the institution of sacred groves and ethnicity.

The process of peopling of India stretching over indeed a long period brought in not only different human biological traits, but also a variety of cultural, religious and technological characteristics. Contemporary India is an agglomeration of over 40,000 endogamous groups (Malhotra, 1984). An estimated 37,000 groups are structured in the Hindu caste system. Each group (caste) belongs to one of the five *varnas*: Brahmin, Kshatriya, Vaishya, Sudra and Pancham. The remaining 3,000 groups constitute different tribes, religious communities and other communities like Parsis and Siddis who immigrated in recent history. In other words, there is a bewildering heterogeneity in the Indian society in terms of religious beliefs, culture, language and pattern of livelihoods.

A few tentative inferences in terms of association of SGs with different ethnic groups that can be drawn from the materials described earlier are:

(i) *that sacred groves are found among both tribals and non-tribals;*
(ii) *there is regional variation in terms of ethnic association;*
(iii) *the association with castes of different varnas is not clear; and*
(iv) *in States like Andhra Pradesh, Chattisgarh, Jharkhand, Orissa, West Bengal, etc., where we have both tribals and non-tribals the presence or absence of groves in the non-tribal areas is not clear. Deb (unpublished) reports in four blocks of South West Bengal that out of 423 SGs, 148 (36.2%) are maintained by tribals, 248 (60.6%) by Hindus and 13 (3.2%) by Muslims (Table 20).*

Table 20. Number of sacred groves maintained by different ethno-religious communities in southwest Bengal.

Block	Tribal		Hindu*		Muslim		Total
	No.	%	No.	%	No.	%	
Mayureswar-1	2	1.68	105(17)	86.67	13	10.83	120
Neturia	61	61.62	38(10)	38.38	0	0	99
Santuri	58	80.56	14(4)	19.44	0	0	72
Bishnupur	25	18.94	105(48)	79.54	2	1.48	132
Total	**148**	**36.19**	**248(24)**	**60.63**	**13**	**3.18**	**423**

* *Hindu SGs include those maintained exclusively by S.C. communities (in parentheses).*
Source: Deb (unpublished, 2006).

7. Gender and SGs

The role of gender in SGs can be analysed at least at four levels: (a) the gender of the deity associated with the sacred groves, (b) the gender of the priest serving the groves, (c) the nature and extent of access to men and women in various rituals, festivals and ceremonies that take place in the groves, and harvest of biomass from the groves, and (d) the role of gender in the management of the SGs.

A random literature search reveals that by and large a majority of the SGs are associated with female deities. Gadgil and Vartak (1976) found, among 21 SGs in Maharashtra, 15 associated with goddesses and 5 with male deity (phallic worship) and one with ancestor worship. Chandran (1995) reports occurrence of both male (*bhutappa, jatakappa*) and female (*choudamma*) deities associated with sacred groves in Karnataka. In southwest Bengal and in Koraput district of Orissa, the deities are mostly female (Hemam *et al.*, 1997; Malhotra *et al.*, 1998): In Semiliguda 53% deities were females.

Regarding the gender of the priest, it appears that without an exception the priesthood rests with males (see Vartak and Gadgil, 1981; Roy Burman, 1996; Godbole *et al.*, 1998; Sinha, 1989 and others). However, this aspect needs to be further studied, as many studies do not provide explicit details on the gender of priests. Of great interest will be the situation among the matrilineal societies such as Nairs in Kerala, Khasis and Garos in northeast India.

The data in terms of access to sacred groves by women are also very scanty. It appears that generally women are not permitted into the groves after attaining puberty. However, women's entry is not restricted in Wes Bengal SGs (Deb *et al.*, in press). Roy (1912) while describing sacred groves among the *Oraon* of Chotanagpur mentioned that the main festival associated with *sarana* is *Sarhul*. However, women are not allowed in the *sarana*, but take part in dance at the *akhara* which is located close to the grove (also see Fernandes, 1993 for more details). Roy Burman (1996) has reported a similar phenomenon among the Mahadeo Kolis of Pune district and among the Kunbis of Kolhapur district in Maharashtra. Malhotra *et al.* (1998) have observed taboo against entry of women in the sacred groves among the tribes of south-west Bengal and among the tribes of Koraput district of Orissa. However, in 79 SGs studied by Malhotra *et al.* (1998) it was observed that women in some SGs were also allowed (Table 21).

Table 21. Access to sacred groves related taboos in Semiliguda.

Category	Total No. of SGs	Permitted in SGs.	
		No.	%
Menstruating women	79	0	0.0
Husband of Menstruating women	79	10	12.0
Pregnant women	79	13	16.0
Husband of Pregnant women	79	79	100.0
Widow	79	5	6.0
Widower	79	5	6.0

Source: Malhotra *et al.* (1998).

Although many studies have dealt with harvesting of biomass from SGs, it is not clear whether women are allowed to gather the same (see, among others, Unnikrishnan, 1990; Mitra and Pal, 1994; Viji, 1995).

Finally, nothing is known at all about the kind of role women play in decision-making regarding management of SGs. It will be of immense value to examine whether women are represented in the numerous trust bodies that are managing SGs, in particular in Karnataka, Kerala, Himachal Pradesh and Maharashtra. The limited information available from the studies in West Bengal and Orissa (Deb *et al.*, 1997; Deb *et al.*, in press; Malhotra *et al.* (1998) suggests practically no role of women in the management of SGs.

8. INTERFACES BETWEEN PEOPLE AND SACRED GROVES

In this section we examine the role of sacred groves in the lives of the people from three aspects: (i) religious; (ii) socio-cultural; and (iii) economic.

Religious (Pls. 23-25)

There is a category of SGs among many communities that are associated with certain deities. In such groves annual rituals and ceremonies are performed to propitiate the deity. During these rituals sacrifices of animals (such as fowl, goat, pig and buffalo) are made. In other Sanskritized groves offerings of vegetable items are made. These rituals are performed for the well-being of the people, animals, crops, etc. Details of such offerings are available in the anthropological literature.

The presiding deities are believed to look after the well-being of the people, and also protect the groves by administering punishment (mostly death) to the offenders. The practice of oath/vow taking in the groves is fairly widespread in the country (among others see Roy, 1912; Sisodia and Malhotra, 1963; Kalam, 1996). People take vows for wish-fulfilment when there is a crisis, particularly bearing on health, and offerings mostly of terracotta of animals, birds, humans, etc., are made. In some of the groves of West Bengal heaps of such terracotta offerings of elephants and horses are found (Malhotra and Das, 1997). Various animals sacrificed in SGs of Semliguda are given in table 22. As expected, there are some differences between the tribes and other communities in respect of types of animal sacrificed. Table 23 gives different kinds of symbols observed in these groves: over 60% groves depict stones as sacred symbols, while only one grove out of 322 had an idol.

Table 22. Animals sacrificed in SGs of Semliguda.

Animal	Tribal	Non-tribal
Buffalo	+	-
Cow	+	-
Pig	+	(-) (+)
Goat	+	+
Sheep	+	(-) (+)
Fowl	+	+
Duck	+	(-) (+)
Dove	+	-
Pigeon	+	-

(+) indicates present and (-) indicates absence. Source: Malhotra *et al.* (1998).

Table 23. Symbol of worship observed in sacred groves of Semliguda.

Symbol	No. of SG	%
No symbol	18	5.28
Stone	200	62.11
Iron objects	15	4.66
Mud pot	33	10.25
Wooden pole	8	2.48
Mole hill	2	0.62
Idol	1	0.31
Others	45	13.98
Total	**322**	**100.00**

Source: Malhotra *et al.* (1998).

There seems to be a hierarchy of sacred groves in terms of their geographical influence. At least five such hierarchical levels are discernible (Table 24). Inhabitants of a village or even different ethnic groups/ different castes in multi-ethnic situations have their own groves. Roy Burman (1996) reports the existence of such groves for different castes in villages of Kolhapur and Pune districts. Malhotra *et al.* (1997) observed in Kendua village of Jamboni taluk of Midnapore district where Kora and Santhal communities have their separate groves. Such a pattern seems fairly widespread among the tribes of Jharkhand, Chhattisgarh and Orissa. Such groves are mostly managed by the local community(ies), and owned by a family, group of families, or a clan.

A second category of SGs is represented by those managed by the entire village community, regardless of ethnic composition of the village.

The local-level groves are where people from somewhat larger geographical areas, usually a few neighbouring districts come to worship a particular grove. Examples of such groves are *Iringole* in Kerala and *Kantabanshini thakurma* in Orissa. Such groves are usually managed by local community and/or committees.

Table 24. Hierarchical levels of sacred groves in India.[1]

	Levels of sacred groves	Management of sacred groves
V	Pan-Indian	By trust
IV	Regional	By trust
III	Local	By whole village/community/local committees
II	Village	By whole village
I	Intra-village	By separate communities

1. Modified from Malhotra (1998).

The regional-level sacred groves are where people from several districts/States participate. Such an example is the Sabarimala sacred grove in Kerala. Such groves are usually managed by temple trusts.

The next higher level of SGs involves those of Pan-Indian character where people from many parts of the country participate. An example of such groves is the Hariyali sacred grove in Garhwal Himalayas (Sinha and Maikhuri, 1998). Such groves tend to be larger and managed by temple trusts.

Another category of SGs includes those that are believed to be abodes of ancestral spirits. Often these groves are, in fact, burial grounds. Such groves have been reported from a number of places. A few illustrative examples are: *masani* SGs among the Maler of Bihar (Vidyarthi, 1963); SGs in Sangameshwar tehsil of Ratnagiri district in Maharashtra (Godbole *et al.*, 1998); north Kerala SGs where ancestor worship is performed with *theyyam* ritual (Unnikrishnan, 1990); *sasan* SGs as burial grounds in Chotanagpur (Fernandes, 1993); and SGs among the Bhils of Ratanmal (Nath, 1960). It may be mentioned that sometimes a grove may serve both the functions, i.e. deity worship and ancestor worship. Unlike the groves associated with deities, the groves associated with ancestor worship, in particular burial grounds do not seem to have a hierarchical pattern.

Socio-cultural (Pls. 26 & 27)

SGs have important socio-cultural functions, in addition to the religious functions. Several festivals are performed at SGs. The literature on this subject is indeed very vast, and detailed accounts of socio-cultural functions performed are described in several earlier ethnographic studies.

Just to mention a few as illustration: Nath (1960) mentions that once a year on the occasion of Deepavali, offerings of food and liquor are made in groves among the Bhils of Ratanmal; Deb and Malhotra (1997) report that among the tribals of southwest Bengal, social gatherings take place in these groves on the occasion of *Salui* and *Karam* festivals, as well as wedding ceremonies; Vidyarthi and Rai (1997) report that different tribes of Bihar celebrate their major festivals at the SGs; marriage ceremonies of the Mahadeo Koli of Pune district of Maharashtra are held in their SGs. Fernandes (1993) has stressed on the role of sacred groves in the socialization of the youth among the tribes of Chotanagpur; Godbole *et al.* (1998) report that festivals like Holi, Navratri, Dev diwali are performed in sacred groves in Ratnagiri district of Maharashtra; Troisi (1978) mentions that the association of a village with *jaherthan* expresses the unity of the group. No two villages share the same *jaherthan*, and this serves as an important criterion to ascertain village membership and geographical boundary; Paranjapye (1989) highlights that the function of the SGs is to maintain a caste hierarchy within the village. The clan control over resources is signified by the SGs among the Mahadeo Koli of Western Maharashtra (Roy Burman, 1996).

The purpose and meaning attached to various rituals, ceremonies and functions performed in SGs are summarized in Table 25.

Table 25. Services and functions of SGs.[1]

	Types	Functions provided by SGs
1.	Religious	Propitiation of deity/spirits
		Propitiation of ancestral spirits
		Propitiation of totems

contd.

2.	Secular	
	2.1 Cultural	Provides cultural space to the community as a common property resource
	2.2 Political	Assertion of group identity
		Assertion of group solidarity
		Establishing new alliances
	2.3 Health	Fertility and Paternity
		Well-being of individual/family
		Well-being of community
	2.4 Economic	Good rainfall
		Good agricultural production
		Well-being of crops and animals
		Success in hunting, Gift exchange, Eco-tourism
	2.5 Psychological	Moral support and guidance

1. Modified from Malhotra *et al.* (1998).

Many cultural beliefs relating to fertility and paternity find expression in vows and prayers made at SGs. Similarly, moral support and guidance for individuals are derived from the cultural value associated with the SGs.

Economic

Several economic activities take place in SGs. Also, certain community activities with economic implications are associated with the SG (Table 25). SGs also provide a wide range of ecosystem services, in particular water. However, this aspect due to lack of systematic studies, has not been dealt with this book.

Harvesting of Biomass (Pl. 28)

There is a general belief that biomass is not harvested from the SGs. This is certainly true in many SGs found across the country. Gadgil and Vartak (1976), Roy Burman (1995) and Godbole *et al.* (1998) report such groves in the Western Ghats of Maharashtra. Malhotra *et al.* (1998) report such groves in southwest Bengal and in Koraput district of Orissa. Pushpangadan *et al.* (1998) report the existence of numerous groves in Kerala from which plants and animals are not harvested, and Swamy *et al.* (1998) report such groves in Tamil Nadu. Kerkar (personal communication, 2004) report several such groves in Pernem, Bicholim, Sattari, Canacona, Sanguem and Quepem talukas of Goa. Tewari *et al.* (1998) report many such groves from Meghalaya.

However, there are many groves from where biomass is extracted, and thus the local communities derive certain direct economic benefits from the groves (Box 3). A few illustrative examples are: Singh and Saxena (1998) and Jha *et al.* (1998) report that in many *orans* people graze their animals; Godbole *et al.* (1998) report collection of dead wood and dried leaf litter and harvesting of certain species of trees (*Caryota urens* and *Mangifera indica*) from groves in

Ratnagiri district of Maharashtra; Malhotra *et al.* (1998) report 192 out of 322 groves from Koraput district from which dead wood and several non-timber forest products are gathered; Unnikrishnan (1990) observes that certain plants extracted from SGs of Kerala provide livelihood to many artisans; Gadgil and Vartak (1976) report that villagers of Tunbad in Kolaba (now Raigad) district use the bark of *Entada phaseoloides* Merr. for the treatment of cattle against snake bite; wood is also extracted from many groves dedicated to ancestor spirits for cremation (Mitra and Pal, 1994).

Box 3: Rules for harvesting biomass resources from sacred groves of Semiliguda.

Biomass	No. of SGs	Biomass harvesting			
		Allowed		Not allowed	
		No.	%	No.	%
Tree	79	0	0.00	0	0.00
Leaf litter	79	9	11.39	70	88.61
Dry wood	79	62	78.48	11	13.92
NTFP	79	19	24.05	60	75.95
Grasses	79	25	31.65	54	68.35

Source: Malhotra *et al.* (1998).

Gift Exchange

Exchange of gifts is an important social activity, which takes place at SGs during certain festivals. Malhotra *et al.* (1998) report that villagers in Koraput district of Orissa engage in gift exchange at their SGs during the annual festival associated with the SGs.

Eco-tourism

The villagers of Mawphalng village in Meghalaya allow regulated tourists in their sacred groves, and earn substantial money which is used for protection of the grove as well as village development activities.

Activities with Economic Implications

Deities/spirits of SGs are propitiated by devotees with a view to ensuring success in hunting and good harvest. Rituals are also performed in SGs to bring in good rainfall, health of livestock and fending off disasters. Kalam (1996) mentions offering of miniature images of cattle and buffaloes to the SG deity in *Iyappa devarakadu* by villagers in Kodagu district of Karnataka, to keep their livestock healthy.

9. POLITICAL DIMENSIONS OF SGs (Pl. 29)

This section draws heavily on a series of articles by Roy Burman (1992, 1995, 1996), which have demonstrated the political dimensions of SGs in the local and regional context.

Sontheimer (1989) showed linkages of forest deities of the Western Ghats with the pastoral nomads as a means of drawing their territorial affinity. Kosambi (1962) observed that SGs are usually found along the preagrarian trade routes and cross-roads. Sawant (1990) wrote that

SG at Phondaghat in Sindhdurg district of Maharashtra was a resting place for traders and that the troops of Shivaji passed through it while depredating the coastal townships. Roy Burman (1996) described that at Jhinji Mahal sacred grove in Kolhapur district, Shivaji had taken shelter before attacking Shayasta Khan in Pune. This grove has been a hiding place for the troops and also their training centre. Sacred groves have often been supported by the local rulers. Shau Chattrapati, the king of Kolhapur, use to support a sacred grove dedicated to Amba Devi (Roy Burman, 1992). Kalam (1996) has written about the State patronage of sacred groves in Kodagu district of Karnataka.

Roy Burman (1992) mentions the strategic location of SGs along the trade routes in Meghalaya where the moral authority of the priests-chiefs facilitated the flow of commodity. As noted earlier, village membership among the Santhal and the geographical boundary of their village are defined by the SG (Troisi, 1978).

Hembram (1983) states that *sarna dharma* (religion) brought together discrete ethnic groups of Chotanagpur in to a common platform for asserting their rights to self-determination. The *sarna dharma*, in fact, helped them in consolidating their common identity and solidarity between the Christian and non-Christian tribes of the region. Mitra and Pal (1994) observed that *sarana* was one of the basic factors that stalled the Koel-Karo dam project in Bihar a decade ago.

Roy Burman (1995) has also highlighted this aspect of self-assertion among the Gonds of Gadchiroli district of Maharashtra. The Gonds have revived the Danteshwari sacred grove to assert their identity and right of self-determination. Self-assertion of the tribes through sacred groves is not always strong. D.N. (1990) interprets the construction of temples in the groves or replacement of local deities by the idol of Hanuman as reflecting subjugation and marginalisation of the tribal communities by the mainstream Hindu culture.

Stanley (personal communication, 2004) reports that villagers from many villagers of Koraput district successfully stalled tourist related activities to be undertaken by Orissa Tourism Department in Deomali hills by declaring and ritualizing the entire hill as a sacred grove.

There are more than 364 sacred areas and groves of *Umang Lais* reported to have existed in Manipur which have got royal patronage. The Pandit Loishang (the institution of the royal pandits) and the Pandit Achouba (head royal pandit/ priest) had the privilege to look after these sites. The delicacy of *Umang Lai* worship is still practised in a large scale but the maintenance of these areas with respect to the earlier form of ecological concern is endangered by progress. Human interventions under the name of development; impassiveness act and negligence towards the customary laws and practices; alarming change in attitude to life and beliefs; unwanted policies of the Government and lack of patronage are some of the factors responsible for the poor condition of Laikons or sacred groves in Manipur.

The folk tradition which—considered to be the storehouse of knowledge becomes much more pertinent in the context of modern way of life coupled with the forces of globalization. A special attention to this treasure has now been paid by some scholarly agencies to uplift its threatening position and to recognize its important aspects.

In this regard the Indira Gandhi Rashtriya Manav Sangrahalaya, Bhopal, in collaboration with Manipur State Museum jointly organized a programme on "Audio-visual documentation of 33 sacred groves of Manipur.

Fourteen members including officials from Manipur State Museum and IGRMS, ethno-botanist, environmentalists, freelance writer accompanied with video and photography team undertook the programme successfully. It was fortunate that the documentation was held under the guidance of Sri Ng. Kulachandra Singh, Pandit Achouba (royal head priest), who in fact is the person looking after the *Umang Lai* Laikons (sacred shrines and groves) in Manipur (IGRMS, 2002).

10. SACRED GROVES AS COMMON PROPERTY RESOURCES

This section is based on a paper published by Malhotra (2002) where in the author has examined the SGs from the point of view of Common Property Resources (CPRs).

In order to analyse SGs from the CPRs perspective it is essential that we briefly describe the salient features of CPRs. Although CPRs have been defined quite differently in literature, the following features seem to have wider acceptance:

(i) *Use rights*: That the resources are controlled by an identifiable group and are not privately owned by individuals or managed by government;

(ii) *Boundary condition or exclusion principle*: That there exist rules. Concerning who may use the resource as against who may not use the resource; and

(iii) *Use Rules*: That there exist rules regarding how a resource is used by the group.

In the vast literature that exists on CPRs, there seems to be an emphasis on resources that accrue economic benefits to the community (group of people that collectively use a resource). The examples of CPR often cited are water, wildlife, fish, forests and pastures. The concept has, however, been extended to some other resources like public parks, highways and oil pools (Oakerson, 1986), radio wavelengths (Ostrom, 1986). The deep seabed and Antarctica are cited as examples of global commons.

Let us now examine whether the traditional institution of SGs satisfies the above mentioned features of CPRs:

(i) *Use rights*: As noted earlier, a wide variety exists in terms of ownership of SGs in the country;

(a) *SGs owned and managed by single or joint family*: Such groves are found mostly in Karnataka, Kerala and Bastar district of Chhattisgarh. It may be noted here that in these groves both land and fauna and flora belong to the families. These are thus examples of privately owned and managed groves and, therefore, cannot be treated as CPRs.

(b) *SGs owned and managed by temple trusts*: There are groves that are associated with temples. Usually like in (a) above, both land and fauna and flora are privately owned and managed by the temple trusts. Such groves are found in Maharashtra, Kerala, Karnataka, and Himachal Pradesh, etc. Like (a) above, these groves are also privately owned and managed and, therefore, do not fall under the category of CPRs.

(c) *SGs managed by communities*: There are numerous SGs where although the land usually is owned by the Forest Department or Revenue Department, or other State agencies, the right of use of resources and management rest with the communities. Such groves could be owned and managed by a clan, different ethnic group in a village or the entire village. These are the classic examples of community-managed SGs. Such groves are found throughout the country, but especially in Andhra Pradesh, Bihar, Karnataka, Meghalaya, parts of Maharashtra, Orissa, Rajasthan, Tamil Nadu, West Bengal, etc.

Although the number of such groves is not known, based on the limited data available, it is certain that their number is several times greater than the types mentioned in (a) and (b) above. It may be mentioned that just in one block of Semiliguda of Koraput district there are 322 such groves (Malhotra *et al.*, 1998); in Kodagu district of Karnataka there are over 1,000 (Kalam, 1966); a majority of the 953 groves reported from Maharashtra belong to this category (Deshmukh *et al.*, 1998).

It is of immense interest here to point out that there seems to be a strong association between the three types of SGs mentioned above and the ethnicity; type (a) and (b) are mostly associated with Hindu castes, while type (c) is most often associated with numerous tribal communities.

It is thus evident that based on the use rights, some SGs do not fall under CPRs, whereas a large number of them, primarily found among different tribal communities, confirm to the definition of CPRs. Therefore, the other two features of CPRs have been examined only for those SGs that conform to CPRs.

(ii) *Boundary condition or the exclusion principle*: On the basis of this principle at least three types of SGs are observed (Fig. 18).

(a) A village having only one SG. In such cases the whole village is affiliated to the grove. Occasionally a village may have more than one grove (serving different purposes), in such situations also the whole village is affiliated to both (or more) the groves. Persons from other villages cannot be affiliated to such village-owned and managed groves;

(b) Sometimes in multi-ethnic villages each ethnic group may have a separate grove of its own. In other words, each ethnic group manages its own SG; and

(c) Sometimes people from neighbouring villages may participate in a village having SG. Such a situation occurs when the neighbouring villages do not have their own SGs and have moved out from the parent village to establish new villages/hamlets.

It is thus seen that all SGs have well-defined boundary rules.

(iii) *Use rules*: There are well-established rules in terms of use of resources from SGs. Broadly speaking two types (although there is scope to further refine this) of use patterns are witnessed: (a) groves from where collection of any form of biomass is forbidden, and (b) groves from where dead wood, leaf litter, medicinal plants and other NTFP are harvested. In other words, from groves of type (a) no tangible economic benefits are derived, while from the type (b) some tangible economic benefits are derived. It is thus evident that the (c) type of SGs confirm to all the three characteristic features of CPRs.

From the foregone description and analysis, it is evident that the institution of sacred groves is not a homogeneous category, and instead encompasses a variety of systems ranging from truly privately owned and managed groves to community-owned and managed groves. Therefore, further discussion will be limited only to those SGs that are community-owned and managed.

Unlike many CPRs studies reported in the literature like pastures, forests, fisheries, water, etc., which provide tangible economic benefits to the communities, not all SGs in contrast provide such tangible economic benefits. In this regard SGs, therefore, differ markedly from other CPRs. In fact, a majority of SGs provide a variety of, strictly speaking, non-economic functions-cultural, social, political and religious to the individuals, clan and communities. It is highly noteworthy that a number of ceremonies are performed and festivals held annually in the groves. All households affiliated to a grove contribute their share in cash for the purchase of sacrificial animal (s) and other materials. Thus, in fact, instead of deriving any economic benefits the community spends a considerable amount to propitiate the deity.

Therefore, SGs should not be viewed as CPRs providing tangible economic benefits to the community but instead providing a common socio-religious space which the community uses to establish cohesiveness, identity, solidarity and well-being of the inhabitants as also of crops and animals.

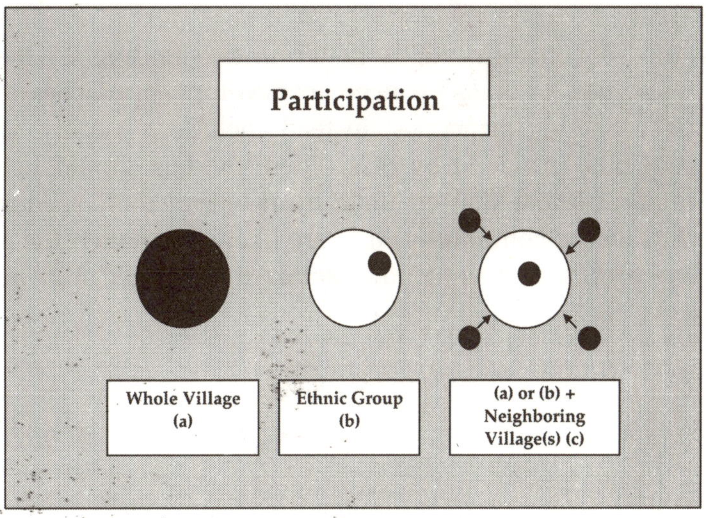

Fig. 18. Showing three types of villages with boundary condition in Semiliguda, Orissa. Source: Malhotra *et al.* (1998).

As noted earlier, irrespective of the type, all SGs harbour varying degrees of natural biodiversity. The biodiversity in the groves is preserved on religious grounds and not because of economic benefits. However, several studies show that because of the weakening of traditional religious beliefs, the cultural and biological integrity of many groves is threatened. However, it is not always clear as to which type of groves are under threat, i.e. the privately owned (family-owned or owned and managed by temple trusts) or the community-owned (the ones from where biomass is harvested or the ones from where biomass cannot be harvested). It is often also not explicitly stated whether the degree of threat is associated with the hierarchical levels of SGs. In order to develop suitable intervention strategies for the conservation of SGs, it is abundantly clear that no single approach or strategy will be applicable to all the groves. Instead grove-type specific approaches will have to be developed. In this context it is appropriate that we briefly examine the analytical models developed in relation to CPRs. It is outside the scope of this chapter to examine critically the various models, so we shall limit our observation to the overall relevance of such models to SGs. Also, it is not the purpose of this chapter to suggest any alternative models appropriate to SCs, instead the purpose is to raise issues and look for major constraints in the existing models.

Singh (1994) gives an excellent account of theories of collective action in managing common pool resources. Some of the theories and models mentioned are: Prisoner's dilemma game, the chicken or the hawk-dove game, tender trap game, threat to survival theory, theory of participative behaviour, Olson's theory, Buchanan and Tullock's theory, etc. All these theories are based on an important assumption that CPRs provide economic benefits to the group managing a CPR. Since a majority of SCs do not provide tangible economic benefits, instead provide a variety of non-economic services, most of these theories in their present form cannot be applied to analyse the threats faced by SGs.

Similarly the seven principles of design for self-organized systems of resource management advanced by Ostrom (1990, 1992) cannot be applied in their present form to an analysis of SGs.

To conclude, for a better understanding of the changes that are taking place in the institution of SGs, we need to develop approaches and models that are primarily not based on economic principles, instead include a variety of services—cultural, social, political and religious, provided by SGs. These models should help us analyse the nature of threats, both internal (those that emanate from within the community) and external (those that come from outside the community) that are likely to weaken the institution of SGs. We need to understand the processes, identify the factors that trigger shift in the traditional value and belief system.

2

BIOLOGICAL AND ECOLOGICAL DIMENSIONS

A number of scholars have studied biological and ecological value of SGs in the country. The literature is too vast to be described here. We shall, therefore, mention only some of the main findings as illustration. The materials are described under the following heads:

2.1 Biological Value
- Ecological refugia
- Storehouse of biodiversity

2.2 Ecological Services
- Recharge of aquifers
- Soil conservation and nutrient cycling.

2.1 BIOLOGICAL VALUE (Pl. 30)

As noted in chapter 1, the institution of SGs is very ancient in the country. Access to and interference with SGs has been culturally restricted and, thereby, reduced the human impact in terms of harvesting of natural resources. The consequence of such restriction has been that SGs have evolved as important reservoirs of biological diversity and permitted the complex and diverse array of ecological processes to continue uninterruptedly over long period of time (Malhotra *et al.*, 2001 b). In the context of biological value two main functions sacred groves carry lot of importance, namely, ecological refugia and storehouse of the biodiversity. The ecological refugia serve as the last remnants for the gene pool whereas the storehouse function reiterates the continued importance of the sacred grove system in biological cycle.

Ecological Refugia (Pl. 31)

The role of sacred groves as ecological refugia in terms of species of importance has been discussed by several researchers. Studies carried out in the SGs of areas like the Western Ghats, have clearly demonstrated the ecological importance of these vegetation patches. These are providing several insights for scientists and policy makers.

The concept of refugia has not become restricted only at the level of the species but also at the level of larger ecosystems such as tropical forests in the Western Ghats, which is one of the biodiversity hotspots in the world.

The biological spectrum of sacred groves of Kerala closely resembles normal spectrum of tropical forest, except in the case of therophytes. Sacred groves comprised 45% phanerophytes, 8% chameophytes and 6% geophytes comparable to values generalized by Raunkiar's system of classification. The other lifeforms are 3% epiphytes and 15% lianas. SGs in the high lands of Kerala have typical Western Ghats forest type vegetation. Dominant flowering species include *Hopea parviflora, Antiaris toxicaria* and *Anacolosa densiflora*. On the other hand, the SGs of midland region are dominated by *Artocarpus hirsutus, Hopea ponga, Hydnocarpus pentandra, Holigarna arnottiana, Vateria indica*, etc. The coastal Kerala is characterized by *Calophyllum inophyllum, C. calaba, Carallia brachiata, Artocarpus hirsutus, Samadera indica, Holigarna arnottiana*, etc.

The pantropical families are megathern families that are exclusively found in SGs of Kerala. These are Anonaceae, Bombacaceae, Combretaceae, Connaraceae, Cyperaceae, Dichapetalaceae, Dilleniaceae, Clusiaceae, Myristicaceae, Pandanaceae, Rhizhophoraceae and Zingiberaceae. There are some families very common in SGs which are tropical with sub-tropical and temperate outlines. They include Ebenaceae, Icacinaceae, Lauraceae, Fabaceae, Caesalpiniaceae, Mimosaceae, Oleaceae, Passifloraceae, Piperaceae, Rubiaceae, Rutaceae, Sapindaceae, Urticaceae, Verbenaceae and Vitaceae. The cosmopolitan families in sacred groves are Moraceae, Rubiaceae, Euphorbiaceae, Loganiaceae, Rutaceae, Bixaceae, Lauraceae and Fabaceae.

Among the inter-tropical elements like mangrove family Rhizophoraceae one genus viz., Carallia is somewhat widespread. Another element is Dipterocarpaceae of which two genera *Hopea* and *Vateria* show wide distribution in sacred groves. Pandanaceae with one genus is a palaeotropical family found mostly in sacred groves located in swampy coastal areas (Pushpangadan *et al.*, 1998).

From the species enumerated from the SGs of Tamil Nadu, 42 species are endemic to Western Ghats and Southern Western Ghats and 12 are of endangered, rare and threatened categories. Six species of pteridophytes also come in the above categories. The plant *Tectaria zeylanica* (pteridophyte) which is highly endemic particularly in the Silent valley is preserved in one of the groves studied. This gives a clue that even climax vegetation of various altitudes and latitudes can be conserved in-situ in the sacred groves (Sukumaran *et al.*, 2005).

Kunstleria keralensis, a climbing legume, reported from a sacred grove in southern Kerala, is a species found only in that SG (Mohanan and Nair, 1981). *Belpharistemma membranifolia, Buchanania lanceolata* and *Syzygium travancoricum* are rare species found only in some SGs of Kerala (Nair and Mohanan, 1995). Mohanan also discovered a rare species of cinnamon, *Cinnamomum quilonensis*, in some of the *kavus* of Alapuzha district in Kerala (Unnikrishnan, 1995). The Kallabbekan SG in Kumta taluk, Karnataka, over 50 hectares in extent, despite being in the midst of arecanut-spice gardens of a populated village, is rich in endemics like wild nutmegs (*Myristica malabarica*), cinnamon, *Garcinia gummi-gutta* and wild pepper (Chandran *et al.*, 1998). A new species of frog, *Philautus sanctisilvaticus*, has recently been reported from Amarkantak sacred grove, Madhya Pradesh (Das and Chanda, 1997).

With the continuing destruction of forest all around them, the SGs have become fragmented habitats housing a variety of genetic pools and became the last refuge for many

Pl. 30. The star tortoise is protected in a sacred grove, Andhra Pradesh.

Pl. 31. Protected roosts of fruit bats in a grove, Maharashtra.

Pl. 32. *Gymnacranthera canarica* – a threatened plant protected in a Kerala grove.

Pl. 33. *Pinaga dicksonii* – a rare endemic palm in a grove of Karnataka.

Pl. 34. Chinkara in *oran* of Rajasthan.

Pl. 35. A sacred grove conserving water in Kerala.

Pl. 36. Pond in a sacred grove of Rajasthan.

Pl. 37. Untouched fallen wood in sacred grove, Karnataka.

Pl. 38. Decay of litter in a grove, S. Orissa.

threatened endangered and endemic plant and animal species. Tree species like *Phoeba hainsiana* (vulnerable), *Rhus hookeri* (endangered) and *Flacourtia cataphracta* (endangered) have been found to be well-represented in two sacred groves in Manipur valley. *Syzygium travancoricum,* an endemic tree, reported from the low-level evergreen forests of Kulathupuzha (South Kerala) has been totally eliminated from its type locality. Today, only a few plants are reported thriving in some sacred groves of Pathanamthitta district and in the marshlands of Quilon-Asramam in the southern Western Ghats of India. Haridasan and Rao (1985) reported at least 50 endangered and rare species in SGs of Meghalaya. Sacred groves of Kerala are also found to harbour a number of plant species that are wild relatives of many crop species. These wild relatives are important for improving the cultivated varieties of plants.

Many animal species including birds that are otherwise threatened or becoming rare find a safe refuge in many sacred groves. The *orans* in Rajasthan, managed by the Bishnoi community, provide protection to the Indian gazelle (*Gazella*), blackbuck (*Antelope cervicarpa*) and to the migratory bird Demoiselle crane (*Anthropoides virgo*). A similar study by Deb *et al.* (1997) has shown that a number of local bird species find refuge exclusively in relict SGs of West Bengal. Many SGs in Goa shelter rare snake species such as Golden Vine snakes and other animals like Shield tails, flying lizards, Dreco, etc.

Storehouse of Biodiversity (Pls. 32-34)

In this section an attempt has been made to compile published inventories of floral and faunal diversity observed in SGs of the country. Unlike numerous cultural studies that have covered various dimensions of SGs, unfortunately only limited studies have documented biodiversity in the groves. Further, most of the studies are not comprehensive. Each scholar has focused often on certain components of the biodiversity in the groves they have studied. In respect of floral diversity emphasis has often been given only to the tree species. Except for a few studies, most of the scholars have hardly paid any attention to the animal diversity. Even where animals have been studied, focus has mostly been on the birds.

In table 26, readily available data on plant and animal diversity found in SGs of seven States of the country have been presented. Despite the limited nature of the data, it is evident from the table that rich biodiversity occurs in the SGs. Altogether 2767 species of plants have been recorded in the groves of seven States.

In order to facilitate scholars to undertake further comparative analytical studies in respect of biodiversity occurring in SGs in different parts of the country, in Appendices 1 to 9 detailed inventories of species together with families and wherever available other details such as habit and status have been presented for the seven States in the country for which summary data are given in table 26.

Many SGs constitute pristine vegetation, and are particularly rich in trees and associate groups of organisms, like epiphytes, amphibia, reptiles, birds, butterflies, etc.

A number of studies have emphasized that many SGs are climax forests, and probably constitute the only representative of near-natural vegetation in many parts of India. Such island of climax vegetation amidst a degraded landscape can be seen in many parts of the Western Ghats, Koraput and Kalahandi districts of Orissa and south-west Bengal.

Several studies have shown that many groves in Meghalaya (Tiwari *et al.*, 1998), Kerala (Chandrashekara and Sankar, 1998), Maharashtra (Gadgil and Vartak, 1976), Himachal Pradesh (Singh *et al.*, 1998) and Goa harbour rich floral and faunal biodiversity. Pushpangadan *et al.* (1998) demonstrated that the biological spectrum of groves in Kerala closely resembles the typical spectrum of tropical forest biodiversity. For example, the SGs occupying only 1.4 sq. km contained 722 species of angiosperm, compared with 960 species occurring in 90 sq. km of the Silent valley forest. *nirankarachi Rai* SG in Goa is abode of rare medicinal plants. Achar and Naik (2006) reports that SGs in Dakhshina Kannada and Udupi district of Karnataka are veritable sanctuary of flora and fauna and may be considered as biodiversity hotspots. 294 species of flowering plants, 22 species of mammals, 55 species of birds, 18 species of reptiles have been recorded in 1111 SGs of just 15 villages.

Sacred groves, in general, act as a nursery and storehouse of many of the ayurvedic, tribal and folk medicines. Species not under any immediate risk of extinction, if preserved in SGs, may have great potential of diverse uses in the future. The SGs may also serve to preserve genotypes which may be useful in forest tree-breeding programmes.

The sacred forests are also of great forestry interest as indicators of the natural productivity of the region. Ecologically valuable species like *Albizia lebbeck* and *Ficus glomerata*, which conserve high amount of nitrogen, phosphorous, magnesium and calcium in their leaves, are found in several SGs of Manipur. Keystone species that contribute to the maintenance and enhancement of biodiversity are also species that are socially valued by local communities for cultural or religious reasons, and often found in SGs. In *orans* of Rajasthan, the khejari (*Prosopis cineraria*) is a keystone species, inseparably linked to the survival of many other species, and occupies a special position in Rajasthani culture.

Table 26. Inventories of plant and animal spices reported in sacred groves.

Sl. No.	State	No. plant species	No. animal species	Fungi	References
1.	Andhra Pradesh	118			WWF – Andhra Pradesh, 1996
2.	Karnataka (1)		86	163	Bhagwat *et al.*, 2005
	(2)	291			Gokhale, 2005
	(3)	294	95		Achar and Naik, 2006
3.	Kerala	139	220		Sashikumar, 2005 Subramanian *et al.*, 2005
4.	Maharashtra	1040			Deshmukh, 1999
5.	Manipur	90			Khumbongmayum *et al.*, 2005
6.	Meghalaya	416			Tiwari *et al.*, 1999
7.	Tamil Nadu	216			Sukumaran *et al.*, 2005 Amrithalingam, 2005

As shown in Fig. 19 the species checklist (SG-1) and the list of species based on the quadrat sampling (SG-2) was compared with the species found in other management regimes in Siddapur taluk of Uttara Kannada district of Karnataka for various species attributes such as timber, RET (Rare, Endemic and Threatened), NTFP (Non Timber Forest Produce), endemic and evergreen species. Almost 80% of the species in the SGs can be considered as "important" species because these are evergreen, endemic and RET species. There is a overlap of species between endemic and evergreen species. Nearly 25% species are evergreen in SGs and almost 30% of the total species are endemic in SGs (Gokhale, 2002).

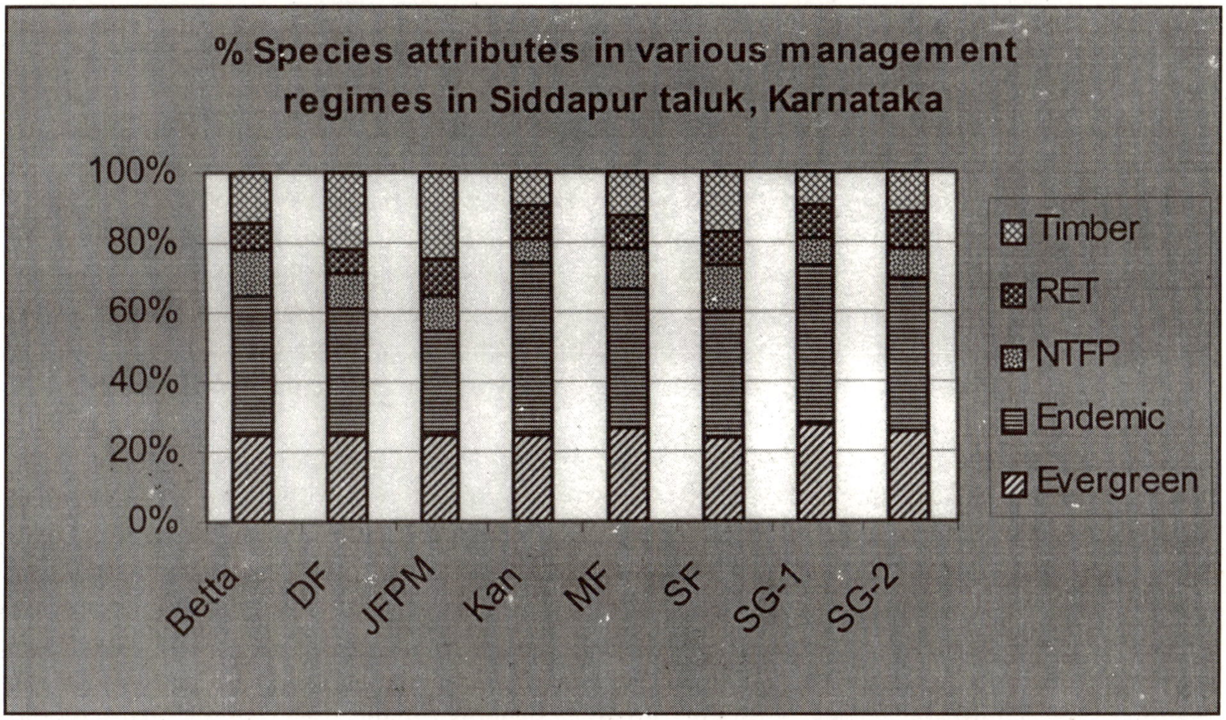

Fig. 19. Species attributes in various management regimes in Siddapur taluk, Karnataka (Gokhle, 2002).

2.2 ECOLOGICAL SERVICES

Some of the important ecological services provided by the SGs that have been reported in the literature are summarized below.

Recharge of Aquifers (Pls. 35 & 36)

Many SGs hold water resource in the form of springs, ponds, lakes, streams or rivers. Not only that, but the vegetative mass of the grove itself retains water, soaking it up like a sponge during wet periods and releasing it slowly in times of drought. It is evident that one of the important ecological roles of these groves is to provide a more dependable source of water for the organisms living in and around the SGs (Puspangadan *et al.*, 1998). The ponds and streams adjoining the groves are often perennial and in some cases, act as the last resorts to many of the animals and birds for their water requirements, especially during dry seasons. Another function may be to reduce the incidence and intensity of forest fire, at least in some climates. In addition, transpiration from the SGs vegetation would increase atmospheric humidity and reduce temperature in the immediate vicinity and produce a more favourable microclimate for many organisms (Khiewtam and Ramakrishnan, 1989).

Soil Conservation and in Nutrient Cycling (Pls. 37 & 38)

As an ecosystem, the environmental significance of the sacred groves lies in their stellar role in soil and water conservation, besides preserving the rich and diverse biological wealth. The *Mawsmai* sacred groves in the Cherrapunji ecosystem experience very high rainfall and with rapid litter decomposition rate, comparable to lower montane rainforests elsewhere, nutrient release rate in these groves is very high. The soil itself has little nutrient to offer to support a large biomass of the sacred grove. The fine root mat developed on the surface layers of the soil is important for supporting the large above ground biomass and for tight cycling of nutrients. The nutrients, released from the decomposing litter, is short circuited back into living biomass through surface root mat even before the nutrients could leach out. The sharp boundary between these sacred groves and the surrounding balded landscape indicates that the fragile system is never to recover (Khiewtam and Ramakrishnan, 1989). When forest litter is allowed to accumulate, organic material builds the soil and is returned to the biomass of the standing forest. In the process, many micro-organisms, invertebrates, fungi, etc. flourish and a vast array of species, not hitherto indigenous to the groves, may also colonies and thrive. Deforestation is usually found to accelerate the local extinction of species, and along with the associated micro-organisms, ultimately this paves the way for the ecological degradation of the sacred grove.

The humid sub-tropical forests in Cherrapunji in Meghalaya in northeast India have developed highly leached nutrient deficient soils and are, therefore, very fragile. This extremely fragile ecosystem suffered deforestation largely due to the practice of shifting agriculture and is now represented only by a relict sacred grove forest at *Mawsmai*, protected by the local Khasi tribe for religious/cultural reasons.

All of these factors indicate that the preservation of sacred groves is of key importance in maintaining biodiversity, the continuity of evolutionary process and the comprehensive health of a landscape. They provide greater benefits than their small size would otherwise indicate.

3

THREATS

This ancient and widespread institution, as revealed by several studies, shows signs of weakening in terms of both cultural and biological integrity in many parts of the country. The nature and extent of threats and pressures are often region and even grove-specific (Pls. 39-44). The magnitude of these threats therefore varies from region to region as well as from one type of grove to another. In this chapter we summarize the nature of threats reported in the literature. The reported threats can be grouped under the following heads, and contain only illustrative examples rather than complete enumeration.

Commercial Forestry: Over the past two centuries, in many parts of the country the local people have lost their customary rights of forest management to the government. Many sacred groves were destroyed under commercial forestry operations (Box 4).

> Box 4. The degradation of *kans* in Siddapur seem to have the following three major reasons:
>
> 1) ***Loss of rights of local people in Bombay Presidency*** The forest department established by British Government in the Bombay Presidency denied right of local people on their 'Sacred kan lands' (Chandran and Gadgil, 1993; Buchanan, 1870). This decision had very adverse impact on the local management of not only *kans* but also overall natural resources in Malnaad area.
> 2) ***Plantations of Acacia auriculiformis*** – During the period 1966 to 1985, selective falling was done in the evergreen *kan* forests in Siddapur taluk. The plantations of Acacia auriculiformis were done in place of clear-fell areas. People had dependence on these *kans* for several needs like dry leaves, several non-timber forest produces like pepper, wild nutmegs, etc. apart from the daily requirements like firewood. The plantations were unable to complete the needs of people. Obviously the earlier untouched *kans* became the only available resources to complete the daily requirements of the growing population.
>
> *contd.*

The village Kadkeri lost its *kans* to plantations of *Acacia auriculiformis*; hence, people of the village turned to the *kan* land of the neighbouring villages to complete their requirements.

3) ***Areca nut cultivation*** – The last decade of 20th century saw the huge market prices for the Areca nuts from the Malnaad region. It prompted even the marginal farmer to convert the paddy land or encroach the *kans* in the valleys for the cultivation of Areca nut without official *soppinabettas*. The vegetation in these encroached *kans* could be easily distinguished from undisturbed *kans* due to the selective protection to Hopea ponga.

Also in many *kans* selective protection has been given to *Garcinia gummi-gutta, G. morella* and *G.indica* due to the economic value; especially to the first species in last few years (Gokhale, 2002).

Development Projects: Some of the sacred groves that fell under government vested lands were destroyed when townships grew. Railways and highways have also taken their toll of many sacred groves. Others were flooded by big dam projects (Box 5).

Box 5. Loss of sacred groves due to Panshet dam in Maharashtra

Pressures for alternative uses from outside the local community may also affect sacred sites due to government intervention. These include construction of reservoirs for hydroelectric or irrigation projects, leading to submergence of lands, including sacred groves. A large number of sacred groves have thus submerged under the Panshet dam west of Pune city (Velhe taluk, Pune district, Maharashtra). Many other sacred groves that remained above the submersion zone were cut down by farmers whose cultivated lands were submerged and who expected to be settled in alternative sites several kilometers away (Gadgil and Vartak, 1976). Similarly in Mayurbhanj district of Orissa, Subarnarekha Irrigation Project has destroyed about 62 'Jahiras' sacred groves recently. The main canal of the project is also going to threaten many more lahiras (Gokhale *et al.*, 1998).

Shift in Belief System: In some cases, conversion to other religions has resulted in the degradation of sacred groves. The erection of temples in the sacred groves have often reduced the vegetation cover in the groves. Below is given an account of the status of SGs in Meghalaya, the primary region for the degradation of the SGs being change in religion.

STATUS OF SACERD GROVES OF MEGHALAYA

Tiwari *et al.* (1999) studied the status of 56 sacred groves in Meghalaya. They were categorized into four broad classes depending upon their canopy cover. Sacred groves having 100% canopy cover were categorized as undisturbed groves (Table 27), and those having canopy cover more than 40% but less than 100% were classified as dense groves (Table 28). The sacred groves with canopy cover more than 10% but less than 40% were categorized as sparse groves (Table 29) and those having canopy cover less than 10% are included in open category (Table 30).

Out of 56 sacred groves studied, 12.5% were undisturbed, 25% were dense, 20% were sparse and as much as 42.5% were in the open category.

Pl. 39. Monoculture plantations.

Pl. 40. Sanskritisation.

Pl. 41. Development work.

Pl. 42. Tree falling in Karnataka.

Pl. 43. Pilgrimage

Pl. 44. Over exploitation.

When calculated on the basis of area it was found that out of the total area of 10,511.7 ha under sacred forests, 138.1 ha area which constitutes a little over 1 % of the total, is still undisturbed and traditional rituals are still performed in accordance with the customary belief. The sacred grove of Mawphlang in East Khasi Hills district and sacred groves at Raliang in Jaintia Hills district are the examples of this category. Another 4,420 ha of sacred groves are under dense category and it constitutes about 42% of the total area. Here too, the rituals are performed but not as rigidly as in the first category. Sparse sacred groves covering an area of 2,765 ha constitute 26% of the total area. This type of sacred groves was mainly found in West Khasi Hills district and Ri Bhoi district. The open category of sacred groves cover 3,188 ha area, which is 30% of the total area under sacred groves. Tree canopy in this type of grove is discontinuous and at times trees are almost absent. Only a few intermittent old-growth trees are found in such groves as representatives of the past thick canopied vegetation that might have been in existence on the same habitats when the religious beliefs were stronger and biotic pressure on these sacred forests was minimal.

In Table 31 degree of disturbance in SGs of Semiliguda block is given. Over 64% of groves show medium to high levels of disturbance.

Table 27. List of undisturbed (canopy 100%) sacred groves studied.

Sl.No.	Sacred grove	Area (ha)
1.	Law Lyngdoh, Mawphlang	75
2.	Blai law, Raliang	0.1
3.	Poh Puja Ka Patti, Raliang	4
4.	Poh Moorang, Raliang	20
5.	Ka Pun Lyngdoh, Raliang	15
6.	Lyngdoh Lawlieng, Sohra rim	20
7.	Umkatnit, Diengksiar	4
	Total	**138.1**

Source: Tiwari *et al.* (1999).

Table 28. List of dense (canopy more than 40% but less than 100%) sacred groves studied.

Sl. No.	Sacred grove	Area (ha)
1.	Khlaw Byrsan, Shangpung	50
2.	Poh Lyngdoh, Shangpung	30
3.	Law Kyntang, Shangpung	400
4.	Trepale Jowai, Jowai	70
5.	Khloo Paiu Ram Pyrthai, Jowai	150
6.	Khloo Lyngdoh	90
7.	Khlaw Blai, Khliehriat	15
8.	Khlaw Suidnoh, Laitryngew	15

contd.

9.	Phyllaw U Blei, Mawsmai	600
10.	Lai Umtong, Umwai	400
11.	Diengkain, Umwai	400
12.	Mawthoh, Umwai	600
13.	Mawkyrngah, Umwai	1200
14.	Law Adong, Mawsmai	400
	Total	**4420**

Source: Tiwari *et al.* (1999).

Table 29. List of sparse (canopy more than 10% but less than 40%) sacred groves studied.

S.l No.	Sacred grove	Area (ha)
1	Pahampdem, Pahampdem	900
2	Nonglyngdoh, Nongkhrah	90
3	Pdengshnong, Cherrapunjee	400
4	Khliehshnong, Cherrapunjee	600
5	Lewthymmai, Cherrapunjee	200
6	Rangbaksaw, Cherrapunjee	100
7	Mawphalor Diengdoh, Cherrapunjee	100
8	Mawkadnia, Cherrapunjee	25
9	Wahsohmaw, Cherrapunjee	100
10	Lawmapsaptur, Sohra rim	50
11	Law Dymmiew, Sohra rim	200
	Total	**2765**

Source: Tiwari *et al.* (1999).

Table 30. List of open (canopy less than 10%) sacred groves studied.

Sl. No.	Sacred grove	Area (ha)
1	Kyllai Lyngngun, Mariam	80
2	Mokhain Sacred Grove, Jowai	45
3	U Law Lyngdoh, Nonglyngkien	90
4	U Lum Sanglia, Nonglyngkien	45
5	U Law Blei, Nonglyngkien	55
6	Law Lyngdoh, Nonglang	200
7	Law Kyntang, Mawlamwir	300
8	Law Kyntang, Mawther	600

contd.

9	Law Lyngdoh, Rangmaw	400
10	Law Kyntang, Mawthawiaw	100
11	Pohsurok, Cherrapunjee	150
12	Ingkhrong, Cherrapunjee	25
13	Siangkatlot, Cherrapunjee	200
14	Law Umiong, Cherrapunjee	100
15	Arwah, Cherrapunjee	200
16	Tih-u-jir-bah, Cherrapunjee	200
17	Ri-iaw Khaiti, Wahlong	20
18	Lum Mawryot, Wahlong	4
19	Niangdoh, Wahlong	4
20	Mawsawa, Mawsmai	100
21	Lawnongshim, Mawmih thied	100
22	Law-u-niang, Laitryngew	50
23	Madan Jadu, Laitryngew	20
24	Law ar liang, Laitryngew	100
	Total	**3188**

Source: Tiwari *et al.* (1999).

Sanskritisation: In many places, local folk deities have been, and continue to be, replaced with Hindu gods and goddesses. This has often resulted in reduction of the vegetation area in the groves.

Pilgrimage and Tourism: The integrity of many groves with regional or pan-Indian character, has suffered due to the influx of large number of pilgrims and tourists.

Removal of Biomass: In many sacred groves, removal of biomass and cattle grazing is permitted. Continuation of these practices over generations has resulted in the dwindling of the groves.

Table 31. Degree of disturbance in SGs of Semiliguda block.

Panchayat	**No. of villages**	**No. of SGs**	**Degree of Disturbances***		
			Nil	**Medium**	**High**
Kunduli	11	21	21	—	—
Sadam	20	33	2	—	27
Rajput	20	15	—	7	3
Subai	18	58	37	—	13
Dudhari	14	16	—	—	14
Guntaput	19	10	2	5	2

contd.

Dalaiguda	14	39	9	28	2
Mutal	18	11	—	10	1
Pakujola	16	33	26	5	2
Khudi	24	27	—	—	27
Renga	16	12	3	7	1
Hatguda	17	35	1	25	8
Kanti	13	13	3	—	5
Total	**220**	**322**	**104**	**87**	**105**
Percentage	—	—	35.14	29.39	35.47

* Information on degree of disturbances not available for 26 SGs.
Source: Malhotra *et al.* (1998).

Encroachment: Many instances are reported where the groves have been encroached by local communities and/or by various government line departments as well as by people migrating from outside.

Modernization and Market Forces: The most recent threat to sacred groves comes from the process of mordernisation. Local traditions are being challenged by westernised urban cultures. Modern education system fails to instill respect for local traditions. As a result, the institution of sacred groves is losing its cultural importance for the younger generation of local people. The spread of market economy has resulted in the denial and erosion of separate identities of local communities. The lure of short-term commercial gains has prompted destruction of traditional resource base, including the sacred groves (Boxes 6 and 7).

Box 6. Why sacred groves dwindled in eastern India

Distribution of sacred groves is the richest in the southern and the northeastern States (Gadgil and Vartak 1976, 1981; Khiewtam and Ramakrishnan, 1989; Tiwari *et al.*, 1998).

Large sacred groves from these States have been reported to represent climax vegetation and to contain rich floral biodiversity (Mohanan and Nair, 1981; Chandran *et al.*, 1998; Tiwari *et al.*, 1998).

In contrast, sacred groves seem to have the scarcest distribution in States where the British East India Company enforced a novel land use system for maximizing revenue extraction. The zamindars, created by the. 1793 Permanent Settlement Act of 1793, brought all "unproductive" woodlands under cultivation in order to maximize yield of land revenue, for the British East India Company. The oppression by zamindars and moneylenders forced the forest tribals of the western districts of Bengal to migrate en masse to neighbouring districts. Permanent Settlement thus marks a watershed in the ecological history of eastern V.P., Bengal, Orissa and Bihar, which sealed the fate of the pristine forest tracts including sacred groves. While there is no concrete documentary evidence, it can be summarized that at least some of the sacred groves were cleared for revenue generation.

contd.

The next phase of destruction of the sacred groves began with the passage of the 1876 Forest Act, which brought most of the pristine forests, including sacred groves (SGs), under the Forest Working Plans for extracting valuable timber, first for the Empire and then, after Independence, for the state government. Brandis (1897, p. 14-15) acknowledged the existence of SGs "in nearly all provinces" since pre-colonial ages. Most of them disappeared after the enclosure of forests by the state.

After Independence, the waves of urban-industrial development marked the third phase of destruction, which expunged most of the remnants of SGs from the village landscapes. Coal mines, steel plants, and big river projects took their toll on vast tracts of forest and tribal hinterlands, including their SGs.

In spite of these phases of destruction, numerous patches of SGs still exist in eastern India (Deb and Malhotra, 1997, 2001; Malhotra and Das, 1997). Deb *et al.* (1997) reported existence of "remnants of SG in almost every tribal village" in the southwestern districts of West Bengal, and showed that these SGs still served as important bird refugia. Although severely fragmented and decimated, these SGs clearly account for a large area under vegetation cover outside the State forests. An inventory of local land birds in five forest ranges of Medinipur district revealed a distinct preference of 18 birds for the sacred groves. Four of these birds were sighted exclusively in the sacred groves (Deb *et al.*, 1997).

Box 7. Killing of SGs for development: instances from West Bengal

The process of fragmentation of SGs is spectacularly instanced by an ancient SG at Chhandar village of Barjora block, Bankura district, where it has been criss-crossed by a busy road from Beliatore to Vishnupur town and a road to Bardhaman town. A small Kali temple with a clump of trees at the tri-juncture maintains the sanctity of the place. A century-old sprawling banyan (Ficus benghalensis) tree, and an old Saraca indica tree survive across from the temple. Along the road, about 10 m away from the temple, another couple of banyan trees constitute another small SG, where a newly-built Shiva shrine was recently built. The area covered by these tiny SGs around the tri-juncture of roads as well as the age of a banyan tree suggests the large area and rich species composition of the original grove.

In many places, local people reported that a SG had existed there before it was expunged by a governmental agency. All such cases related to roads, power transmission lines, dam, irrigation canal, or public buildings. A large SG in Baghmara village of Neturia block, for example, was destroyed in the 1960's by the National Thermal Power Corporation in a bid to extend power lines over the area: the SG was too dense to extend the line through it. The Panshet and Maithon dams of Damodar Valley Project submerged several SGs in dozens of villages upstream. In Garia village of Mayureswar-I block in Birbhum district, a small SG, along with the adjoining agricultural lands, was engulfed about 10 years back by a stone quarry.

contd.

Although SGs are by and large immune from extractive exploitation of plants and animals sheltered there, wood required for construction and repair of a temple is in some cases harvested from its grove. In the absence of regeneration or replacement of trees, timber removal, even at a low frequency, eventually leads to dwindling of the grove. In Bankura district, images of Shiva and other Hindu deities have been erected in a number of ancient SGs, and most of the trees in the groves have been cleared to make room for temple structures (Deb, 2003).

Fragmentation and Perforation: Many of the SGs are fragmented and perforated by roadways, extension of power lines, or reclaimed land for agriculture. Such fragmentation leads to loss of species, and disruption of ecological functions.

4

OPPORTUNITIES

Despite all the threats described in chapter 3, SGs are still alive in many parts of the country. Local people maintain these groves as a part of the culture. This fact indicates that there are ample opportunities for strengthening this institution. In this chapter are given details of some of the initiatives undertaken by various stakeholders in the country to revive and strengthen this multi-dimensional institution.

In some areas especially Manipur, the institution has in recent years been revived. Elsewhere, especially in Rajasthan, West Bengal, Chattisgarh and Jharkhand new groves have been established. The concept has been extended, especially in Karnataka to establish through plantations of *pavitra vana* (sacred forest); groves have also been established around temples and schools. In Kerala new partnerships have been developed among the grove trustees, NGOs and local people to protect the forest. In Madhya Pradesh, Forest Department, in collaboration with local people, has fenced sacred groves.

In Ratnagiri district, Maharashtra and Semiliguda block of Koraput district in Orissa, through the efforts of NGOs, networks among functionaries of SGs are being created. An increasing number of scientists from different disciplines are studying various aspects of the groves. A lot more opportunities are being created to provide fora inside and outside the country in the form of workshops, conferences, publications for exchange of views among a wide range of people. International agencies like UNESCO, the World Bank and Ford Foundation have included SGs in their agenda. The media is currently devoting a lot more space to this institution than before. The level of awareness among different sections of the population regarding the cultural and biological importance of SGs is increasing.

It is heartening to note that in the Environmental Education book for class 10 of ICSE and CBSE a section on SGs has been included (Box 8).

Below are given illustrative examples of revival of SGs from different parts of the country.

DUVARIA' SARAN

Kui village in Garu block of Palamau district is a new habitation separated from the neighbouring village. The village did not have "Duvaria sarna", which consists of mainly bamboo. The local priest identified the place for "Duvaria sarna". The new place was not having bamboo. But the priest planted a bamboo sapling at new place now considered as "Duvaria sarna" (Gokhale, 1998, unpublished).

Box 8. Sacred Groves

Some environment conservation practices have become part of the culture and were developed as a religious taboo or religious sanction. In almost all the cultures, some animal species and plant species are protected by the respective religions. Some mountains are considered sacred and are worshipped. The activity of deforestation and hunting is strictly protected by the local culture or religion. The Bible is filled with many such injunctions that govern the use of land and other resources which perform a conservation function. Many tribal people have emotional and spiritual relationship with nature. Therefore, they view rivers, mountains, forests, etc. as having spiritual essence. Such beliefs led to the establishment of certain groves which rural or tribal people worship and get spiritual protection.

In the polytheistic (that believe in several deities) the Earth is worshipped as a goddess and associated with the god of heaven as her spouse. That is why many people practise the ceremony of laying down the new born babies on earth.

Most of the mountains are worshipped in the world by the local people because of their that they lie close to sky and are treated as heavenly ladders. The mountains are considered as abode of gods. They are treated as the first land to appear on earth. In Zimbabwe pilgrimages are made to mountain sanctuaries that are considered as seats of gods. In India, the Vedic gods and their wives are believed to have their abodes in the Himalayas. Associating mountains with the religion make them sacred groves. Even the origins of earthquakes are associated with the deities beneath the ground.

Among the animals of magic and religion the wild animals of jungles, water animals and a few birds are significant. Tribes that worship the animals often do not hunt them. In several other tribes the animal that has been killed is also worshipped as a sense of respect because it fulfilled their needs.

In Ghana the enthronement of chief among many tribes is performed in the sacred forests. Some forests are protected as the burial place of their chiefs. Therefore, some communities like Sefwi Anwiaso, Atwereboanda, Kubi and many others are resisting mining in forest reserves.

The Japanese mountain deity yama-no-kami is demonstrated to have been a deity of the hunt, i.e. god of the forest, lord of the animals in ancient Japan.

Totemism is a belief in which humans are believed to have kinship with a totem. A mystical relationship is said to exist between an individual and a totem. A totem is normally an object, like an animal or plant that serves as the symbol of a kinship.

(Deepak *et al.*, 2006).

MIZORAM: SAFETY FORESTS IN MANIPUR AND MIZORAM

Some of the most interesting cases of such revival come from northeastern states like Manipur and Mizoram where the once extensive network of sacred groves was largely destroyed in 1950's on development of a transport network and a lucrative market for timber coupled to conversion to Christianity. But in this tract where shifting cultivation prevailed, some of the sacred groves encircling the settlements served as firebreaks during the slash and burn operations. In several villages inhabited by Gangte tribals of Churchandpur district of Manipur such revival of sacred groves encircling habitation has taken place. Since now the community has embraced Christianity, the groves are no longer being viewed as abodes of deities. In communication with outsiders they are called "forest reserves", or as Malhotra (1990) reports for Mizoram "safety forests". The term used for the grove in their own language, however, remains as before "Gamkhal".

Protection to these gamkhals continues to be organized through monitoring by local community members and implemented through sanctions for violation imposed by the community leaders. This is possible because in the more remote Gangte villages traditional community level organization is still functional. There is, however, a clear pattern in the spatial distribution of villages where such revival has occurred. In villages close to the market town of Churchandpur the whole land use pattern has changed with all land now belonging to individuals; terraced and bought under permanent cultivation of commercial crops like pineapple. In these villages the function of sacred groves as a firebreak is irrelevant, nor do these villages retain the community level organization capable of monitoring and enforcing protection. In such villages there has been no revival. The cases of revival become more frequent as one moves to the interior, away from the market town and roads, to settlements which continue the practice of shifting cultivation and retain more traditional forms of community organization.

Similarly in Mizoram, Mizo tribes had a system of keeping safety reserves around the habitation to prevent intrusion of fire while burning for shifting cultivation. Before Christianization of the area, a worship of deity was associated with these safety reserves. But the practice could continue in remote areas of Mizoram without sacred belief mainly due to the need. At the same time the state government order to maintain safety and supply reserves after regrouping of about 450 villages in 1960 (personal communication: Roy Burman) also might have helped the revival (Gokhale, 2000).

MEGHALAYA: KI LAW LYNGDOH SACRED GROVE

In case of Meghalaya, the chieftains and local priests were having a control over sacred forest called as "Ki Law Kyntang" and "Ki Law Lyngdoh" respectively. But Christianity wiped out the sacred beliefs and so to say the community protection. But at Cherrapunji the "Siem", i.e. chieftain and his ministry is maintaining the "Ki Law Kyntang" forest because of biodiversity and ecological concerns (Gokhale, 2000).

Many of the sacred groves have lost their religious significance (Tiwari *et al.*, 1998). However, in many villages, the headman with the concurrence of the village council has protected patches of forests and declared them as protected groves. Many such reserve forests exist in the region. Limited extraction of timber is permitted. Further, all the families in the village share the extracted timber. However, removal of dead biomass from these reserve forests is still strictly prohibited. Such a traditional restriction of removal of litter would help in maintaining soil fertility through nutrients released from it. Therefore, this practice has a conservatory role.

The trees cut down often are very old ones so that regeneration in these gaps helps in maintaining the stability of these forests. After removal of the older trees, re-vegetation using seeds from the forest is done intentionally by the villagers (Khiewtam and Ramakrishnan, 1989).

KESAR CHIRKAV PRACTICE IN RAJASTHAN

A case study carried out by Sevamandir of Udaipur, Rajasthan discusses the process of establishing a sacred protected area in 1994. The practice is called as Kesar Chirkav (sprinkling of saffron). It is based on traditional system of forest protection, wherein saffron is sprinkled on boundary of the forests and the falling of green wood is prohibited in the area. This tradition finds it origin from the temple of "Kesariyaji" a place of worship for the local communities living in Udaipur district. Kesariyaji is worshipped by offerings of saffron and when that saffron is sprinkled, it is believed that God has now come to reside in the trees and he would punish anyone indulging in cutting of green wood.

The villages Shyampura and Bada Bhilwara in Bichiwara panchayat of Jhadol block in Udaipur district were having Forest Protection Committees (FPCs) under Joint Forest Management Programme. In spite of having rules and regulations framed by Forest Protection Committees of both the villages, the forest was getting degraded day by day. Hence, they ultimately decided to sprinkle saffron after learning about it (Gandhi, 1994).

Villagers for the first time learnt about Kesar Chirkav when they interacted with workers and other village groups of Sevamandir working in this area. They had heard about Sagwara village where local people had sprinkled Kesar and protected their forests for about 40 years while the other forests in the vicinity became degraded. Sagwara village being situated nearer to Kesariyaji, the tradition has stayed alive and has been used by the villagers to protect their forests (Gandhi, 1994).

Villagers framed certain regulations for Kesar Chirkav which were to be strictly maintained. They decided that:

1. *The forests will be closed for a period of five years.*
2. *Taking an axe or any spiky tool to the forest is forbidden.*
3. *Collection of gum and musli (medicinal plant) is prohibited.*
4. *Collection of fruits, flowers, seeds, honey, grass, medicinal plants, leaves, dry wood is allowed.*
5. *The dry wood collected as fuelwood should be tied into a bundle using a rope, instead of the bark of a tree.*
6. *Open grazing is permitted in the forests, except in the Joint Forest Management area.*
7. *Four villagers will patrol the forest everyday; the duty will be rotated among all the households in the village. Those who fail to carry out their duty will have to pay fine as decided by the FPC.*

A villager from Bada Bhilwara went and collected saffron from Kesariyaji. Villagers contributed money to bring saffron. The part of the offered saffron was brought back to the village. Meanwhile, the local priest—Bhopa was contacted who went from house to house asking people to come for a ritual "Ratri Jagaran", a method of worship followed by the local people where all the villagers gather at one place at night and sing songs about the forests and their forefathers. While the singing is going on the spirit of goddess "Mataji" enters the priest and people then ask questions about their problems. That night at Ratri Jagran, when the spirit of goddess Mataji entered the body of the priest, gave blessing and said that the villagers were doing a good deed by sprinkling saffron and closing the forests for 5 years. Mataji, also said that she would punish anyone who would destroy the forest. After this, the villagers watched the picture made on Sagwara Kesar Chirkav (Gandhi, 1994). Next day morning villagers took the saffron to the Gopeshwar Mahadev temple located in Bichiwara and the priest offered the same to God. Then they mixed saffron in water and carried it in an earthen pot (kalash) to the meeting place.

Both the FPCs organized a big programme in Bichiwara with help from Sevamandir. People from both the villages, i.e. Shyampura and Bada Bhilwara and few from Sevamandir attended this function. Speaking on this occasion the President of Shyampura FPC said that Kesar Chirkav is a belief of the tribals. It is now upto the people of the two villages to uphold this belief. He narrated an incident happened in Sagwara where a woman who had collected green wood as fuelwood wandered in the forests the entire day. It was only when she left the fuelwood that she found her way back to the village.

The priest of Gopeshwar Mahadev temple said that Kesar, which had been offered to God, would now be sprinkled in the forests which will hence be the sacred abode of God and anyone damaging forests would be punished by Him. Chief executive of Sevamandir while addressing the people called this a historical day. The villagers had taken a step in accordance with their culture and religion. The most significant thing was that they were willing to practice self-discipline in order to protect their forests. It was decided that 6th April, i.e. the day of Kesar Chirkav would be celebrated every year as forest day and a fair would be held in Bichiwara.

Then came the sacred moment when the sound of beating drums the villagers moved towards the forests. Before starting Kesar Chirkav they paid homage to the idol of Mataji. The Bhopa who had accompanied the villagers went into a trance (the spirit of Mataji entered his body) and said that the forest would be closed for 7 years, thereby increasing the time period earlier decided by the people. Also before deciding to reopen the forests, they would have to consult her. The villagers then formed 4 groups and to the sound of beating drums and chanting of slogans, sprinkled saffron water along the boundaries of the forest. Thus, 700 hectares of forests came under the protection of Kesar (Gandhi, 1994).

PAVITRAVANAS IN KARNATAKA

Karnataka Forest Department (K.F.D) which in early 1970's, clear-fell large sacred groves, such as one at Mensi of 21 ha. to supply softwood to plywood industry, is having programmes of establishment of sacred groves called "Pavitravanas". In 1988, KFD established a Pavitravana called as "Sridharvana" in village Salkani of Sirsi Tahsil of district Uttara Kannada. The youth organization in the village took initiative in the process. They planted species used for ritual performances like *yajnas* on 1 ha land on the hill top. Now in the same village people are demanding for afforestation of other barren hill tops with useful species for NTFP, fuel, fodder, etc. The later proposal is getting support from villagers because the plantation will serve as wind break and the areca and coconut gardens will be saved from heavy winds.

In another experiment in the village Bakkal in Sirsi taluka of Uttara Kannada district, KFD has established a Pavitravana spread over 28 ha. Earlier KFD was planning to have an Acacia plantation on that area. But people opposed it; hence the Pavitravana was established with local support.

This Pavitravana is based on Hindu scriptures. As a result we find in this garden grown together *Acacia catechu* (Mrigashira star) and *Calotropis gigantea* (Shravana star) from dry open on rocky habitats in the company of evergreens *Artocarpus heterophylia* (Uttarashada star) and *Mesua ferrea* (Ashlesha star) and *Pinus longifolia* (Jyestha star). They are intermingled with various deciduous tree species like *Butea monosperma* (Hubba star) and *Spondias mangifera* (Hastha star). This synthetic sacred forest is then no substitute for natural vegetation. Nevertheless these groves can be of educative value as well as re-emphasize man's bonds with plants (Gokhale *et al.*, 1998).

INITIATIVES FOR STRENGTHENING SGs

There are numerous initiatives undertaken by different stakeholders for strengthening SGs in the country. Some of the intitaives have been described below.

CHHATTISGARH

Divisional Forest Officer of the Forest Department of the erstwhile Madhya Pradesh in the Jaspur Forest Division of Raigad district in Chhattisgarh, in response to local people and in collaboration with them has fenced 24 SGs to protect them from illegal falling of trees in the groves from outsiders (Pandey, 2000).

KARNATAKA

A Sacred Forest Festival (Devarakadu Habba) was organized to protect the sacred groves in Kodagu district of Karnataka in October, 2000. We produce here salient features of the festival. This festival and subsequent developments have great bearing on the management of SGs in Kodagu and perhaps elsewhere in the country.

The Sacred Forest Festival was held in October, 2000 at Kodava Samaj, Virajpet, Kodag district, Karnataka. It was organized jointly by:

1. *Forestry College, Ponnampet*
2. *Centre for Environmental Education, Coorg Field Office, Virajpet*
3. *Indira Gandhi Rashtriya Manav Sangrahalaya, Bhopal*
4. *Coorg Foundation, Pollibetta*
5. *Kodava Samaj, Virajpet and*
6. *Karnataka Forest Department, Kodagu Circle.*

The festival was attended by over 630 persons: 348 from 85 Devarakadu committees, 38 scientists, 12 government officials, 22 community leaders, 67 students, 109 artisans and 34 media persons.

Summary of Recommendations of the sacred forest festival:

1. *Devarakadu should not be considered as a means for generating revenue, but should be conserved as an important element in the bio-cultural landscape.*

2. *Existing temple committees and community leaders will initiate the process of forming a federation of the committees with the support of the working group on Devarakadu for conservation of the Devarakadu tradition.*
3. *The community leaders will ensure the furtherance of cultural traditions of the respective communities with respect to Devarakadus.*
4. *Forest department in consultation with temple committees will devise a mechanism for the joint management of Devarakadus.*
5. *Forestry College Ponnampet will take an initiative in establishing a working group involving the government, NGOs, community leaders, researchers, academicians and media.*

KERALA

The young and active members among the owners of the SN Puram Kavu have formed a committee to protect the sacred grove. In 1997, they organized a workshop involving local people and resource persons from outside for creating awareness about the functional role and importance of SGs. Local youth clubs, schools, forest departments, municipality and panchayats are now actively involved in the protection and management of the grove (Chandrashekhara and Sankar, 1998).

MAHARASHTRA

In Sagameshwar taluk of Ratnagiri district, Maharashtra, through the efforts of an NGO Applied Environmental Research Foundation, Pune, a network among the functionaries of a large number of SGs has been formed to protect the groves (Godbole *et al.*, 1998).

ORISSA

Struggle to protect Deomali—The Sacred Deomali Hill, the highest peak in the state of Orissa is located near the village of Barakotni, which is under Dudhari Gram Panchayat of Semiliguda Block, in Koraput district of Orissa. The height of the hill is 5585 feet above sea level. Since time immemorial this hill was revered as sacred by the indigenous communities particularly, the Kondh Adivasis.

The Adivasi goddess called "Nisani Munda" lives on the top of the hill. Most of the Adivasis festivals have been celebrated in this hill by the inhabitants, living far and near. The entire belts of the hill serve as a source of livelihood for the indigenous people. Besides, the forest products, the perennial streams serve as a source of irrigation for their agricultural fields.

The Government of Orissa recently declared the place to be developed as a tourist resort without consulting the people. The announcement was made in the month of October 2000 by the local Member of Legislative Assembly (MLA). The first visit to the area by the concern authorities took place on 22nd October 2000. Later, after the survey was completed, it was followed by road construction covering a distance of 4 kilometers, starting from Arlimula ghati towards the hill. An amount of Rs. 2 crores (20 millions) was allocated at the initial stage. More is to flow, yet. Also, they tried to convince the people by promising employment for 500 persons from the area. On the other hand, the indigenous communities are not ready to easily succumb to this kind of intrusion in their soil without a cause. As the first step to resist to such kind of illegal intrusion of the State the Adivasis called an emergency meeting in the month of November 2000. All together 6000 people from 60 villages participated in the meeting. The meeting took place at Barakotni village. During the meeting the consequences and implications that are likely to befall on the people as a result of the proposed tourist resort were discussed.

The details are given as follows:

1. *Ecology of the region will be disturbed.*
2. *Loss of valuable biodiversity species.*
3. *Cattle grazing and NTFP collection in the area will be prohibited.*
4. *Their economic sustenance will be at stake.*
5. *Their culture will be hampered.*
6. *Their socio-religion practices will be precarious.*
7. *The flow perennial streams would be affected due to water mining for the resort*
8. *Some villages will be displaced.*

Meanwhile, a committee known as "Deomali Banabasi Prakruti Surakshya Kuvi Jatu", was unanimously formed by the participants. From each village five persons consisting of 3 females and 2 males were nominated as members of the committee. Subsequently, the committee adopted resolutions, which are given below:

1. *To oppose any kind of development works that are against Adivasis interest implemented in the schedule area if the people are not consulted.*
2. *Not to sell off even a single piece of land, not withstanding any compensation of any kind including the common lands.*
3. *They will preserve their existing culture at any cost, no matter what may happen.*
4. *They will try any means to protect their land, water and forest.*

Till to date, the committee has taken a number of agitation to express their disapproval against the proposed plan of the government.

Firstly, an awareness meeting was organized to strengthen the unity among the people, protection of natural resources, rights on land, water, forest, and fight against injustice.

Secondly, Adivasi Rally Central Team meeting was held to review the survey conducted on the matter.

Thirdly, the construction of road was stopped indefinitely by the people. Another agitation is yet to follow if the government do not heed to their problems. One of the action that is likely to be taken is a public rally covering a distances of 30 kms.

It is high time that every concern individual takes note of their ceaseless sufferings. If we want humanity to prevail in this part of the world, one ought to speak up instead of being a mere spectator. A robust effort needs to be emphasized immediately if justice is to be achieved as granted under the Indian Constitution.

IN THE WORDS OF PEOPLE

Tikai Disari with innocence shares that, "we get everything what we need for our livelihood from the Deomali, Deomali is where our brother and sister live". Komuti Khillo says that, "Deomali is like a source of light, our ancestors lived, we live now and our children and the generations to come will live, we may come and go but Deomali will live forever providing

Pl. 45. Installation of a sacred grove of Arunachal Pradesh in IGRMS.

Pl. 46. Deities being carved out for replica of sacred grove from Kerala.

Pl. 47. Indoor exhibition at IGRMS, 2000.

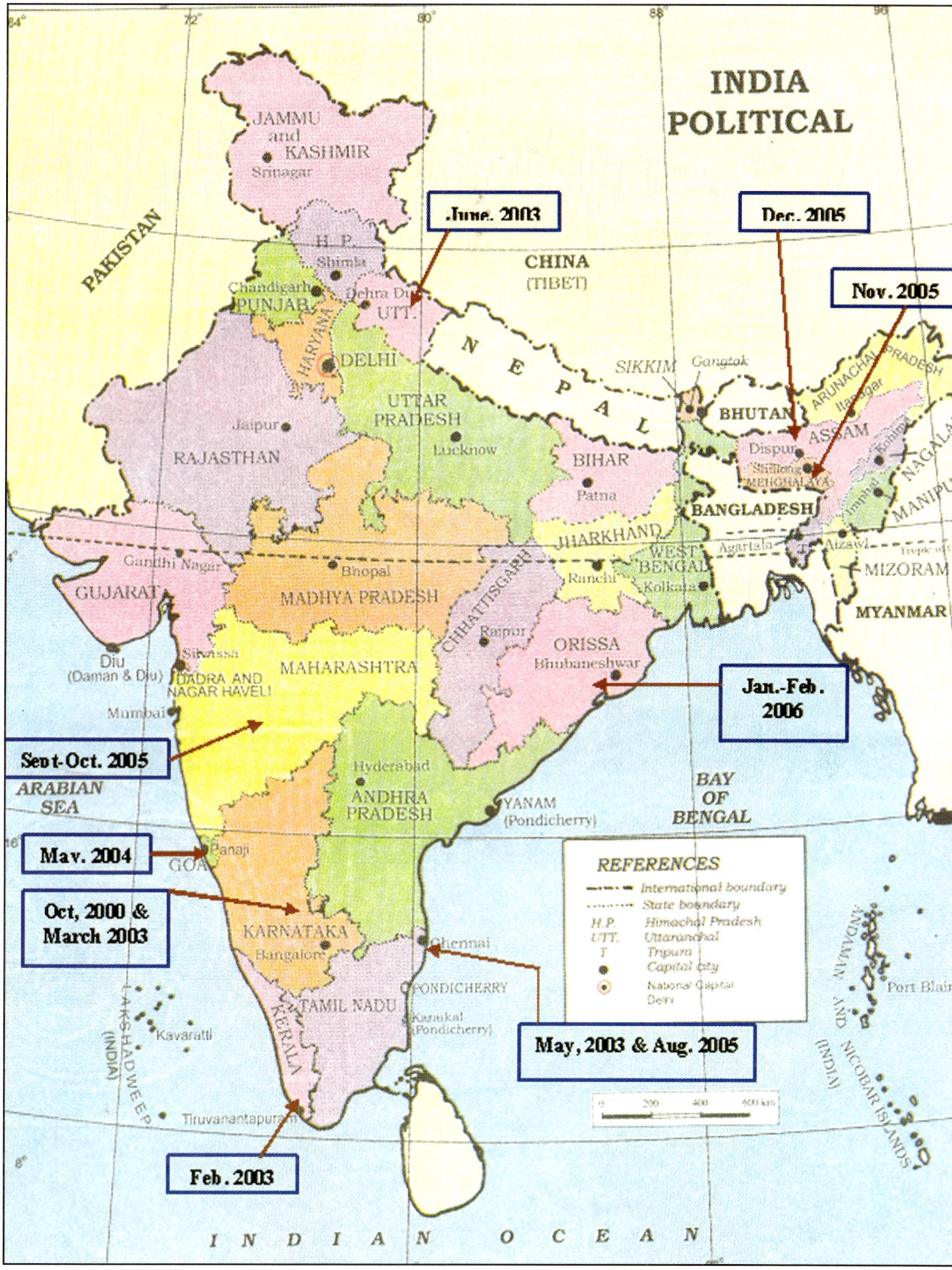

Fig. 20. Map of India showing the States where Travelling Exhibition was displayed.

Sacred Grove Festival, 2000

Interaction among participants.

*Ritual performance at *sarana*.

Lai Haraoba dance of Manipur.

Cultural performance, Maharashtra.

Cultural performance, Orissa.

Glimpses of Travelling Exhibition

Karnataka, 2000.

Tamil Nadu, 2005.

Meghalaya, 2005.

Glimpses of Travelling Exhibition

Maharashtra, 2005.

Orissa, 2006.

life and hope for every one, why should we disturb our sacred hill, what ever may happen, we will see that Deomali is not murdered."

An old man from Barakotni says, "The Deomali is a source not only for people but for animals, birds, and different species of plants take abode here, how can I see and keep quiet while Deomali is invaded."

Lodda Disari a young man with anger expresses, "Koraput a hill country was invaded by the kings of other communities, the White rulers, the non-adivasis after the independence and now in the name of Adivasi Development the State and the invisible enemies. Deomali is our life, our land, our water, our forests, our air, it is we who have to protect Deomali – our mother goddess. He continues to say that, after independence the Adivasis lost their right to their livelihood resources. Deomali does not belong to us but we belong to Deomali."

In conclusion, it is necessary to respect and understand the relationship between the nature and the Adivasis cannot be separated. Adivasis in Koraput have already experienced and suffer by the aggressive development for decades, it is the hope for the future that the Adivasis are the Communities of Hope, they may look underdeveloped but that is how they have kept the natural resources not only for themselves but also for the future generations—a lesson to learn is how we can live with less and not more and more! (William Stanley, personal communication, 2004).

RAJASTHAN

The groves of Rajasthan provide biodiversity refuges in an arid region; there the religious law of the Bishnois protects all khejari trees (*Prosopis cineraria*) and the blackbuck (*Antilope cervicapra*). A grove of 363 khejari was planted in 1978 in a village in honour of Amrita Devi and the other Bishnois who sacrificed their lives defending their trees in 1731 against the axe-men of the Maharaja of Jodhpur, who wanted the timber for a palace.

INITIATIVES UNDERTAKEN BY INDIRA GANDHI RASHTRIYA MANAV SANGRAHALAYA (IGRMS)

Realizing the cultural, biological and ecological importance of the SGs in our country and the threats faced by this ancient institution, the Indira Gandhi Rashtriya Manav Sangrahalaya (IGRMS), Bhopal has undertaken a number of activities in collaboration with many academic institutions and NGOs like the Indian Statistical Institute, Calcutta; Centre for Inter-disciplinary Studies, Barrackpore; Dept. of Anthropology, University of Pune; Indian Institute of Science, Banglore; Kerala Institute for Research and Training in Anthropology and Development Studies, Kozhikode; St. Joseph's College, Thiruchirapalli; Applied Environmental Research Foundation, Pune; Indian Institute of Forest Management, Bhopal; North Eastern Hill University, Shillong; World Wide Fund for Nature-India; The Energy Resources Institute; Orissa Development Action Forum (ODAF), Bhubanswar; WIDA, Koraput; RANWA, Pune; Forestry College, Poonampet, and many others.

These initiatives are a part of the IGRMS effort to put in place an ecological history exhibition at the museum in Bhopal; to demonstrate an important dimension of the natural resource management strategies adapted by different communities. Some of the initiatives and activities undertaken are:

(I) Installation of Replicas of SGs (Pls. 45 & 46)

The museum has installed in 1999, on its 200-acre campus at Bhopal replicas of SGs from Arunachal Pradesh, Chhattisgarh, Kerala, Maharashtra, Manipur, Meghalaya, Rajasthan, Tamil Nadu and West Bengal. Plants from groves of these States were planted in their respected replicas on IGRMS campus, after a very careful selection, taking into consideration the geo-climatic condition of Bhopal. For more details see Appendices 10 and 11.

These groves were ritually established, accompanied by dances and ceremonies performed by the local communities of the respective States. Installation of a SG from south Orissa is in progress.

These SG replicas are meant to serve as living nurseries of ancestral and community identity, purity and longevity in the community habitats.

(II) Indoor Exhibition (Pl. 47)

An indoor exhibition has been developed on SGs, using photographs, maps and charts, etc. depicting various aspects of SGs.

(III) Sacred Groves Festival

A Three-days Sacred Grove Festival was organized in January 2000, involving 185 participants from 15 States. The festival provided for the first time – a platform to different stakeholders like grass-roots level functionaries associated with SGs, foresters, scientists and media persons to discuss various aspects of the SGs including formation of a network of stakeholders, developing region/grove specific field based activities, publication of workshop proceedings, etc.

(IV) Publications on SGs

Some of the publications brought out by IGRMS in collaboration with other institutions are:

- Sacred Groves in India: An Overview, 2000 (Malhotra *et al.*, 2000a).
- Sacred Groves in India: A Travelling Exhibition, 2000 (Malhotra *et al.*, 2000b).
- Sacred Groves in India: An Annotated Bibliography, 2001 (Malhotra *et al.*, 2001a).
- Cultural and Ecological Dimensions of Sacred Groves in India, 2001 (Malhotra *et al.*, 2001b).
- A Field Report on Documentation of 33 Sacred Groves in Manipur, 2002 (IGRMS).

A number of brochures in different languages on replicas of SGs installed at IGRMS and travelling exhibition have been developed, published and widely distributed.

(V) Travelling Exhibition

A travelling exhibition has also been created during 1999–2000, using 67 panels of photographs and maps (Malhotra *et al.*, 2000b). The objective of this travelling exhibition is to interact with local people and different organizations to learn more about SGs of the country, and to strengthen the diverse SG-related local management practices and knowledge systems.

ABOUT THE EXHIBITS

The exhibition presents a set of pictures, maps and artifacts pertaining to various dimensions of sacred groves. They are arranged in accordance with the following themes:

- Concept
- Distribution
- Evolution
- Religious & Socio-cultural functions
- Ecosystem functions
- Threats
- Opportunities

Table 32 and Fig. 20 lists the places where Travelling exhibition has been displayed in different part of the country and gives details of the collaborating institution and the main activities undertaken. So far it has been displayed in Eight States involving Twenty Four locations. At each location the organizers made all efforts to involve school children, SG functionaries, local communities, forest and other government departments, academicians, etc. in the various activities undertaken.

Table No. 32. Travelling exhibition displayed in different parts of the country.

Display duration	State	Location	Collaborating Institution with IGRMS	Activities held
October 2000	Karnataka	Coorg	Forestry College and Kodava Samaj Poonampet	Exhibition, Workshop, Documentation, Cultural performances, Community meeting.
February 2003	Kerala	Quilon	District Administration and Deptt. of tourism	Exhibition, Artist meets.
February-March 2003	Karnataka	Mysore	IGRMS	Exhibition, Cultural performances.
April-May 2003	Tamil Nadu	Chennai	State Archaeology Museum	Exhibition, Meeting of stalk holders.
June 2003	Uttaranchal	Nainital	HSVS Nainital	Exhibition, Seminar.
May 2004	Goa	Panaji	Archaeological Survey of India Kala Academy	Exhibition, Documentation.
August 2005	Tamil Nadu	Chennai	Sharma Centre for Heritage Education and Children Garden School Society	Exhibition, Painting competition, Lecture on Environment.
September 2005	Maharashtra	Pune	RANWA	Exhibition, Film shows, Lecture on Environment.

contd.

Display duration	State	Location	Collaborating Institution with IGRMS	Activities held
September 2005	Maharashtra	Bhor	RANWA and Anant Rao Thopte college	Exhibition, Film shows, Documentation, Lecture on Environment.
September 2005	Maharashtra	Ajeevali	RANWA	Exhibition, Film shows, Documentation, Lecture on Environment, Painting competition.
October 2005	Maharashtra	Nasik	RANWA, Mahila Utkarsh Mandal and GDPS Sanstha	Exhibition, Film shows, Documentation, Lecture on Environment, Painting competition.
October 2005	Maharashtra	Malegoan	RANWA, Mahila Utkarsh Mandal and GDPS Sanstha	Exhibition, Film shows, Lecture on Environment.
November 2005	Meghalaya	Shillong	North Eastern Hill University	Exhibition, Workshop, Film shows.
November 2005	Meghalaya	Mawphalang	North Eastern Hill University	Exhibition, Film shows, Documentation, Workshop.
November 2005	Meghalaya	Jowai	North Eastern Hill University	Exhibition, Film shows, Documentation, Workshop.
December 2005	Assam	Guwahati	S.S. Kalashetram Society	Exhibition.
January 2006	Orissa	Semiliguda	IRDWSI & ODAF	Exhibition, Film shows, Documentation, Workshop.
January 2006	Orissa	Umerkote	SEDP & ODAF	Exhibition, Film shows, Documentation, Workshop.
January 2006	Orissa	Narela	SEDP & ODAF	Exhibition, Film shows, Documentation, Workshop.
January 2006	Orissa	Baliguda	Seva Bharati, TSRD & ODAF	Exhibition, Film shows, Documentation, Workshop.
February 2006	Orissa	Bhubaneswar	Gram Vikas, SVK & ODAF	Exhibition, Film shows.

contd.

Display duration	State	Location	Collaborating Institution with IGRMS	Activities held
February 2006	Orissa	Chakapal	PIPAR & ODAF	Exhibition, Documentation, Workshop, Oath taking ceremony.
February 2006	Orissa	Pllahara	SEDP & ODAF	Exhibition, Workshop, Oath taking ceremony.
February 2006	Orissa	Rasgovindpur	ACM & ODAF	Exhibition, Documentation, Workshop, Oath taking ceremony.

FUTURE STRATEGY AND ACTION PLAN

Under the coordinatorship of Kailash C. Malhotra, a Thematic Group on Culture and Biodiversity was constituted with Mr. Feisal Alkazi, Ms. Seema Bhatt, Dr. Debal Deb, Mr. Yogesh Gokhale, Dr. Tiplut Nongbri, Dr. D.N. Pandey, and Shri Shekhar Pathak as members. The group prepared a report entitled "Culture and Biodiversity" (Malhotra, 2003). It was prepared under National Biodiversity Strategy and Action Plan, executed by Ministry of Environment and Forests (Government of India), technical implementation by Technical and Policy Core Group coordinated by Kalpavriksh, and administrative coordination by Biotech Consortium India Ltd., funded by Global Environment Facility through United Nations Development Programme. The group made following suggestions in respect of strengthening the SGs in the country.

1. *It is recommended that an inventory of sacred groves should be prepared urgently for all the States in the country. The inventory among other aspects should include location, area under the grove, ownership and management, cultural and biological dimensions, nature and extent of degradation and nature and extent of threats.*

Action: The MoEF is best suited to undertake this task. All state forest departments should be advised to prepare such inventories in their respective states. In view of the multi-dimensional nature of SGs, a multi-disciplinary team needs to be set up. The institutions that could contribute significantly are Anthropological, Botanical and Zoological Surveys of Government of India. Besides state level NGOs, leading colleges/schools and Panchayati Raj Institutions may also be involved in this process.

2. *It is recommended that efforts should be made to map the nature and extent of vegetation cover in the SGs through out the country.*

Action: The Forest Survey of India should be advised to develop suitable methodologies for mapping the vegetation cover in the SGs. For ground truthing support from a number of institutes, NGOs and communities currently working on biodiversity related issues could be elicited.

3. *In absence of a policy on SGs, it is recommended that the MoEF develop a policy document on SGs. In this context it may be noted that in the document—National Policy and Macro-level Strategy on biodiversity - The MoEF, GOI, 1999 under section 1.4 Approach, item vii (pp. 13) writes "Sacred groves are the rich heritage of India. Occuring in various parts of the country sacred groves harbour ecosystems at pristine level. These would be treated as special areas deserving full protection and conservation".*

Action: MoEF may constitute a Working Group for this purpose involving forest departments, environmental lawyers, anthropologists, ecologists and representatives of Panchayati Raj institutions and communities. Experience learnt in Kodagu will be of immense help in this regard.

4. *There are many groves that face threats, internal as well as external. It is recommended that in such cases campaigns should be undertaken to strengthen the SGs. The campaign could be in the form of yatras, exhibitions, workshops, printed literature, etc. especially aimed at people who live in the vicinity of the SGs who may be made aware of the ecological functions performed by the SG and motivated to protect them.*

Action: The existing networks of NGOs, functionaries of SGs and academicians could be entrusted with this responsibility. The travelling exhibition on SGs and several publications on SGs prepared by Indira Gandhi Rashtriya Manav Sangrahalaya, Bhopal could be used effectively for this purpose. The experience learnt in Kodagu as described earlier could be widely shared with such networks, institutions and individuals.

APPENDICES

APPENDIX 1. SPECIES DIVERSITY FOUND IN SACRED GROVES OF ANDHRA PRADESH (AFTER WWF-ANDHRA PRADESH, 1996).

Sl. No.	NAME OF PLANTS
1.	*Adhatoda vasica*
2.	*Asparagus racemosus*
3.	*Abutilon indicum*
4.	*Achyranthes aspera*
5.	*Actionopteris dichotoma*
6.	*Adina cordifolia*
7.	*Aegle marmelos*
8.	*Aerva lanata*
9.	*Ailanthus excelsa*
10.	*Alangium salvifolium*
11.	*Albizia sikharamensis*
12.	*Andrographis paniculata*
13.	*Argyreia nervosa*
14.	*Azadirachta indica*
15.	*Boswellia ovalifoliata*
16.	*Boswellia serrata*
17.	*Bupleurum andhricum*
18.	*Butea monosperma*
19.	*Caesalpinia bonduc*
20.	*Cajanus cajanifolia*
21.	*Calotropis gigantia*
22.	*Cardiospermum halicacabum*
23.	*Cassia auriculata*
24.	*Cassytha filiformis*
25.	*Catharanthus roseus*
26.	*Chloroxylon sweitenia*
27.	*Cissampelos pareira*
28.	*Cissus vitiginea*
29.	*Citrus medica*
30.	*Clematis gouriana*
31.	*Clerodendron inerme*
32.	*Clitorea ternatea*

Sl. No.	NAME OF PLANTS
33.	*Cocculus hirsutus*
34.	*Colebrookea oppositifolia*
35	*Commiphora caudate*
36.	*Costus speciosus*
37.	*Crataeva magna*
38.	*Crotalaria paniculata*
39.	*Curculigo orchioides*
40.	*Curcuma amarissima*
41.	*Cyathea gigantean*
42.	*Cycas beddomei*
43.	*Cymbopogon flexuosus*
44.	*Datura stramonium*
45.	*Dillenia pentagyna*
46.	*Dioscorea glabra*
47.	*Drosera burmanii*
48.	*Eclipta prostrate*
49.	*Ensete glaucum*
50.	*Eriolaena lushingtonii*
51.	*Erythroxylon monogynum*
52.	*Euphorbia hirta*
53.	*Garuga pinnata*
54.	*Gloriosa superba*
55.	*Gymneme sylvestre*
56.	*Helicteres isora*
57.	*Holarrhena antidysenterica*
58.	*Hybanthus enuaespermus*
59.	*Kalanchoe cherukondensis*
60.	*Lecuas aspera*
61.	*Limonia acidissima*
62.	*Ocimum tenuiflorum*
63.	*Urena lobata*
64.	*Vanilla wightiana*
65.	*Mallotus philippensis*
66.	*Phyllanthus amarus*
67.	*Vrginea nagarjunae*
68.	*Mimosa prainiana*
69.	*Pimpinella tirupatiensis*
70.	*Woodfordia fruticosa*
71.	*Moringa concanensis*
72.	*Musa Rosacea*

Sl. No.	NAME OF PLANTS
73.	*Prosopis cineraria*
74.	*Pterocarpus marsupium*
75.	*Randia dumetorum*
76.	*Rauvolfia sarpentina*
77.	*Sanseveria roxburghiana*
78.	*Scaevola taccada*
79.	*Semecarpus anacardium*
80.	*Solanum nigrum*
81.	*Sphaeranthus indicus*
82.	*Stychnos nuxvomica*
83.	*Syzygium cumini*
84.	*Terminalia arjuna*
85.	*Terminalia chebula*
86.	*Thalictrum foliolusum*
87.	*Trianthema decandra*
88.	*Tridax procumbens*
89.	*Tylophora asthmatica*
90.	*Leucas molissima*
91.	*Luffa acutangula*
92.	*Marsdenia volubilis*
93.	*Morinda tinctoria*
94.	*Murraya koenigi*
95.	*Oberonia falconeri*
96.	*Oxystema lanceolatus*
97.	*Phyllanthus emblica*
98.	*Pongamia pinnata*
99.	*Psilotum nudum*
100.	*Pterocarpus santalinus*
101.	*Rauvolfia canescens*
102.	*Rhizophora apiculata*
103.	*Sarcostemma acidum*
104.	*Scyphyphota hydrophillacea*
105.	*Shorea tumbaggaia*
106.	*Soymida febrifuga*
107.	*Sterculia urens*
108.	*Strychnos potatorum*
109.	*Tephrosia purpurea*
110.	*Terminalia bellirica*
111.	*Terminalia tomentosa*
112.	*Tinospora cordifolia*

Sl. No.	NAME OF PLANTS
113.	*Tribulus terrestris*
114.	*Triphasia reticulate*
115.	*Tylophora indica*
116.	*Yanda tissellata*
117.	*Vitex negundu*
118.	*Withania somnifera*

APPENDIX 2. SPECIES DIVERSITY FOUND IN SACRED GROVES OF KARNATAKA (AFTER GOKHALE, 2005).

Sl. No.	NAME OF PLANTS	FAMILY
1.	*Acacia auriculiformis* A. Cunn.	Fabaceae
2.	*Acacia concinna* (Willd.) DC.	Fabaceae
3.	*Acanthaceae spp.*	Acanthaceae
4.	*Acronychia laurifolia Bl.*	Rutaceae
5.	*Actinodaphne angustifolia* (Bl.) Nees	Lauraceae
6.	*Adhatoda zeylanica Medic*	Acanthaceae
7.	*Aegle marmelos Corr.*	Rutaceae
8.	*Aglaia elaegnoidea* (Juss.) *Benth var. bourdillonii* (Gamble) K.K.N. Nair	Meliaceae
9.	*Ailanthus triphysa* (Dennst.) Alston	Meliaceae
10.	*Alangium salvifolium var hexapetalum Wang.*	Alangiaceae
11.	*Albizzia chinensis*	Fabaceae
12.	*Albizzia procera Benth.*	Fabaceae
13.	*Allophylus cobbe* (L.) Raeuch.	Sapindaceae
14.	*Alseodaphne semicarpifolia Nees*	Lauraceae
15.	*Alstonia scholaris* (L.) R. Br.	Apocynaceae
16.	*Amorphophallus spp.*	Araceae
17.	*Anacardium occidentale L.*	Anacardiaceae
18.	*Ancistrocladus heyneana Wall. Ex Graham*	Ancistrocladaceae
19.	*Antidesma menasu Miq. Ex Tul.*	Euphorbiaceae
20.	*Apama siliquosa Lam.*	Aristolochiaceae
21.	*Aphanamyxis polystachya Parker*	Meliaceae
22.	*Aphanathe cuspidata* (Bl.) Plan.	Ulmaceae
23.	*Aporosa lindleyana Baill.*	Euphorbiaceae
24.	*Ardisia solanacea Roxb.*	Myrsinaceae
25.	*Areca catechue Linn.*	Arecaceae
26.	*Arisaema sp.*	Araceae
27.	*Artocarpus gomezianus Wall. Ex Trecul ssp. Zeylanicus Jarrete*	Moraceae
28.	*Artocarpus heterophyllus Lam.*	Moraceae
29.	*Artocarpus hirsuta Lamk.*	Moraceae
30.	*Asparagus racemosus Willd.*	Liliaceae

Sl. No.	NAME OF PLANTS	FAMILY
31.	*Atlantia racemosa Wt. & Arn.*	Rutaceae
32.	*Bambusa arundinacea* (Retz.) Roxb.	Poaceae
33.	*Bauhinia racemosa Lam.*	Fabaceae
34.	*Beilschmiedia dalzellii Kost.*	Lauraceae
35.	*Blachia denudata Benth.*	Euphorbiaceae
36.	*Blepharistema membranifolia* (Miq.) Ding Hou	Rhizophoraceae
37.	*Bombax ceiba L.*	Bombacaceae
38.	*Breynea patens* (Roxb.) Rolfe	Euphorbiaceae
39.	*Bridelia stipularis Bl.*	Euphorbiaceae
40.	*Buchnania lanzan Sprengel*	Anacardiaceae
41.	*Butea frondosa Roxb.*	Fabaceae
42.	*Calamus spp.*	Arecaceae
43.	*Callicarpa tomentosa* (l.) Murray	Verbenaceae
44.	*Calophyllum apetalum Willd.*	Clusiaceae
45.	*Calophyllum polyanthum Wall. Ex Choisy*	Clusiaceae
46.	*Calotropis gigantea* (L.) Dryand.	Asclepiadaceae
47.	*Calycopteris floribunda* (Roxb.) Poir.	Combretaceae
48.	*Canarium strictum Roxb.*	Burseraceae
49.	*Canthium angustifolium Roxb.*	Rubiaceae
50.	*Canthium dicoccum* (Gaertn.) Merr. Var umbellatum Wt.	Rubiaceae
51.	*Carallia brachiata* (Lour.) Merr.	Rhizophoraceae
52.	*Careya arborea Roxb.*	Lecythidaceae
53.	*Carissa carandas L.*	Apocynaceae
54.	*Carissa congesta Wt.*	Apocynaceae
55.	*Caryota urens L.*	Arecaceae
56.	*Cassia fistula L.*	Fabaceae
57.	Cassine glauca (Rottb.)	Celastraceae
58.	*Celtis cinnamomea Lindl.*	Ulmaceae
59.	*Celtis philippensis Decne. var philippensis*	Ulmaceae
60.	*Chasalia curviflora auct.*	Rubiaceae
61.	*Chrysophyllum lanceolatum* (Bl.) DC.	Sapotaceae
62.	*Chukrasia tabularis A. Juss.*	Lauraceae
63.	*Cinnamomum malabathrum* (Burm. f.)	Lauraceae
64.	*Cissus discolor Bl.*	Vitaceae
65.	*Clerodendron viscosum Vent.*	Verbenaceae
66.	*Colocacia spp.*	Araceae
67.	*Combretum ovalifolium Roxb.*	Combretaceae
68.	*Connarus ritchiei J. Hk.*	Connaraceae
69.	*Connarus wightii J. Hk.*	Connaraceae
70.	*Cryptocarya bourdillonii Gamble*	Lauraceae

Sl. No.	NAME OF PLANTS	FAMILY
71.	*Cryptocarya wightiana Thw.*	Lauraceae
72.	*Cucurbitacea spp*	Cucurbitaceae
73.	*Cucurbitacea spp-2*	Cucurbitaceae
74.	*Cucurbitacea spp-3*	Cucurbitaceae
75.	*Curcuma psuedomontana Graham*	Zingiberaceae
76.	*Cyclea peltata Kh. & Th.*	Menispermaceae
77.	*Dalbergia horrida* (Dennest.) Mab.	Fabaceae
78.	*Dalbergia latifolia Roxb.*	Fabaceae
79.	*Dalbergia species*	Fabaceae
80.	*Dalbergia sympathetica Nimmo*	Fabaceae
81.	Debregeasia longifolia (Burm.) Wedd.	Urticaceae
82.	*Derris scandens* (Roxb.) Benth.	Fabaceae
83.	*Dichapetalum gelonioides Engl.*	Dichapetalaceae
84.	*Dillenia pentagyana Roxb.*	Dilleniaceae
85.	*Dimocarpus longan Lour.*	Sapindaceae
86.	*Dioscoria spp*	Dioscoreaceae
87.	*Diospyros angustifolia* (Miq.) Kosterm.	Ebenaceae
88.	*Diospyros assimilis Bedd.*	Ebenaceae
89.	*Diospyros buxifolia* (Bl.) Hiern	Ebenaceae
90.	*Diospyros candolleana Wt.*	Ebenaceae
91.	*Diospyros crumenata Thw.*	Ebenaceae
92.	*Diospyros montana Roxb.*	Ebenaceae
93.	*Diospyros paniculata Dalz.*	Ebenaceae
94.	*Diospyros saldanhae Kosterm.*	Ebenaceae
95.	*Diospyros spp-1*	Ebenaceae
96.	*Diospyros spp-2*	Ebenaceae
97.	*Diploclisia glaucescence* (Bl.) Diels.	Menispermaceae
98.	*Dipterocarpus indicus Bedd.*	Dipterocarpaceae
99.	*Dryneria quercifolia* (L.) J. Smith	Drynariaceae
100.	*Drypetes malabarica* (Bedd.) A. Shaw	Euphorbiaceae
101.	*Dysoxylum malabaricum Bedd.*	Meliaceae
102.	*Elaegnus latifolia L.*	Elaeagnaceae
103.	*Elaeocarpus serratus L.*	Elaeocarpaceae
104.	*Elaeocarpus tuberculatus Roxb.*	Elaeocarpaceae
105.	*Embelia ribes Burm.*	Myrsinaceae
106.	*Emblica officinalis Gaertn.*	Euphorbiaceae
107.	*Entada pursaetha DC.*	Fabaceae
108.	*Erythrina srticta Roxb.*	Fabaceae
109.	*Eugenia jambos L.*	Myrtaceae
110.	*Eugenia macrocepala Duthie*	Myrtaceae

Sl. No.	NAME OF PLANTS	FAMILY
111.	*Euonymous indicus Heyne ex Wall.*	Celastraceae
112.	*Eupatorium odoratum L.*	Asteraceae
113.	*Evodia lunu-ankenda* (Gaertn.) Merr.	Rutaceae
114.	*Fagraea ceilanica Thunb.*	Loganiaceae
115.	*Ficus arnottiana* (Miq.) Miq.	Moraceae
116.	*Ficus asperrima Roxb.*	Moraceae
117.	*Ficus beddomei King*	Moraceae
118.	*Ficus benghalensis L.*	Moraceae
119.	*Ficus callosa Willd.*	Moraceae
120.	*Ficus hispida L.f.*	Moraceae
121.	*Ficus microcarpa L.f.*	Moraceae
122.	*Ficus mysorensis Roth*	Moraceae
123.	*Ficus nervosa Roth*	Moraceae
124.	*Ficus religiosa L.*	Moraceae
125.	*Ficus species*	Moraceae
126.	*Ficus tsjahela Burm.*	Moraceae
127.	*Flacourtia montana Graham*	Flacourtiaceae
128.	*Fluggea leucopyrus Willd.*	Euphorbiaceae
129.	*Garcinia gumi-gatta* (L.) Robson	Clusiaceae
130.	*Garcinia indica* (Thouras) Choisy	Clusiaceae
131.	*Garcinia morella* (Gaertn.) Desr.	Clusiaceae
132.	*Garcinia xanthochymus, Ander.*	Clusiaceae
133.	*Glochidion hohenackeri Bedd.*	Euphorbiaceae
134.	*Glochidion malabaricum Bedd.*	Euphorbiaceae
135.	*Glochidion spp*	Euphorbiaceae
136.	*Glochidion tomentosum Dalz.*	Euphorbiaceae
137.	*Glochidion velutinum Wt.*	Euphorbiaceae
138.	*Glycosmis pentaphyla* (Roxb.) DC.	Euphorbiaceae
139.	*Gmelina arborea Roxb.*	Verbenaceae
140.	*Gnetum ula Brong.*	Gnetaceae
141.	*Goniothalamus cardiopetalus J. Hk. & Thw.*	Annonaceae
142.	*Grewia spp-1*	Tiliaceae
143.	*Grewia tiliaefolia Vahl*	Tiliaceae
144.	*Gymnosporia rothiana* (Walp.) Lawson	Celastraceae
145.	*Haldinia cordifolia* (Roxb.) Ridsdale	Rubiaceae
146.	*Helicteres isora L.*	Sterculiaceae
147.	*Hemidesmus indicus* (L.) R. Br.	Asclepiadaceae
148.	*Hibiscus rosa-sinensis L.*	Malvaceae
149.	*Hippocratea grahami Wight*	Hippocrateaceae
150.	*Holarrhena antidysenterica* (Roth.) DC.	Apocynaceae

Sl. No.	NAME OF PLANTS	FAMILY
151.	*Holigarna ferruginea March.*	Anacardiaceae
152.	*Holligarna arnottiana J Hk.*	Anacardiaceae
153.	*Holligarna beddomei J. HK.*	Anacardiaceae
154.	*Hopea ponga* (Dennst.) Mabberly	Dipterocarpaceae
155.	*Hoya wightii Hk.*	Asclepiadaceae
156.	*Hulimajjige* (local)	
157.	*Hydnocarpus pentandra* (Buch - Ham.) Oken	Flacourtiaceae
158.	*Hymenodictyon excelsum Wall.*	Rubiaceae
159.	*Ixora brachiata Roxb.*	Rubiaceae
160.	*Ixora nigricans R. Br. Ex Wt. & Arn.*	Rubiaceae
161.	*Jasminum malabaricum Wt.*	Oleaceae
162.	*Knema attenuata* (J. Hk. & Thw.) Warb.	Myristicaceae
163.	*Lagerstroemia lanceolata Clarke*	Lythraceae
164.	*Lagerstroemia parviflora Roxb.*	Lythraceae
165.	*Lannea coromandelica* (Houtt.) Merr.	Anacardiaceae
166.	*Lantana camara L.*	Verbenaceae
167.	*Lasiosiphon eriocephalus* (Grah.) Decaisne	Thymeleaceae
168.	*Leea indica* (Burm.) Merr.	Leeaceae
169.	*Leptonychia moacurroides Bedd.*	Sterculiaceae
170.	*Linociera malabarica Don*	Oleaceae
171.	*Litsea chinensis Lam.*	Lauraceae
172.	*Litsea ghatica Saldanha*	Lauraceae
173.	*Litsea mysorensis Gamble*	Lauraceae
174.	*Litsea stocksii J. Hk. Var glabrescens J. Hk.*	Lauraceae
175.	*Lophopetalum wightianum Arn.*	Celastraceae
176.	*Loranthus capitellatus W. & A.*	Loranthaceae
177.	*Loranthus spp-1*	Loranthaceae
178.	*Loranthus wallichianus Schultes*	Loranthaceae
179.	*Luvanga sarmentosa* (Bl.) kurz	Rutaceae
180.	*Macaranga peltata* (Roxb.) Mueller	Euphorbiaceae
181.	*Madhuca indica Gmelin*	Sapotaceae
182.	*Madhuca neriifolia* (Moon.) Lam.	Sapotaceae
183.	*Maesa indica* (Roxb.) DC.	Myrsinaceae
184.	*Mallotus philippensis* (Lam.) Muell.	Euphorbiaceae
185.	*Mallotus stenanthus M. Arg.*	Euphorbiaceae
186.	*Mammea suriga* (Buch. - Ham. Ex Roxb.) Kosterm.	Clusicaeae
187.	*Mangifera indica L.*	Anacardiaceae
188.	*Margaritaria indica* (Dalz.) A. Shaw	Euphorbiaceae
189.	*Mastixia arborea (Wt.) Bedd.*	Cornaceae
190.	*Meiogyne pannosa* (Dalz.) Sinclair	Annonaceae

Sl. No.	NAME OF PLANTS	FAMILY
191.	*Melastoma malabathricum L.*	Melastomaceae
192.	*Melia azadirachta L.*	Meliaceae
193.	*Meliosma pinnata* (Roxb.) Walp.	Sabiaceae
194.	*Memecylon malabaricum* (Cl.) Cogn	Melastomaceae
195.	*Memecylon talbotianum Brandis*	Melastomaceae
196.	*Memecylon terminale Dalz.*	Melastomaceae
197.	*Mesua ferrea L.*	Clusicaeae
198	*Microcos paniculata Linn*	Tiliaceae
199.	*Milliusa totmentosa* (Roxb.) Sinclair	Annonaceae
200.	*Mimusops elengi L.*	Sapotaceae
201.	*Mitragyna parviflora* (Roxb.) Korth.	Rubiaceae
202.	*Modecca palmata Lam.*	Cucurbitaceae
203.	*Murraya koenigi Spr.*	Rutaceae
204.	*Mussaenda frondosa L.*	Rubiaceae
205.	*Myristica dactyloides Gaertn.*	Myristicaceae
206.	*Myristica malabarica Lam.*	Myristicaceae
207.	*Neolitsea zeylanica* (Nees) Gamble	Lauraceae
208.	*Nothapodytes foetida* (Wt.) Sleumer	Icacinaceae
209.	*Nothopegia colebrookiana Bl.*	Anacardiaceae
210.	*Nothopegia spp*	Anacardiaceae
211.	*Ochlandra spp*	Poaceae
212.	*Olea dioica Roxb.*	Oleaceae
213.	*Oroxylum indicum Vent.*	Bignoniaceae
214.	*Pajanalia longifolia* (Willd.) Schum.	Bignoniaceae
215.	*Pandanus species*	Pandanaceae
216.	*Paramignya monophylla Wt.*	Rutaceae
217.	*Persea macrantha* (Nees) Kosterm.	Lauraceae
218.	*Phoenix spp.*	Arecaceae
219.	*Phyllanthus sp.*	Euphorbiaceae
220.	*Pinanga dicksonii* (Roxb.) Scheffer	Arecaceae
221.	*Piper species*	Piperaceae
222.	*Pithecellobium monadelphum* (Roxb.) Kosterm.	Fabaceae
223.	*Pittosporum dasycaulon Miq.*	Pittosporaceae
224.	*Plumeria acutifolia poiret*	Apocynaceae
225.	*Pongamia pinnata* (L.) Pierre	Fabaceae
226.	*Pothos scandens L.*	Araceae
227.	*Psidium guajava L.*	Myrtaceae
228.	*Psychotria dalzelli Hk.*	Rubiaceae
229.	*Psychotria flavida Talbot*	Rubiaceae
230.	*Psychotria truncata Wall.*	Rubiaceae

Sl. No.	NAME OF PLANTS	FAMILY
231.	*Pterocarpus marsupium Roxb.*	Fabaceae
232.	*Pterospermum acerifolium Willd.*	Sterculiaceae
233.	*Pterospermum reticulatum Wt. & Arn.*	Sterculiaceae
234.	*Randia dumetorum* (Retz.) Poir.	Rubiaceae
235.	*Raphidophora laciniata* (Burm.) Merr.	Araliaceae
236.	*Rubia cordifolia L.*	Rubiaceae
237.	*Santalum album L.*	Santalaceae
238.	*Sapindus laurifolia Vahl*	Sapindaceae
239.	*Sapium insigne var.* malabaricum (Wt.) Hook. f.	Euphorbiaceae
240.	*Saraca asoca* (Roxb.) De Wilde	Fabaceae
241.	*Schefflera venulosa* (W. & A.) Harms	Araliaceae
242.	*Schleichera oleosa* (Lour.) Oken	Sapindaceae
243.	*Scolopia crenata* (W. & A.) Clos	Flacourtiaceae
244.	*Scutia myrtina* (Burm.) Kurz	Rhamnaceae
245.	*Semecarpus anacardium L.f.*	Anacardiaceae
246.	*Sida acuta Burm.*	Malvaceae
247.	*Smilax spp*	Smilacaceae
248.	*Spondias pinnata L.f.* (Kurz)	Anacardiaceae
249.	*Sterculia guttata Roxb.*	Sterculiaceae
250.	*Stereospermum personnatum* (Hassk.) Chatt.	Bignoniaceae
251.	*Streblus asper Lour.*	Moraceae
252.	*Strombosia ceylanica Gardn.*	Olacaceae
253.	*Strychnos colubrina L.*	Loganiaceae
254.	*Strychnos dalzelli Clarke*	Loganiaceae
255.	*Strychnos nux-vomica L.*	Loganiaceae
256.	*Strobilathes spp*	Acanthaceae
257.	*Symplocos macrocarpa Wt. Ex Cl. ssp. kanarana* (Talbot) Noot.	Symplocaceae
258.	*Symplocos racemosa Roxb. var. racemosa*	Symplocaceae
259.	*Syzygium caryophyllatum* (L.) Alston	Myrtaceae
260.	*Syzygium cumini* (L.) Skeels	Myrtaceae
261.	*Syzygium gardeneri Thw.*	Myrtaceae
262.	*Syzygium hemisphericum* (Walp.) Alston	Myrtaceae
263.	*Syzygium heyneanum* (Duthie) Wall. ex Gamble	Myrtaceae
264.	*Syzygium jambos* (L.) Alston	Myrtaceae
265.	*Syzygium laetum* (Buch. - Ham.) Gandhi	Myrtaceae
266.	*Tabernaemontana heyneana* Wall.	Apocynaceae
267.	*Terminalia arjuna* (DC.) Wt. & Arn.	Combretaceae
268.	*Terminalia bellirica* (Gaertner) Roxb.	Combretaceae
269.	*Terminalia chebula* (Gaertner) Retz.	Combretaceae

Sl. No.	NAME OF PLANTS	FAMILY
270.	*Terminalia crenulata* Roth.	Combretaceae
271.	*Terminalia paniculata* Roth.	Combretaceae
272.	*Thevetia peruviana* (Persoon) Schum.	Apocynaceae
273.	*Toddalia asiatica* (L.) Lam.	Rutaceae
274.	*Toona ciliata* Roemer	Meliaceae
275.	*Trema orientalis* (L.) Bl.	Ulmaceae
276.	*Trichilia connaroides* (W. & A.) Bent.	Meliaceae
277.	*Tylophora spp*	Asclepiadaceae
278.	*Unona species*	Annonaceae
279.	*Uvarium narum* (Dunal) Wt. & Arn.	Annonaceae
280.	*Vateria indica L.*	Dipterocarpaceae
281.	*Ventilago bombainsis Dalz.*	Rhamnaceae
282.	*Vitex altissima L.f.*	Lamiaceae
283.	*Vitex leucoxylon L.f.*	Lamiaceae
284.	*Vitex negundo L.*	Lamiaceae
285.	*Wrightia tinctoria R. Br.*	Apocynaceae
286.	*Xantolis tomentosa* (Roxb.) Raf.	Sapotaceae
287.	*Xylia xylocarpa* (Roxb.) Taub.	Fabaceae
288.	*Zanthoxylum ovalifolium Wt.*	Rutaceae
289.	*Zanthoxylum rhetsa* (Roxb.) DC.	Rutaceae
290.	*Zingiberacea spp*	Zingiberaceae
291.	*Zizyphus oenoplea Miller*	Rhamnaceae

APPENDIX 3. SPECIES DIVERSITY FOUND IN SACRED GROVES OF KERALA (AFTER SUBRAMANIAN *et al.*, 2005).

Sl. No.	NAME OF PLANTS	FAMILY
1.	*Abrus precatorius*	Fabaceae
2.	*Acampe praemorsa*	Orchidaceae
3.	*Adiantum caudatum*	Adiantaceae
4.	*Ageratum conyzoides*	Asteraceae
5.	*Alloteropsis cimicina*	Poaceae
6.	*Alstonia scholaris*	Apocyanaceae
7.	*Amorphophalus sylvaticus*	Araceae
8.	*Anacardium occidentale*	Anacardiaceae
9.	*Apluda mutica*	Poaceae
10.	*Artocarpus heterophyllus*	Moraceae
11.	*Artocarpus lakoocha*	Moraceae
12.	*Arylosia sp.*	Fabaceae
13.	*Asparagus racemosus*	Liliaceae
14.	*Bothriochloa pertusa*	Poaceae
15.	*Brachiaria reptans*	Poaceae
16.	*Bridelia retusa*	Euphorbiaceae
17.	*Bridelia scandens*	Euphorbiaceae
18.	*Calotropis gigantea*	Asclepiadaceae
19.	*Calycopteris floribunda*	Combretaceae
20.	*Canthium parviflQrum*	Rubiaceae
21.	*Carallia brachiata*	Rhizophoraceae
22.	*Caryota urells*	Arecaceae
23.	*Cassia fistula*	Fabaceae
24.	*Cassia mimosoides*	Fabaceae
25.	*Cassia tora*	Caesalpiniaceae
26.	*Cayratia trifolia*	Vitiaceae
27.	*Centella asiatica*	Apiaceae
28.	*Chasalia curviflora*	Rubiaceae
29.	*Cheilanthus jarinosa*	Adiataceae
30.	*Chromolaena odorata*	Asteraceae
31.	*Cinnamomum malabathrum*	Lauraceae
32.	*Cissus glauca*	Vitaceae

Sl. No.	NAME OF PLANTS	FAMILY
33.	*Cissus sp.*	Vitaceae
34.	*Cleome viscosa*	Capparidaceae
35.	*Clerodendrum viscosum*	Verbenaceae
36.	*Commelina nodiflora*	Commelinaceae
37.	*Connarus monocarpus*	Connaraceae
38.	*Connarus paniculatus*	Connaraceae
39.	*Costus speciosus*	Zingiberaceae
40.	*Crotalaria labernifolia*	Fabaceae
41.	*Cryptocoryne spiralis*	Araceae
42.	*Curculigo orchioides*	Liliaceae
43.	*Curcuma oligantha*	Zingiberaceae
44.	*Curcuma oligantha var.lutea*	Zingiberaceae
45.	*Cyanotis axillaris*	Commelinaceae
46.	*Cyathula prostrata*	Amaranthaceae
47.	*Cyclea peltata*	Menispermacee
48.	*Cynodon dactylon*	Poaceae
49.	*Cyperus rotundus*	Poaceae
50.	*Dactyloctenium aegyptium*	Poaceae
51.	*Dalbergia horrida*	Fabaceae
52.	*Desmodium triflorum*	Fabaceae
53.	*Desmodium triquetrum*	Fabaceae
54.	*Drynaria quercifolia*	Polipodiaceae
55.	*Echinochloa colonum*	Poaceae
56.	*Elephantopus scaber*	Asteraceae
57.	*Eleusine indica*	Poaceae
58.	*Emilia sonchifolia*	Asteraceae
59.	*Eragrostis tenella*	Poaceae
60.	*Eragrostis unioloides*	Poaceae
61.	*Eragrostis viscosa*	Poaceae
62.	Eriocaulon sp.	Eriocaulaceae
63.	*Erycibe paniculata*	Convolvulaceae
64.	*Erythrina indica*	Fabaceae
65.	*Euphorbia hirta*	Euphorbiaceae
66.	*Evolvulus alsinoides*	Con vol vulaceae
67.	*Evolvulus nummularius*	Convolvulaceae
68.	*Ficus benghalensis*	Moraceae
69.	*Ficus religiosa*	Moraceae
70.	*Garcinia sp.*	Clusiaceae
71.	*Gloriosa superba*	Liliaceae
72.	*Gnetum uia*	Gnetaceae

Sl. No.	NAME OF PLANTS	FAMILY
73.	*Hedyotis corymbosa*	Rubiaceae
74.	*Heteropogon contortus*	Poaceae
75.	*Hibiscus hispidissimus*	Malvaceae
76.	*Holigarna arnottiana*	Anacardiaceae
77.	*Hopea ponga*	Dipterocarpaceae
78.	*Hybanthus ennaespermus.*	Violaceae
79.	*Hydnocarpus pentandra*	Flacourtiaceae
80.	*Ichnocarpus frutescens*	Apocyanaceae
81.	*Isachne sp.*	Poaceae
82.	*Ischaemum indicum*	Poaceae
83.	*Ixora coccinia*	Rubiaceae
84.	*Lannea coromandelica*	Anacardiaceae
85.	*Laportea interupta*	Urticaceae
86.	*Leucas aspera*	Lamiaceae
87.	*Litsea glutinosa*	Lauraceae
88.	*Lygodium pinnatifidum*	Schizaeaceae
89.	*Macaranga indica*	Euphorbiaceae
90.	*Mangifera indica*	Anacardiaceae
91.	*Memecylon umbellatum*	Melastomaceae
92.	*Merremia tridentata*	Convolvulaceae
93.	*Mimosa pudica*	Fabaceae
94.	*Mimusops elengi*	Sapotaceae
95.	*Mucuna pruriens*	Fabaceae
96.	*Murdannia paniculata*	Commelinaceae
97.	*Mussaenda frondosa*	Rubiaceae
98.	*Naregamia alata*	Meliaceae
99.	*Ochna squarosa*	Ochnaceae
100.	*Oldenlandia auriculata*	Rubiaceae
101.	*Oplismenus burmannii*	Poaceae
102.	*Pavetta indica*	Rubiaceae
103.	*Pennisetum polystachyon*	Poaceae
104.	*Perotis indica*	Poaceae
105.	*Phyllanthus simplex*	Euphorbiaceae
106.	*Phyllanthus urinaria*	Euphorbiaceae
107.	*Plumeria rubra*	Apocyanaceae
108.	*Polygala elongata*	Polygalaceae
109.	*Pothos scandens*	Araceae
110.	*Pouzolzia indica*	Urticaceae
111.	*Premna latifolia*	Verbenaceae
112.	*Rauvolfia serpentina*	Apocyanaceae

Sl. No.	NAME OF PLANTS	FAMILY
113.	*Santalum album*	Santalaceae
114.	*Sapium insigne*	Euphorbiaceae
115.	*Scoparia dulcis*	Scrophulariaceae
116.	*Selaginella sp.*	Salaginellaceae
117.	*Setaria glauca*	Poaceae
118.	*Sida acuta*	Malvaceae
119.	*Sida cordifolia*	Malvaceae
120.	*Smilax zeylanica*	Liliaceae
121.	*Spermaccse hispida*	Rubiaceae
122.	*Stachytarpheta indica*	Verbenaceae
123.	*Strychnos nux-vomica*	Loganiaceae
124.	*Syzygium caryophyllatum*	Myrtaceae
125.	*Syzygium cumini*	Myrtaceae
126.	Tabernaemontana heyneana	Apocyanaceae
127.	*Tinospora cordifolia*	Menispermaceae
128.	*Toxocarpus sp.*	Asclepiadaceae
129.	*Tragia involucrata*	Euphorbiaceae
130.	*Trema orientalis*	Ulmaceae
131.	*Triumfetta rhomboidea*	Sterculiaceae
132.	*Urena lobata*	Malvaceae
133.	*Uvaria narum*	Annonaceae
134.	*Vateria indica*	Di pterocarpaceae
135.	*Vernonia cinerea*	Asteraceae
136.	*Zanthoxylum rhetsa*	Rutaceae
137.	*Zingiber zerumbet*	Zingiberaceae
138.	*Ziziphus oenoplia*	Rhamnaceae
139.	*Zornia gibbosa*	Fabaceae

APPENDIX 4. SPECIES DIVERSITY FOUND IN SACRED GROVES OF MAHARASHTRA (AFTER DESHMUKH, 1999).

T= Tree, S = Shrub, C = Climber, CS = Climbing shrub, Cl = Climber, H= Herb, E= Epiphyte, HG = Herb grass L = Liana, RET = Rare, endangered and threatened category

Sl. No.	NAME OF PLANTS	FAMILY	HABIT
1.	*Abelmoschus esculentus (L.) Moench.*	Malvaceae	S
2.	*Abelmoschus ficulneus (L.) Wall. Wt. & Am.*	Malvaceae	S
3.	*Abelmoschus manihot (L.) Medic.*	Malvaceae	S
4.	*Abrus precatorius* L.	Fabaceae	C
5.	*Abutilon persicum (Burm. f.) Merrill.*	Malvaceae	S
6.	*Acacia auriculiformis A. Cunn.*	Mimosaceae	T
7.	*Acacia catechu* Willd.	Mimosaceae	T
8.	*Acacia chundra* (Roxb.) Willd.	Mimosaceae	T
9.	*Acacia concinna* DC.	Mimosaceae	C
10.	*Acacia leucocephala Link.*	Mimosaceae	T
11.	*Acacia leucophloea* Willd.	Mimosaceae	T
12.	*Acacia nifotica* (L.) Del.	Mimosaceae	T
13.	*Acacia pennata* (L.) Willd.	Mimosaceae	T
14.	*Acacia sinuata* (Lour.) Merr.	Mimosaceae	T
15.	*Acacia suma* Buch.& Ham.	Mimosaceae	T
16.	*Acacia torta* (Roxb.) Craib.	Mimosaceae	T
17.	*Acalypha hispida* Burm.f.	Euphorbiaceae	H
18.	*Acampe praemorsa (Roxb.) Blatt.*	Orchidaceae	E
19.	*Acanthospermum hispidum DC.*	Asteraceae	H
20.	*Acanthus i/icifolius* L.	Acanthaceae	S
21.	*Achyranthes apera* L.	Amaranthaceae	H
22.	*Achyranthes coynei Santapau*	Amaranthaceae	H
23.	*Acrocarpus fraxinifolius Benth.*	Caesalpiniaceae	T
24.	*Actinodaphne angustifolia Nees.*	Lauraceae	T
25.	*Adansonia digitata* L.	Bombacaceae	T
26.	*Adelocaryum coelestinum (Lind!.) Brand*	Boraginaceae	H
27.	*Adhatoda zeylanica Medic.*	Acanthaceae	S
28.	*Aegiceras majus* Gaertn.	Myrcinaceae	T
29.	*Aeginetia indica* L.	Orobanchaceae	P
30.	*Aeg/e marmalos* Corr.	Rutaceae	T

Sl. No.	NAME OF PLANTS	FAMILY	HABIT
31.	*Aerides maculosum Lind!.*	Orchidaceae	E
32.	*Aeschynomene indica* L.	Fabaceae	H
33.	*Agave ingens* Berger.	Agavaceae	H
34	*Ageratum conyzoides* L.	Asteraceae	H
35.	*Ag/aia lawii (W.) Saldhana*	Meliaceae	T
36.	*Ailanthus excelsa* Roxb.	Simaroubaceae	T
37.	*A/bizzia chinensis* (Osb.) Merrill.	Mimosaceae	T
38.	*Albizzia lellbeck* Benth.	Mimosaceae	T
39.	*Albizzia odoratissima (L.) Benth.*	Mimosaceae	T
40.	*Albizzia procera* (Roxb.) Benth.	Mimosaceae	T
41.	*A/bizzia st;pulata* Boiv.	Mimosaceae	T
42.	*Alcea rosea* (L.) Cav.	Malvaceae	H
43.	*Aleuritopteris farinosa (Frost.) Fee.*	Sinopteridaceae	HF
44.	*Allamanda cathartica* L.	Apocynaceae	C
45.	*Allophyllus cobbe* (L.) Raeu.	Sapindaceae	S
46.	*Allophyllus rheedii* (Wt.) Radlk.	Sapindaceae	S
47.	*Aiseodaphne semicarpifolia Nees.*	Lauraceae	T
48.	*Alstonia scho/aris* (L.) R.Br.	Apocynaceae	T
49.	*Altemanthera sessilis (L.) R.Br.*	Amaranthaceae	H
50.	*Altemanthera triandra Lamk.*	Amaranthaceae	H
51.	*Alysicarpus glumaceus (Vahl.) DC.*	Fabaceae	H
52.	*Alysicarpus monilifer DC.*	Fabaceae	H
53.	*Alysicarpus pubescens Laws.*	Fabaceae	H
54.	*Alysicarpus tetragonolobus Edgw.*	Fabaceae	H
55.	*Amaranthus hybridus* L.	Amaranthaceae	H
56.	*Amaranthus spinosus* L.	Amaranthaceae	H
57.	*Ammania baccifera* L.	Lythraceae	H
58.	*Amorphophallus commutatus (Schott.) Engler.*	Araceae	H
59.	*Amoora lawii* (Wt.) Bedd.	Meliaceae	T
60.	*Ampelocissus latifolia (Roxb.) Planch.*	Vitaceae	C
61.	*Ampelocissus tomentosa (Roth.)Planch.*	Vitaceae	C
62.	*Anacardium occidentale L.*	Anacardiaae	T
63.	*Anagallis arvensis* L.	Primulaceae	H
64.	*Ancistrcladus heyneanus Wall.*	Ancistrocladaceae	S
65.	*Andropogon pumilis Roxb.*	Poaceae	HG
66.	*Aneilema paniculata Wall.*	Commelinaceae	H
67.	*Annona reticulata* L.	Annonaceae	T
68.	*Annona squamosa* L.	Annonaceae	T
69.	*Anodendron paniculata.Jm A. DC.*	Apocynaceae	S
70.	*Anogeissus latifolia* Wall.	Combretaceae	T

Sl. No.	NAME OF PLANTS	FAMILY	HABIT
71.	*Anthoceros* sp.	Anthocerotaceae	
72.	*Antidesma bunius* (L.) Spr.	Euphorbiaceae	T
73.	*Antidesma diandra* Roth.	Euphorbiaceae	T
74.	*Antidesma ghasembilla Gaertn.*	Euphorbiaceae	T
75.	*Antidesma menasu* Miq. exTul.	Euphorbiaceae	T
76.	*Antigonon leptopus Hook. & Am.*	Polygonaceae	C
77.	*Apluda mutica* L.	Poaceae	HG
78.	*Aporosa lindleyana* (Wt.) Bail.	Euphorbiaceae	T
79.	*Arachis hypogea* L.	Fabaceae	H
80.	*Ardisia solanacea* Roxb.	Myrsinaceae	S
81.	*Argemone maxicana* L.	Papaveraceae	H
82.	*Argyreia boseana* Sant. & Patel	Convolvulaceae	C
83.	*Argyreia elliptica* (Roth.) Chois.	Convolvulaceae	C
84.	*Argyreia nervosa (Burm.f.) Boj.*	Convolvulaceae	C
85.	*Argyreia sericea* Dalz.	Convolvulaceae	C
86.	*Arisaema murrayi (Graham.) Hook.*	Araceae	H
87.	*Aristida funiculata* Trin.	Poaceae	HG
88.	*Artabotrys hexapetala (L.f.) Bhandri*	Annonaceae	S
89.	*Artemisia nilagiricia (Clarke) Pamp.*	Asteraceae	S
90.	*Artemisia pallens* Wall.	Asteraceae	H
91.	*Artemisia parviflora Buch. & Ham. ex Roxb.*	Asteraceae	S
92.	*Arthraxon lancifolius (Trin.) Hochst.*	Poaceae	HG
93.	*Artocarpus heterophyllus Lamk.*	Moraceae	T
94.	*Arundinella metzii Hoechst.*	Poaceae	HG
95.	*Arundinella pumila (Hoschst) Steud.*	Poaceae	HG
96.	*Asclepias curassavica* L.	Asclepiadaceae	S
97.	*Asparagus racemosus Willd.*	Lillaceae	S
98.	*Aspidopterys cordata* A. Juss.	Malpighiaceae	C
99.	*Asplenium* sp.	Aspleniaceae	E
100.	*Asystasia violacea* Dalz.	Acanthaceae	S
101.	*Alalantia monophylla* DC.	Rutaceae	T
102.	*Atalantia racemosa Wt. & Am.*	Rutaceae	T
103.	*Azadiracta indica A. Juss.*	Meliaceae	T
104.	*Azanza lampas* (Cav.) Alef.	Malvaceae	H
105.	*Bacopa monnieri* (L.) Pennell	Scrophulariaceae	H
106.	*Balanophora abbreviata Muell.*	Balanophoraceae	P/H
107.	*Baliospemum solanifolium (Burm.f.) Suresh*	Euphorbiaceae	S
108.	*Bambusa arundinacea Willd.*	Poaceae	T
109.	*Barleria gibsoni* Dalz.	Acanthaceae	S
110.	*Barleria lawii T. Anders.*	Acanthaceae	S

Sl. No.	NAME OF PLANTS	FAMILY	HABIT
111.	*Bar/eria prionitis.* L.	Acanthaceae	H
112.	*Barringtonia acutangula Forst. & Forst.*	Barringtoniaceae	T
113.	*Barringtonia racemosa (L.) Spr.*	Barringtoniaceae	T
114.	*Bassia latitolia* Roxb.	Sapotaceae	T
115.	*Bauhinia purpurea* L.	Caesalpiniaceae	T
116.	*Bauhinia racemose Lamk.*	Caesalpiniaceae	T
117.	*Bauhinia vahlii Wt.& Am.*	Caesalpiniaceae	Cl/*L*
118.	*Begonia crenate* Drvand.	Begoniaceae	H
119.	*Beilschmledie dalzellii (Meissn.) Kosterm.*	Lauraceae	T
120.	*Benincasa hispida* Cogn.	Cucurbitaceae	C
121.	*Bergia ammanioides Roxb.*	Elatinaceae	H
122.	*Bidens bitemata* (Lour.) Merr.	Asteraceae	H
123.	*Biophytum sensitivum (L.) DC.*	Geraniaceae	H
124.	*Blainvillea acmella* (L.) Philipson	Asteraceae	H
125.	*Blepharis asperrima Nees.*	Acanthaceae	H
126.	*Blepharis molluginifolia Pers.*	Acanthaceae	H
127.	*Blumea lacera* (N.Burm) DC.	Asteraceae	H
128.	*Blumea amplectens* DC.	Asteraceae	H
129.	*Blumea malcolmii (Clarke) Hook. f.*	Asteraceae	H
130.	*Blumea membranacea DC.*	Asteraceae	H
131.	*Blumea mollis* (Don) Merrill.	Asteraceae	H
132.	*Blumea oxyodonta* DC.	Asteraceae	H
133.	*Boehmeria scabrella (Roxb.) Gaud.*	Urticaceae	S
134.	*Boerhavia diffusa* L.	Nyctaginaceae	H
135.	*Bolbitis presliana* (Fee) Ching	Lomariopsidaceae	H/F
136.	*Bolbitis subcrenata (Hook. et Grew.) Ching ex. Christ.*	Lomariopsidaceae	H/F
137.	*Bombax ceiba* L.	Bombacaceae	T
138.	*Bombax insigne* Wall.	Bombacaceae	T
139.	*Bonamia semidigyna Hall.f.*	Convolvulaceae	C
140.	*Borreria articularis (L. f.) F. N. Will.*	Rubiaceae	H
141.	*Borreria stricta (U.)Schum.*	Rubiaceae	H
142.	*Boswellia serrata* Roxb. ex Coleb.	Burseraceae	T
143.	*Bothriochloa pertusa (L.) A.Camus.*	Poaceae	HG
144.	*Bougainvillea spectabilis Willd.*	Nyctaginaceae	S
145.	*Brachiaria ramosa* (L.) Stapf.	Poaceae	HG
146.	*Brassica juncea* Hook.	Brassicaceae	H
147.	*Brassica oleracea* var. botrytis L.	Brassicaceae	H
148.	*Brassica oleracea* var. capitata L.	Brassicaceae	H
149.	*Breweria cordata* Blume	Convolvulaceae	C
150.	*Bridelia hamiltoniana Wall.*	Euphorbiaceae	S

Sl. No.	NAME OF PLANTS	FAMILY	HABIT
151.	*Bridelia scandens* (L.) Spr.	Euphorbiaceae	C
152.	*Bridelia* squamosa (lamk.) Gehrm.	Euphorbiaceae	T
153.	*Bridelia stipularis* Blume	Euphorbiaceae	T
154.	Buchanania lanzan Spreng.	Anacardiaceae	T
155.	Buchanania latifolia	Anacardiaceae	T
156.	Buchnera hispida Buch. A.Ham.	Scrophulariaceae	PH
157.	*Bulbostylis densa* (Wall.) Hand.A Maz.	Cyperaceae	H
158.	*Burmannia pusilla* Wall. ex. Miers	Burmanniaceae	H
159.	*Butea monosperma (lamk.) Jaub.*	Fabaceae	T
160.	*Butea superba* Roxb.	Fabaceae	T
161.	*Cadaba fruticasa* (L.) Druce.	Capparaceae	S
162.	*Caesalpinia bonducella Flem.*	Caesalpiniaceae	S
163.	*Caesalpinia nuga* (l.) Ait.	Caesalpiniaceae	C
164.	*Caesalpinia pulcherrima Swartx.*	Caesalpiniaceae	S
165.	*Caesalpinia sepiaria Roxb.*	Caesalpinaceae	S
166.	*Caesulia axillaris* Roxb.	Asteraceae	H
167.	*Cajanus cajan (L.) Millsp.*	Fabaceae	H
168.	*Cajanus scarabaeoides (L.) Van der Meusen*	Fabaceae	C
169.	*Calamus pseudotennuls Baccari*	Arecaceae	Rattan
170.	*Celastrus paniculatus Willd.*	Celastraceae	C
171.	*Callicarpa tomentosa (L.) Alston*	Verbenaceae	S
172.	*Callistemon citriatus (Curtis) Stapf.*	Myrtaceae	T
173.	*Calophyllum inophyllum L.*	Clusiaceae	T
174.	*Calotropis gigantea* (L.) R. Sr.	Asclepiadaceae	S
175.	*Calotropis procera* R. Br.	Asclepiadaceae	S
176.	*Calycopteris floribunda* L.	Combretaceae	C
177.	*Canarium strictum* Roxb.	Burseraceae	T
178.	*Canavalia ensifolia* DC.	Fabaceae	C
179.	*Canavalia gladiata (Jacq.) DC.*	Fabaceae	C
180.	*Cannabis sativa* L.	Cannabaceae	H
181.	*Canscora decurrens Dalz.*	Gentianaceae	H
182.	*Canscora diffusa* (Vah!.)R. Sr.	Gentianaceae	H
183.	*Canscora pauciflora Dalz.*	Gentianaceae	H
184.	*Cansjera rheedii* Gmel.	Oleaceae	C
185.	*Canthium amarum* Oken.	Rubiaceae	S
186.	*Canthium decocum* var. umbellatum (Wt.) Sant. & March.	Rubiaceae	T
187.	*Capillipedium huegelii (Hack.) Stapf.*	Poaceae	H
188.	*Capparis aphyl/a* Roth.	Capparaceae	S
189.	*Capparis moonii* Wt.	Capparaceae	S

Sl. No.	NAME OF PLANTS	FAMILY	HABIT
190.	*Capparis rotundifolia Rattle.*	Capparaceae	S
191.	*Capparis sepiaria* L.	Capparaceae	S
192.	*Capparis spinosa* L.	Capparaceae	S
193.	*Capparis zeylanica* L.	Capparaceae	CS
194.	*Capsicum annuum* L.	Solanaceae	H
195.	*Caralia brachiata* (Lour.) Merr.	Rhizophoraceae	T
196.	*Carelamine trichocarpa Hoch.*	Brassicaceae	H
197.	*Cardiospermum helicacabum* L.	Sapindaceae	CH
198.	*Careya arborea* Roxb.	Myrtaceae	T
199.	*Carica papaya* L.	Caricaceae	T
200.	*Carissa carandas* L.	Apocynaceae	S
201.	*Carissa congesta* Wt.	Apocynaceae	S
202.	*Carissa'inermis* Vahl.	Apocynaceae	S
203.	*Carvia callosa* (Nees.) Brem.	Acanthaceae	S
204.	*Caryota urens* L.	Arecaceae	T
205.	*Casearia elliptica* Willd.	Flacourtiaceae	S
206.	*Casearia esculanta Roxb.*	Flacourtiaceae	S
207.	*Casearia graveolens Dalz.*	Flacourtiaceae	S
208.	*Casearia ovata* (Lamk.) Willd.	Flacourtiaceae	S
209.	*Casearia rubescens Dalz.*	Flacourtiaceae	S
210.	*Cassia absus* L.	Caesalpiniaceae	H
211.	*Cassia auriculata* L.	Caesalpiniaceae	S
212.	*Cassia fistula* L.	Caesalpiniaceae	T
213.	*Cassia kolabensis* Kothari *et al.*	Caesalpiniaceae.	H
214.	*Cassia mimosoides* L.	Caesalpiniaceae	H
215.	*Cassia occidentalis* L.	Caesalpiniaceae	H
216.	*Cassia pumila* Lamk.	Caesalpiniaceae	H
217.	*Cassia siamea* Lamk.	Caesalpiniaceae	T
218.	*Cassia tora* L.	Caesalpiniaceae	H
219.	*Cassia uniflors* Muen.	Caesalpiniaceae	H
220.	*Cassine glauca* (Rottb.) Kuntze.	Celastraceae	T
221.	*Casuarina equisetifolia J.R. & G. Forst*	Casuarinaceae	T
222.	*Catharanthus roseus* (L.) G. Don.	Apocynaceae	H
223.	*Catunaregum spinosum* (L.) Thiruveng.	Rubiaceae	T
224.	*Catunaregam uliginosum (Rell.) Sivarajan.*	Rubiaceae	S
225.	*Cayratia camosa Gagnep.*	Vitaceae	CS
226.	*Celastrus paniculatus Willd.*	Celastraceae	CS
227.	*Celosia argentea* L.	Amaranthaceae	H
228.	*Celtis trinervia* Roxb.	*Urticaceae*	T
229.	*Centaurium roxburghii (Don.) Druce.*	Gentianaceae	H

Sl. No.	NAME OF PLANTS	FAMILY	HABIT
230.	*Centella asiatica* (L.) Urban	Apiaceae	H
231.	*Centranthera indica* (L.) Gamble.	Scrophulariaceae	H
232.	*Cerbera manghas* L.	Apocynaceae	S
233.	*Ceriops tagal* (Perr.) Roxb.	Rhizophoraceae	S
234.	*Ceropegia attenuata Hook.*	Asclepiadaceae	H
235.	*Ceropegia evansii McCann.*	Asclepiadaceae	H
236.	*Ceropegia lawii* Hook. f.	Asclepiadaceae	H
237.	*Ceropegia tuberosa Roxb.*	Asclepiadaceae	H
238.	*Cestrum noctumum* L.	Solanaceae	C
239.	*Chenopodium ambrosioides L.*	Chenopodiaceae	H
240.	*Chloris barbata* Sw.	Poaceae	H
241.	*Chloris dolichostachya Lagasca*	Poaceae	HG
242.	*Chloris virgata* Sw.	Poaceae	H
243.	*Chlorophytum glaucum Dalz.*	Liliaceae	H
244.	*Chlorophytum tuberosum (Roxb.) Baker*	Liliaceae	H
245.	*Christisonia lawii* Wight	Orobanchaceae	H
246.	*Chrysophyllum acuminatum Roxb.*	Sapotaceae	T
247.	*Chrysopogon fulvus (Spr.) Chiov.*	Poaceae	HG
248.	*Cicer arietinum* L.	Fabaceae	H
249.	*Cinnamomum verum* J. Presl.	Lauraceae	T
250.	*Cirrhopetalum fimbriatum Lind!.*	Orchidaceae	H
251.	*Cissampelos pareira* L.	Menispermaceae	C
252.	*Cissus camosa* Lamk.	Vitaceae	CS
253.	*Cissus discolor* Blume.	Vitaceae	CS
254.	*Cissus elongata* Roxb.	Vitaceae	CS
255.	*Cissus pallida (Wt. & Am.) Planch.*	Vitaceae	CS
256.	*Cissus repanda* Vahl.	Vitaceae	CS
257.	*Cissus repens* Lamk.	Vitaceae	CS
258.	*Cissus woodrowi Santapau*	Vitaceae	S
259.	*Citrus grandis* Osb.	Rutaceae	T
260.	*Citrus limon* Baney.	Rutaceae	T
261.	*Citrus medica* L.	Rutaceae	T
262.	*Clematis hedysarifolia DC.*	Ranunculaceae	C
263.	*Cleome viscosa* L.	Cleomaceae	H
264.	*Clerodendrum inerme (L.) Gaertn.*	Verbenaceae	S
265.	*Clerodendrum infortunatum L.*	Verbenaceae	S
266.	*Clerodendrum serratum L.*	Verbenaceae	S
267.	*Clitoria binora* Dalz.	Fabaceae	C
268.	*Clitoria tematea* L.	Fabaceae	CH
269.	*Coccinia indica* Wt. & Am.	Cucurbitaceae	CS

Sl. No.	NAME OF PLANTS	FAMILY	HABIT
270.	*Cocculus hirsturs* (L.) Diels	Menispermaceae	CS
271.	*Cocos nucifera* L.	Arecaceae	T
272.	*Coix lachryma-jobi* L.	Poaceae	HG
273.	*Coldenia procumbens* L.	Boraginaceae	H
274.	*Colebrookea oppositifolia Smith*	Lamiaceae	S
275.	*Coleus blumei* Bth.	Lamiaceae	S
276.	Colocasia esculanta (L.) Schott	Araceae	H
277.	*Combretum albidum* D.Don.	Combretaceae	CS
278.	*Combretum latifolium* Blume	Combretaceae	CS
279.	*Combretum ovalifolium* Roxb.	Combretaceae	CS
280.	*Commelina benghalensis* L.	*Commelinaceae*	H
281.	*Commelina diffusa* Burm. f.	Commelinaceae	H
282.	*Commelina nudiflora* L.	Commelinaceae	H
283.	*Commelina sufructicosa* Bl.	Commelinaceae	H
284.	*Connarus ritchiei* Hk. F.	Connaraceae	S
285.	*Conocarpus* sp.	Periplocaceae	CH
286.	*Convolvulus arvensis iL.*	Convolvulaceae	H
287.	*Conyza stricta* Willd.	Asteraceae	H
288.	*Corchorus aestuans* L.	Tiliaceae	H
289.	*Corchorus olitorius* L.	Tiliaceae	H
290.	*Cordia dichotoma* Forst. f	Boraginaceae	T
291.	*Coriandrum sativum* L.	Apiaceae	H
292.	*Cosmostigma racemosum* Wight	Asclepiadaceae	CS
293.	*Costus speciosus* (Koen.) smith	Costaceae	S
294.	*Craeteva religiosa* Auct. Non Frost.	Capparaceae	T
295.	*Cressa cretica* L.	Convolvulaceae	H
296.	*Crinum latifolium* L.	Amaryllidaceae	H
297.	*Crossandra infundibuliformis (L.) Nees.*	Acanthaceae	S
298.	*Crotalaria leptostachya Benth.*	Fabaceae	H
299.	*Crotalaria albida* Heyne	Fabaceae	H
300.	*Crotalaria fitipes* Benth.	Fabaceae	H
301.	*Crotalaria juncea* L.	Fabaceae	H
302.	*Crotalaria leschenaultii DC.*	Fabaceae	S
303.	*Crotalaria tinifolia* L.	Fabaceae	H
304.	*Crotalaria retusa* L.	Fabaceae	H
305.	*Crotalaria venvcosa* L.	Fabaceae	H
306.	*Croton tightium* L.	Euphorbiaceae	S
307.	*Crozophora prostrataDalz.*	Euphorbiaceae	H
308.	*Cryptolepis buchanani Roem. & Schult.*	Asclepiadaceae	CS
309.	*Cryptostegia grandiflora R. Br.*	Asclepiadaceae	CS

Sl. No.	NAME OF PLANTS	FAMILY	HABIT
310.	*Cucumis caffosus* (Rottl.) Cogn.	Cucurbitaceae	CH
311.	*Cucumis meta* L.	Cucurbitaceae	CH
312.	*Cucumis meta* var. agrestis L.	Cucurbitaceae	CH
313.	*Cucumis sativus* L.	Cucurbitaceae	CH
314.	*Cucurbita maxima* Ouch.	Cucurbitaceae	CH
315.	*Curculigo orchioides Gaertn.*	Hypoxidaceae	H
316.	*Curcuma aromatica Salisb.*	Scitaminaceae	H
317.	*Cuscuta reflexa* Roxb.	Convolvulaceae	CH
318.	*Cyamposis tetragonolobus (L.) Taub.*	Fabaceae	H
319.	*Cyanotis cristata* (L.) D. Don.	Commelinaceae	H
320.	*Cyanotis fasiculata (Heyne. ex Roth.) Schult.f.*	Commelinaceae	H
321.	*Cyanotis papilionacea Schultes*	Commelinaceae	H
322.	*Cyanotis tuberosa (Roxb.) Schult.*	Commelinaceae	H
323.	*Cyathocline lutea* Law. ex Wight.	Asteraceae	H
324.	*Cyathocline purpurea (Don) Kuntze*	Asteraceae	H
325.	*Cyathula prostrata* (L.) BI.	Amaranthaceae	H
326.	*Cyclea burmanii* Miers	Menispermaceae	CS
327.	*Cyclea peltata* (Lamk.) Hk. f. & Thoms.	Menispermaceae	CS
328.	*Cynanchum callialatum Buch. A. Ham.*	Asclepiadaceae	CH
329.	*Cynoctonum mitreola* (L.) Britton	Loganiaceae	H
330.	*Cynodon dactylon* Pers.	Poaceae	HG
331.	*Cynoglossum wallichii* G. Don.	Boraginaceae	H
332.	*Cynometra iripu* Kostel	Caesalpiniaceae	S
333.	*Cyperus triceps* (Rob.) Progr.	Cyperaae	H
334.	*Cyperus exaltatus* Retz.	Cyperaceae	H
335.	*Cyperus kyllingia* End!.	Cyperaceae	H
336.	*Cyperus metzii* (Hochst.) Mattf.	Cyperaceae	H
337.	*Cyperus rotundus* L.	Cvperaceae	H
338.	*Cyperus squarrosus* L.	Cyperaceae	H
339.	*Cyrtococcum patens (L.) A. Camus*	Poaceae	H
340.	*Dactyloctenium aegyptiaca (L.) Beauv.*	Poaceae	HG
341.	*Dalbergia horrida (Dannst) Mabberley*	Fabaceae	CS
342.	*Dalbergia lanceolaria* Lt.	Fabaceae	T
343.	*Dalbergia /atifolia* Roxb.	Fabaceae	T
344.	*Dalbergia paniculata Roxb.*	Fabaceae	T
345.	*Dalbergia sissoo* Roxb.	Fabaceae	T
346.	*Dalbergia sympathetica Nimmo.*	Fabaceae	CS
347.	*Dalbergia torta* Grah.	Fabaceae	S
348.	*Dalbergia volubilis* Roxb.	Fabaceae	CS
349.	*Datura metel* L	Soranaceae	S

Sl. No.	NAME OF PLANTS	FAMILY	HABIT
350.	*Delonix regia* (Boj.) Raf.	*Caesalpinaceae*	T
351.	*Dendrobium barbatulum Lindl.*	Orchidaceae	EH
352.	*Dendrobium microbulbon Rich.*	Orchidaceae	EH
353.	*Dendrocalamus strictus Nees.*	Poaceae	G
354.	*Dendrophthoe falcata (U.) Etting*	Loranthaceae	PS
355.	*Dendrophthoe trigona (Wt. & Am.) Dans.*	Loranthaceae	PS
356.	*Derris indica* (Lam.) Bennett.	Fabaceae	T
357.	*Derris scandens* (Roxb.) Benth.	Fabaceae	CS
358.	*Dems trifoliata* Lour.	Fabaceae	CS
359.	*Desmodium umbellatum DC.*	Fabaceae	S
360.	*Desmodium gangeticum DC.*	Fabaceae	S
361.	*Desmodium heterocarpon (L.) DC.*	Fabaceae	S
362.	*Desmodium laxiflorum DC.*	Fabaceae	S
363.	*Desmodium triangulare (Retz.) Merr.*	Fabaceae	S
364.	*Desmodium triflorum* DC.	Fabaceae	H
365.	Desmodium triquetrum (L.) DC.	Fabaeeae	S
366.	*Desmodium velutinum (Willd.) DC.*	Fabaceae	S
367.	*Dianthus caryophyllus* L.	Carvophyllaceae	H
368.	*Dichanthium annulatum (Forsk.) Stapf.*	Poaceae	HG
369.	*Dichanthium aristatum (Poi.) C.E.Hubbard*	Poaceae	HG
370.	*Dichrostachys cinerea (L.) DC.*	Mimosaceae	S
371.	*Dicliptera zeylanica Nees.*	Acanthaceae	S
372.	*Digitaria ciliaris* (Retz.) Koeler	Poaceae	HG
373.	*Digitaria longiffora* (Reiz.) Pers.	Poaceae	HG
374.	*Digitaria marginata var.fimbriata Stapf.*	Poaceae	HG
375.	*Digitaria stricta* Roth. Ex R.& S.	Poaceae	HG
376.	*Dillenia pentagyna* Roxb.	Dilleniaceae	T
377.	*Dimeria omithopoda* Trin	Poaceae	HG
378.	*Dimeria stapfiana* Hub. Ex Pil.	Poaceae	HG
379.	*Dimocarpus longan* Lour.	Sapindaceae	T
380.	*Dinebra retroflexa* (Vahl.) Panz.	Poaceae	HG
381.	*Dioscoria bulbifera* L.	Dioscoreaceae	CS
382.	*Dioscoria oppositifolia* L.	Dioscoreaceae	CS
383.	*Dioscoria pentaphylla* L.	Dioscoreaceae	CS
384.	*Diospyros candolleana WI.*	Ebenaceae	T
385.	*Diospyros embryopteris Pers.*	Ebenaceae	T
386.	*Diospyros melanoxylon Roxb.*	Ebenaceae	T
387.	*Diospyros montana Roxb.*	Ebenaceae	T
388.	*Diospyros oocarpa* Thw.	Ebenaceae	T
389.	*Diploclisia glaucescens (Blume.) Diels.*	Menispermaceae	CS

Sl. No.	NAME OF PLANTS	FAMILY	HABIT
390.	*Dolichos uninorus* Lamk.	Fabaceae	H
391.	*Dracaena teniflora Roxb.*	Liliaceae	S
392.	*Dregea volubliis* (U.) Benth.	Asclepiadaceae	CS
393.	*Drosera indica* L.	Droseraceae	H
394.	*Drynaria quercifolia* (L.) Sm.	Polypodiaceae	EF
395.	*Duranta repeans* L.	Verbenaceae	S
396.	*Dysoxylum binecteriferum (Roxb.) Hook.f.*	Meliaceae	T
397.	*Ecbolium linneanum Kurz.*	Acanthaceae	H
398.	*Echinochloa frumentacea Lamk.*	Poaceae	HG
399.	*Echinochola colonum* (L.) link.	Poaceae	HG
400.	*Eclipta prostrata L. f.*	Asteraceae	H
401.	*Elaeagnus conferta Roxb.*	Elaegnaceae	CS
402.	*E/aeagnus /atifo/ia* L.	Elaegnaceae	CS
403.	*Elaeocarpus oblongus Gaertn.*	Elaeocarpaceae	T
404.	*Elephantopus scaber* L.	Asteraceae	H
405.	*Eleusine coracana Gaertn.*	Poaceae	HG
406.	*Eleusine indica* (L.) Gaertn.	Poaceae	HG
407.	*Embelia basaal (R & S.) A. DC.*	Myrsinaceae	S
408.	*Emblica officinalis Gaerth.*	Euphorbiaceae	T
409.	*Emilia sonchifolia* (L.) DC.	Asteraceae	H
410.	*Ensete superbum* (Roxb.) Cheesman	Musaceae	T
411.	*Entanda pursaetha* DC.	Fabaceae	CS
412.	*Eragrostis ciliaris* (L.) RBr.	Poaceae	HG
413.	*Eragrostis pilasa* (L.) P. Beauv.	Poaceae	HG
414.	*Eragrostis tremula* R & S.	Poaceae	HG
415.	*Eragrostis uniloides (Retz.) Nees.*	Poaceae	HG
416.	*Eranthemum nervosum Br.*	Acanthaceae	H
417.	*Eranthemum roseum (Vahl.) R Br.*	Acanthaceae	H
418.	*Eria dalzellii* Lindl.	Orchidaceae	EH
419.	*Erinocarpus nimmonii Graham.*	Tiliaceae	T
420.	*Eriocaulon diana* Fyson	Eriocaulaceae	H
421.	*Eriocaulon gracile* Mart.	Eriocaulaceae	H
422.	*Eriocaulon sollyanum Rolye*	Eriocaulaceae	H
423.	*Eriolaena hookeriana Wt. & Am.*	Tiliaceae	T
424.	*Eriolaena quinquelocularis Wt.*	Tiliaceae	T
425.	*Ervatamia altemifolia (L.) Almeida*	Apocynaceae	T
426.	*Ervatamia coronaria* stapf.	Apocynaceae	S
427.	*Ervatamia divaricata* (L.) burkil.	Apocynaceae	S
428.	*Erythirna orientalis* L.	Fabaceae	T
429.	*Erythirna variegata* L.	Fabaceae	T

Sl. No.	NAME OF PLANTS	FAMILY	HABIT
430.	*Eucalyptous citridora Hook.*	Myrtaceae	T
431.	*Eucalyptous globulus Hook.*	Myrtaceae	T
432.	*Eululia tricuspidata i(Schult) Henrard*	Poaceae	HG
433.	*Eupatorium repandum* Willd	Asteraceae	S
434.	*Euphorbia antiquorum* L.	Euphorbiaceae	S
435.	*Euphorbia geniculata Ortega*	Euphorbiaceae	H
436.	*Euphorbia hirta* L.	Euphorbiaceae	H
437.	*Euphorbia neriifolia L.*	Euphorbiaceae	S
438.	*Euphorbia nivulia* Buch. A. Ham.	Euphorbiaceae	S
439.	*Euphorbia pycnostegia* Boiss.	Euphorbiaceae	H
440.	*Euphorbia rothiana* Spr.	Euphorbiaceae	H
441.	*Euphorbia tirucalli* L.	Euphorbiaceae	S
442.	*Euphoria longana* Lamk.	Sapindaceae	T
443.	*Eusteralis malabarica (Heyne) Mazumdar*	Lamiaceae	H
444.	*Evolvulus alsinoides* L.	Convolvulaceae	H
445.	*Exacum bico/or* Roxb.	Gentianaceae	H
446.	*Exacum petiolare* Griseb.	Gentianaceae	H
447.	*Feronia elephantum* Corr.	Rutaceae	T
448.	*Ficus amplissima* Sm.	Moraceae	T
449.	*Ficus aarnottiana* (Miq.) Miq.	Moraceae	T
450.	*Ficus benghalensis* L.	Moraceae	T
451.	*Ficus callosa* Willd.	Moraceae	T
452.	*Ficus drupacea* Thunb.	Moraceae	T
453.	*Ficus exasparata* Vahl.	Moraceae	T
454.	*Ficus hispida* Lt.	Moraceae	T
455.	*Ficus microcarpa* L.	Moraceae	T
456.	*Ficus racemosa* L.	Moraceae	T
457.	*Ficus refigiosa* L.	Moraceae	T
458.	*Ficus retusa* L.	Moraceae	T
459.	*Ficus rumphii* Blume.	Moraceae	T
460.	*Ficus tinctoria* var. parasitica (Willd.) Corner	Moraceae	T
461.	*Ficus tsiela* Roxb.	Moraceae	T
462.	*Ficus virens* Ail.	Moraceae	T
463.	*Fimbristylis digitata Boeck.*	Cyperaceae	H
464.	*Firmiana colorata* R.Br.	Sterculiaceae	T
465.	*Flacourtia indica* (Burm.f.) Merrill.	Flacourtiaceae	T
466.	*Flacourtia jungomas (Lour.) Raeusch.*	Flacourtiaceae	T
467.	*Flacourtia montana Graham.*	Flacourtiaceae	T
468.	*Flemingia bracteata Wight.*	Fabaceae	S
469.	*Flemingia macrophylfa (Willd.) Prain.*	Fabaceae	S

Sl. No.	NAME OF PLANTS	FAMILY	HABIT
470.	*Flemingia strobilifera (L.) R. Br.*	Fabaceae	S
471.	*Fluggia leucopyros* Willd.	Euphorbiaceae	S
472.	*Garcinia indica* Choiss.	Clusiaceae	T
473.	*Garcinia talbotii* Raiz. Ex Sant.	Clusiaceae	T
474.	*Gardenia jasminoides Ellis.*	Rubiaceae	S
475.	*Gardenia lucida* Roxb.	Rubiaceae	S
476.	*Gardenia resinifera* Roth.	Rubiaceae	S
477.	*Garuga pinnata* Roxb.	Burseraceae	T
478.	*Geissaspis cristata* Wt. & Arn.	Fabaceae	H
479.	*Geissaspis tenella* Benth.	Fabaceae	H
480.	*Girardinia zeylanica Decne.*	Urticaceae	H
481.	*Girivelia frutescens* (L.) Almeida & Almeida	Periplocaceae	S
482.	*Glinus lotoides* L.	Molluginaceae	H
483.	*Glinus oppositifolius* (L.) A. DC.	Molluginaceae	H
484.	*Gliricidia maculata* H. B. K.	Fabaceae	T
485.	*Glochidion sinicum (Graham) Almeida*	Euphorbiaceae	T
486.	*Glochidion velutinum* Wt.	Euphorbiaceae	T
487.	*Glochidion zeylanicum (Gaertn.) Gehrm.*	Euphorbiaceae	T
488.	*Gloriosa superba* L.	Liliaceae	CH
489.	*Glossocardia bosvallea (L. f.) DC.*	Asteraceae	H
490.	*Glycosmis mauritiana (Lamk.) Tanaka*	Rutaceae	S
491.	*Gmelina arborea* Roxb.	Verbenaceae	T
492.	*Gnaphalium luteo- album L.*	Asteraceae	H
493.	*Gnaphalium polycaulon Pers.*	Asteraceae	H
494.	*Gnetum ula* Roxb.	Gnetaceae	CT
495.	*Gnidia glauca* (Fresen.) Gilg.	Thymeleaceae	S
496.	*Gomphrena globosa* L.	Amaranthaceae	H
497.	*Goniogyne hirla* (Willd.) AIL	Fabaceae	H
498.	*Gossypium heroaceum* L.	Malvaceae	S
499.	*Grangea maderaspatana Poir.*	Asteraceae	H
500.	*Grevillea robusta* Cunn.	Proteaceae	T
501.	*Grewia disperma* Rottl.	Tiliaceae	S
502.	*Grewia navescens* Juss.	Tiliaceae	S
503.	*Grewia laevigata* Vahl.	Tiliaceae	T
504.	*Grewia microcos* L.	Tiliaceae	S
505.	*Grewia paniculata* (L.) Roxb.	Tiliaceae	S
506.	*Grewia salvifolia* Heyne	Tiliaceae	S
507.	*Grewia tiliaefolia* Vahl.	Tiliaceae	T
508.	*Guizotia abyssinica Cass.*	Asteraceae	H
509.	*Gymnema sylvestre (Retz.) Schult.*	Asclepiadaceae	CS

Sl. No.	NAME OF PLANTS	FAMILY	HABIT
510.	*Gymnosporia montata Benth.*	Celastralaceae	S
511.	*Gymnosporia rothiana (Walp.) Laws.*	Celastraceae	S
512.	*Gynura cusimbua* Moore	Asteraceae	H
513.	*Habenaria commelinifolia Wall.*	Orchidaceae	H
514.	*Habenaria grandiflora Lind!.*	Orchidaceae	H
515.	*Habenaria grandifloriforme Blatt. & McC.*	Orchidaceae	H
516.	*Habenaria longicorniculata Graham*	Orchidaceae	H
517.	*Habenaria marginata Coleb.*	Orchidaceae	H
518.	*Habenaria plantaginea Lind!.*	Orchidaceae	H
519.	*Haldinia cordifolia (Roxb.) Ridsdale.*	Rubiaceae	T
520.	*Haplanthodes tentaculatus Muzumdar*	Acanthaceae	H
521.	*Haplanthodes verticillatus (Roxb.) Muzumdar*	Acanthaceae	H
522.	*Hardwickia binata* Roxb.	Caesalpiniaceae	T
523.	*Hedyotis auricularia* L.	Rubiaceae	H
524.	*Helianthus annus* L.	Asteraceae	H
525.	*Helicteres isora* L.	Sterculiaceae	S
526.	*Heliotropium indicum* L.	Boraginaceae	H
527.	*Heliotropium marifolium Retz.*	Boraginaceae	H
528.	*Heliotropium ovalifolium Forsk.*	Boraginaceae	H
529.	*Heliotropium supinum* L.	Boraginaceae	H
530.	*Hemidesmus indicus* (L.) R. Br.	Asclepiadaceae	CS
531.	*Hemigraphis latebrosa Nees.*	Acanthaceae	S
532.	*Hemigyrosa canescens Thw.*	Sapindaceae	T
533.	*Heracleum concanensis Dalz.*	Apiaceae	H
534.	*Heterophragma quadriloculare (Roxb.) Shum.*	Bignoniaceae	T
535.	*Heteropogon contorlus (L.) Beauv.*	Poaceae	HG
536.	*Hetropogon tricticeus (R.Br.) Stapf.*	Poaceae	HG
537.	*Hewittia bicolor* Wt. & Am.	Convolvulaceae	CS
538.	*Hibiscus fureatus* Willd.	Malvaceae	S
539.	*Hibiscus hirlus* L.	Malvaceae	S
540.	*Hibiscus rosa -sinensis* L.	Malvaceae	S
541.	*Hibiscus schizopetalus Hook.*	Malvaceae	S
542.	*Hippocratea grahami* Wt.	Hippocrateaceae	S
543.	*Hippocratea obtusifolia Roxb.*	Hippocrateaceae	CS
544.	*Hiptage benghalensis (L.) Kurz.*	Malpighiaceae	CS
545.	*Hitchenia caulina (Graham) Baker*	Zingiberaceae	H
546.	*Holarrhena antidysenterica (Roth.) A.DC.*	Apocynaceae	S
547.	*Ho/igama amottiana* Hk. f.	Anacardiaceae	T
548.	*Holigama grahami* (Wt.) Kurz.	Anacardiaceae	T
549.	*Holoptelea integrifolia Planch.*	Urticaceae	T

Sl. No.	NAME OF PLANTS	FAMILY	HABIT
550.	*Homonoia riparia* Lour.	Euphorbiaceae	S
551.	*Hoya pendu/a* Wt.	Asclepiadaceae	ES
552.	*Hoya retusa* Dalz.	Asclepiadaceae	ES
553.	*Hoya wight* Hook.	Asclepiadaceae	ES
554.	*Hydnocarpus laurifolia (Dennst.) Sleumer*	Flacourtiaceae	T
555.	*Hydnocarpus pentandra (Ham.) Oken*	Flacourtiaceae	T
556.	*Hydrolea zeylanica* Vahl.	I-iydrophyllaceae	H
557.	*Hygrophila pinnatifida (Dalz.) Sreen.*	Acanthaceae	H
558.	*Hygrophila schulli (Buch.A. Ham.) Almeida & Almeida*	Acanthaceae	S
559.	*Hygrophilla serphyllum (Nees.) Anders.*	Acanthaceae	H
560.	*Hymenodictyon obovatum Wall.*	Rubiaceae	T
561.	*Hypoxis aurea* lour.	Hypoxidaceae	S
562.	*Hyptis suaveolens* (L.) Poit.	Lamiaceae	S
563.	*Ichnocarpus frotescens (L.) R.Br.*	Periplocaceae	S
564.	*Impatiens balsamina* L.	Balsaminaceae	H
565.	*Impatiens kleinii* Wt. & Am.	Balsaminaceae	H
566.	*Impatiens pulchenima Dalz.*	Balsaminaceae	H
567.	*Impatiens rosmarinifolia Dalz.*	Balsaminaceae	H
568.	*Indigofera cassioides Rottl.*	Fabaceae	S
569.	*Indigofera cordifolia Heine.*	Fabaceae	H
570.	*Indigofera glandulosa Willd.*	Fabaceae	H
571.	*Indigofera hirsuta* L.	Fabaceae	H
572.	*Indigofera linifolia* Retz.	Fabaceae	H
573.	*Indigofera prostrata* Willd.	Fabaceae	H
574.	*Indigofera trifoliata* L.	Fabaceae	H
575.	*Indigofera trita* L.	Fabaceae	H
576.	*Indigofera wightii Graham*	Fabaceae	H
577.	*Iphigenia indica* (L.) A. Gray.	liliaceae	H
578.	*Iphigenia pallida* Baker	liliaceae	H
579.	*Ipomoea aquatica* Forsk.	Convolvulaceae	CH
580.	*Ipomoea cairica* (L.) Sweet.	Convolvulaceae	CH
581.	*Ipomoea camea* Jacq.	Convolvulaceae	CH
582.	*Ipomoea diversifolia* RSr.	Convolvulaceae	H
583.	*Ipomoea illusttis* Prain.	Convolvulaceae	H
584.	*Ipomoea leari* Paxt.	Convolvulaceae	H
585.	*Ipomoea longiflora* R Sr-	Convolvulaceae	H
586.	*Ipomoea mauritiana* Jacq.	Convolvulaceae	CH
587.	*Ipomoea nil* (L.) Roth.	Convolvulaceae	CH
588.	*Ipomoea palmata* Forsk.	Convolvulaceae	CS
589.	*Ipomoea pes-caprae* L.	Convolvulaceae	CH

Sl. No.	NAME OF PLANTS	FAMILY	HABIT
590.	*Isachne globosa* (Thunb.) O. Ktze.	Poaceae	HG
591.	*Isachne pifosum* (Klein.) Wight	Poaceae	HG
592.	*Ischaemum indicum (Houtt) Merr.*	Poaceae	HG
593.	*Ixora arborea* Roxb	Rubiaceae	T
594.	*Ixora barbata* Roxb.	Rubiaceae	S
595.	*Ixora brachiata* Roxb.	Rubiaceae	S
596.	*Ixora coccinea* L.	Rubiaceae	S
597.	*Ixora nigricans R. Sr.*	Rubiaceae	S
598.	*Jacquemontia paniculata Hallier.*	Convolvulaceae	C
599.	*Jasminum grandiflorum* L.	Oleaceae	C
600.	*Jasminum malabaricum Wt.*	Oleaceae	S
601.	*Jasminllm pubescens Willd.*	Oleaceae	S
602.	*Jasminllm ritchiei* Clarke.	Oleaceae	S
603.	*Jasminllm sambac* Ait..	Oleaceae	H
604.	*Jatropha curcas* L.	Euphorbiaceae	S
605.	*Justica trinervia* var. arenaria Clarke.	Acanthaceae	H
606.	*Justicia betonica* L.	Acanthaceae	S
607.	*Justicia simplex* D. Don.	Acanthaceae	H
608.	*Justicia wynadensis (Nees.) T. And.*	Acanthaceae	S
609.	*Kalanchoe pinnata (Larnk.) Pers.*	Crassulaceae	S
610.	*Kirganelia reticulata* (SI.) Saill.	Euphorbiaceae	H
611.	*Knema attenuata* (Wall.) Warb	Myristicaceae	T
612.	*Kydia ca/ycina* Roxb.	Malvaceae	T
613.	*Lablab purpureus* (L.) Sweet	Fabaceae	CS
614.	*Lactuca remotiflora* DC.	Asteraceae	H
615.	*Lagasca mo/lis* Cav.	Asteraceae	H
616.	*Lagenaria leucantha (Ouch.) Rusby.*	Cucurbitaceae	CS
617.	*Lagemaria vulgaris Seringe.*	Cucurbitaceae	C
618.	*Lagerstroemia* microcarpa Wt.	Lythraceae	T
619.	*Lagerstroemia parviflora Roxb.*	Lythraceae	T
620.	*Lagerstroemia speciosa (L.) Pers.*	Lythraceae	S
621.	*Lannea coromandelica (Houtt.) Merr.*	Anacardiaceae	T
622.	*Lantana camara* var.aculeata (L.) Mold.	Verbenaceae	S
623.	*Lapisoms nuda* Thumb.	Polypodiaceae	EH
624.	*Lastrea* sp.	Thelypteridaceae	SF
625.	*Launaea pinnatifida* Cass.	Asteraceae.	H
626.	*Lavandula gibsoni* Grah.	Lamiaceae	H
627.	*Lawsonia inermis* L.	Lythraceae	S
628.	*Leea asiatica* (L.) Ridsd.	Leeaceae	H
629.	*Leea indica (Burm. f.) Merr.*	Leeaceae	H

Sl. No.	NAME OF PLANTS	FAMILY	HABIT
630.	*Leea robusta* Roxb.	Leeaceae	H
631.	*Lepidagathis cuspidata Nees.*	Acanthaceae	H
632.	*Lepidagathis rigida* Oalz.	Acanthaceae	H
633.	*Lepisanthes tetraphylla (Vahl.) Radlk.*	Acanthaceae	T
634.	*Leptadenia reticulata Wt. & Am.*	Asclepiadaceae	CS
635.	*Leucaena leucocephala (Lamk.) de Wit.*	Mimosaceae	T
636.	*Leucas aspera* (Willd.) Spr.	Lamiaceae	H
637.	*Leucas ciliata* Benth.	Lamiaceae	H
638.	*Leucas montana* Spreng.	Lamiaceae	H
639.	*Leucas stelligera* Benth,	Lamiaceae	H
640.	*Ligustrum microphyllum (Graham.) Almeida*	Oleacea	S
641.	*Limnophila indica* (L.) Druce.	Scrophulariaceae	H
642.	*Linderina crustacea* (L.) F. Mueller.	Scrophulariaceae	H
643.	*Linderina parvinora (Roxb.) Haines.*	Scrophulariaceae	H
644.	*Lindemia ciliata* (Colsm.) Pennel.	Scrophulariaceae	H
645.	*Lindemia oppositifolia (Retz.) Mukherjee*	Scrophulariaceae	H
646.	*Linociera malabarica Wall.*	Oleaceae	T
647.	*Linum mysorensis Heyne.*	Linaceae	H
648.	*Linum usitatissimum* L.	Linaceae	H
649.	*Litsea chinensis* Lamk.	Lauraceae	S
650.	*Litsea deccanensis Gamble.*	Lauraceae	S
651.	*Lobelia alsinoides* lamk.	Lobeliaceae	H
652.	*Lobelia nicotianaefolia Heyne.*	Lobeliaceae	H
653.	*Loranthus capitellatus Wt.& Am.*	Loranthaceae	PS
654.	*Loranthus stocksii Hook.F.*	Loranthaceae	PS
655.	*Ludwigia octovalvis (Jacq.) Raven.*	Onagraceae	H
656.	*Ludwigia perennis* L.	Onagraceae	H
657.	*Ludwigia suffruticosa* L.	Onagraceae	H
658.	*Luffa acutangula* (L.) Roxb.	Cucurbitaceae	CS
659.	*Luffa acutangula* var. amara Roxb.	Cucurbitaceae	CS
660.	*Luffa aegyptiaca* Mill.	Cucurbitaceae	CS
661.	*Luffa echinata* Roxb.	Cucurbitaceae	CS
662.	*Luvunga sarmentosa (Bl.) Kurz.*	Rutaceae	S
663.	*Lycopersicon lycopersium (L.) Korst.*	Solanaceae	H
664.	*Lygodium flexuosum* (L.) Sw.	Schizaeaceae	CF
665.	*Lygodium mierophyllum (Cav.) R. Sr.*	Schizaeaceae	CF
666.	*Maba angustifolia* Miq.	Ebenaceae	T
667.	*Macaranga peltata (Roxb.) Muell.- Arg.*	Euphorbiaceae	T
668.	*Maekenziea integrifolia (Dalz.) Sremek.*	Acanthaceae	S
669.	*Maesa indica* (Roxb.) DC.	Myrsinaceae	S

Sl. No.	NAME OF PLANTS	FAMILY	HABIT
670.	*Malachra capitata* L.	Malvaceae	H
671.	*Mallotus philippinensis (Lamk.) Muell.-Arg.*	Euphorbiaceae	T
672.	*Mallotus aureo punctatus (Lamk.) Muel.- Arg.*	Euphorbiaceae	S
673.	*Mallotus stenanthus Muell.- Arg.*	Euphorbiaceae	S
674.	*Malvastrum coromandelianum (L.) Garke.*	Malvaceae	H
675.	*Mammea longifolia (Wt. ex Am.) Planch.*	Clusiaceae	T
676.	*Mangifera indica* L.	Anacardiaceae	T
677.	*Manilkara achras* (Mill.) Fosberg.	Sapotaceae	T
678.	*Manilkara hexandra (Roxb.) Dub.*	Sapotaceae	T
679.	*Marsdenia tenaeissima Wt. & Am.*	Asclepiadaceae	CS
680.	*Marsdenia volubilis Cooke.*	Asclepiadaceae	CS
681.	*Martynia diandra* Glox.	Pedaliaceae	H
682.	*Maytenus emarginata (Willd.) Ding.*	Celastraceae	S
683.	*Maytenus rothiana (Walp.) Lobreau -Collen*	Celastraceae	S
684.	*Melanthesa retusa (Dennst.) Kostel.*	Euphorbiaceae	S
685.	*Melia az adirach* L.	Meliaceae	T
686.	*Melia composita* Willd.	Meliaceae	T
687.	*Melothria heterophylla Cogn.*	CuclJrbitaceae	CS
688.	*Memecylon talbotianum Brandis.*	Melastomaceae	T
689.	*Memecylon umbellatum Burm.f.*	Melastomaceae	T
690.	*Merremia tridentata Hallier.f.*	Convolvulaceae	CS
691.	*Merremia turpethum Shah.*	Convolvulaceae	CS
692.	*Merremia umbellata* (L.) Hall. F.	Convolvulaceae	CH
693.	*Merremia vitifolia (Burm.f.) Hall.f.*	Convolvulaceae	CH
694.	*Metilotus indica* All.	Fabaceae	H
695.	*Meyna laxiflora* Robyns.	Rubiaceae	T
696.	*Mezoneuron cucullatum Wt. & Arn.*	Caesalpiniaceae	CS
697.	*Michelia champaca* L.	Magnoliaceae	T
698.	*Microcos peniculata* L.	Tiliaceae	T
699.	*Mil/ingtonia hortensis* L.	Bignoniaceae	T
700.	*Mimosa pudica* L.	Mimosaceae	S
701.	*Mimusops elengi* L.	Sapotaceae	T
702.	*Mirabilis jalapa* L.	Nyctaginaceae.	H
703.	*Mitragyna parvifolia (Roxb.) Korth.*	Rubiaceae	T
704.	*Modecca palmata* Lamk.	Passifloraceae	CS
705.	*Mollugo pentaphyl/a* L.	MoUuQinaceae	H
706.	*Momordica charantia* L.	Cucurbitaceae	CS
707.	*Momordica dioica* Roxb.	Curcurbitaceae	CS
708.	*Momordica subangulata Blume.*	Cucurbitaceae	CS
709.	*Morinda citrifolia* L.	Rubiaceae	T

Sl. No.	NAME OF PLANTS	FAMILY	HABIT
710.	*Morinda tinctoria* Roxb.	Rubiaceae	T
711.	*Moringa pterygosperma Gaertn.*	Moringaceae	T
712.	*Morus alba* L.	Moraceae	S
713.	*Moullava spicata* (Dalz.) Nicols.	Caesalpiniaceae	CS
714.	*Mucuna monosperma DC.*	Fabaceae	CH
715.	*Mucuna pruriens* (L.) DC.	Fabaceae	CH
716.	*Muntingia calabura* L.	Tiliaceae	T
717.	*Murdannia malabarica (L.) Brueckner*	Commelinaceae	H
718.	*Murdannia spirata* (L.) Brueckner	Commelinaceae	H
719.	*Murraya exotica* L.	Rutaceae	T
720.	*Murraya koenigii* (L.) Spr.	Rutaceae	T
721.	*Murraya paniculata* (L.) Jacq.	Rutaceae	T
722.	*Musa parndisiaca* L.	Musaceae	T
723.	*Mussaenda glabrata (HkJ.) Hutch.*	Rubiaceae	S
724.	*Myriophyllum aliganthum Wt. & Am.*	Haloragidaceae	S
725.	*Myristica beddomei* King.	Myristicaceae	T
726.	*Myristica dactyloides Gaertn.*	Myristicaceae	T
727.	*Myrtus communis* L.	Myrtaceae	S
728.	*Naregamia alata* Wt. & Am.	Rutaceae	H
729.	*Neanotis foetida* (Dalz.) Hook.	Rubiaceae	H
730.	*Neanotis meedei* Benth. & Hook.	Rubiaceae	H
731.	*Neolamarkia cadamba (Roxb.) Bosser.*	Rubiaceae	T
732.	*Nerium indicum* Mill.	Apocynaceae	S
733.	*Neuracanthus sphaerostachys (Nees.) Dalz.*	Acanthaceae	S
734.	*Nilgirianthus heyneanus (Nees.) Brem.*	Acanthaceae	S
735.	*Nothopegia racemosa (Oalz.) Ramamurthy*	Anacardiaceae	T
736.	*Nothopodytes nimmoniana .(Grahm.) Mabberley*	Lcacinaceae	T
737.	*Nyctanthus arbortristis* L.	Oleaceae	T
738.	*Nymphaea nauchali* N. Burman.	Nymphaeceae	H
739.	*Nymphaea pubescens Willd.*	Nymph,-eceae	H
740.	*Nymphoides cristatum (Roxb.) O. Kuntze.*	Gentianaceae	H
741.	*Nymphoides indicunl* (L.) O. Kuntze.	Gentianaceae	H
742.	*Oberonia recurva* Lind!.	Orchidaceae	H
743.	*Ochna obtusata* DC.	Ochnaceae	S
744.	*Ocimum americanum* L.	Lamiaceae	S
745.	*Ocimum tenuiflorum* L.	Lamiaceae	H
746.	*Olax psittacorum* (Willd.) Vahl.	Olacaceae	S
747.	*J/denlandia corymbos8* L.	Rubiaceae	H
748.	*Oldenlandia herbacea (L.) Roxb.*	Rubiaceae	H
749.	*Olea dioica* Roxb.	Oleaceae	T

Sl. No.	NAME OF PLANTS	FAMILY	HABIT
750.	*Ophioglossum fibrosum* Schum.	Ophioglossaceae	HF
751.	*Ophioglossum* sp.	Ophioglossaceae	F
752.	*Oplismenus compositus (L.) Beauv.*	Poaceae	HG
753.	*Opuntia dillenii* Raw.	Cactaceae	S
754.	*Oropetium thromaeum (Lt.) Trin.*	Poaceae	HG
755.	*Oroxylum indicum* (L.) Vent.	Bignoniaceae	T
756.	*Oryza sativa* L.	Poaceae	HG
757.	*Osbeckia truncata* Don.	Melastomaceae	H
758.	*Osyris quadripartita* Salz.	Santalaceae	S
759.	*Oxalis comiculata* L.	Geraniaceae	H
760.	*Oxyceros rugulosus (Thw.) Thruveng.*	Rubiaceae	CS
761.	*Oxytenanthera ritchiei (Munro) Nair & Ansari*	Poaceae	*T/B*
762.	*Oxytenanthera stockii Munro.*	Poaceae	*T/B*
763.	*Pancratium sanctae -mariae Blatt. & Hallb.*	Amaryllidaceae	H
764.	*Pandanus furcatus Roxb.*	Pandanaceae	S
765.	*Panicum flavidum* Retz.	Poaceae	HG
766.	*Panicum miliaceum* L.	Poaceae	HG
767.	*Panicum milliare* Lamk.	Poaceae	HG
768.	*Panicum psilopodium Trin.*	Poaceae	HG
769.	*Panicum ramosum* L.	Poaceae	HG
770.	*Panicum trypheron Schult.*	Poaceae	HG
771.	*Paracalyx scariosus (Roxb.) AIL*	Fabaceae	CS
772.	*Paramignya monophylla Wt. ex Graham.*	Rutaceae	S
773.	*Parsonsia alboflavescens (Denhst.) Mabb.*	Apocynaceae	CS
774.	*Paspalidium flacidum (Retz) A. Casso*	Poaceae	HG
775.	*Paspalum distchum.* L.	Poaceae	HG
776.	*Pavetta crassicaulis Sremek.*	Rubiaceae	S
777.	*Pavetta indica* L.	Rubiaceae	S
778.	*Pavetta indica* L. var. tomentosa Roxb.	Rubiaceae	S
779.	*Pedilanthuis tithymeloide (L.) Poir.*	Euphorbiaceae	S
780.	*Peltophorum pterocarpum DC.*	Caesalpiniaceae	T
781.	*Perotis indica* (L.) OK	Poaceae	HG
782.	*Persea macrantha (Nees.) Kosterm.*	Lauraceae	T
783.	*Petalidium barlerioides Nees.*	Acanthaceae	S
784.	*Phoenix humilis* Royle.	Arecaceae	S
785.	*Phoenix sylvestris* (L.) Roxb.	Arecaceae	T
786.	*Phyla nodiflora (L.) Green.*	Verbenaceae	H
787.	*Phyllanthus asperulatus Hutch.*	Euphorbiaceae	H
788.	*Phyllallthus urinaria* L.	Euphorbiaceae	H
789.	*Phyllocephalum fitchii (HookJ) Almeida*	Asteraceae	H

Sl. No.	NAME OF PLANTS	FAMILY	HABIT
790.	*Phyllocephalum scabridum (DC.) Benth.*	Asteraceae	H
791.	*Phyllocephalum tenue (C. B. Clarke) Almeida*	Asteraceae	H
792.	*Physalis minima* L.	Solanaceae	H
793.	*Pimpinella adenascens Dalz.*	Apiaceae	H
794.	*Pimpinella heyneana Wall.*	Apiaceae	H
795.	*Pinda concanense (Dalz.) Mukhop & Constane*	Apiaceae	S
796.	*Piper ma/amiris* L.	Piperaceae	CS
797.	*Piper nigrum* L.	Piperaceae	CS
798.	*Piper trichostachyon (Miq.) DC.*	Piperaceae	CS
799.	*Pithecolobium dulce Benth.*	Mimosaceae	T
800.	*Plectranthus mollis Spreng.*	Lamiaceae	T
801.	*Plectranthus purpurascens Dalz.*	Lamiaceae	H
802.	*Plectranthus stocksii* Hk. f	Lamiaceae	H
803.	*Plectranthus striatus Benth.*	Lamiaceae	H
804.	*Plumbago rosea* L.	Plumbaginaceae	S
805.	*Plumbago zeylanica* L.	Plumbaginaceae	S
806.	*Plumeria acuminata* Ait.	Apocynaceae	S
807.	*Plumeria acutifolia* Poir.	Apocynaceae	S
808.	*Plumeria rubra* L.	Apocynaceae	T
809.	*Pogostemon benghalensis (Burm.f.) O. Kuntze.*	Lamiaceae	S
810.	*Pogostemon parviflorus Benth.*	Lamiaceae	S
811.	*Polyalthia longifolia Benth.& HookJ.*	Annonaceae	T
812.	*Polycarpaea corymbosa Lamk.*	Caryophyllaceae	H
813.	*Polygala chinensis* L.	Polygalaceae	H
814.	*Polygala persicariaefolia DC.*	Polygalaceae	H
815.	*Polygonum chinense* L.	Polygonaceae	H
816.	*Polygonum glabrum Willd.*	Polygonaceae	S
817.	*Polyplerum stylosum (Wight.) Hall.*	Podostemaceae	H
818.	*Porana racemosa* Roxb.	Convolvulace	CH
819.	*Porpax jerdoniana* (WI) Rolfe.	Orchidaceae	E
820.	*Porpax reticulata* Lind!.	Orchidaceae	EH
821.	*Portulaca oleracea* L.	Portulacaceae	H
822.	*Portulaca pilosa* L. var.grandinora (Hook.) Gasink	Portulacaceae	H
823.	*Pothos scandens* L.	Araceae	CS
824.	*Pouteria tomentosa Vaehni.*	Sapotaceae	T
825.	*Premna coriacea* Clarke	Verbenaceae	S
826.	*Premna integrifolia* L.	Verbenaceae	S
827.	*Pseudarthria viscida* Wt. & Arn.	Fabaceae	H
828.	*Psidium gualava* L.	Myrtaceae	T
829.	*Psychotria navida* Talbot.	Rubiaceae	S

Sl. No.	NAME OF PLANTS	FAMILY	HABIT
830.	*Pteris pellucida* Pres!	Pteridaceae	HF
831.	*Pterocarpus marsupium Roxb.*	Fabaceae	T
832.	*Pueraria tuberosa (Roxb.) DC.*	Fabaceae	CS
833.	*Pulicaria wightiana Clarke*	Asteraceae	H
834.	*Pupalia lappacea* Moq.	Amaranthaceae	H
835.	*Putranjiva roxburghii Wall.*	Euphorbiaceae	T
836.	*Quisqualis indica* L.	Combretaceae	CS
837.	*Radermachera xylocarpa (Roxb.) K. Schum.*	Bignoniaceae	T
838.	*Raphanus sativus* L.	Brassicaceae	H
839.	*Rauvoffia densiflora Banth. & Hook. f.*	Apocynaceae	S
840.	*Rauvolfia serpentina (L.) Benth. ex. Kurz.*	Apocynaceae	H
841.	*Rauvolfia tetraphyl/a* L.	Apocynaceae	H
842.	*Reinwardtia trigyna Planch.*	Linaceae	H
843.	*Remusatia vivipara (Roxb.) Schott.*	Araceae	H
844.	*Rhamphicarpa longiflora Benth.*	Scrophulariaceae	H
845.	*Rhinacanthus nasuta* (L.) Kurz.	Acanthaceae	S
846.	*Rhus mysurensis Heyne ex Wt. & Am.*	Anacardiaceae	T
847.	*Rhynchosia cyanospetma Benth.*	Fabaceae	H
848.	*Riccia sp.*	Ricciaceae	
849.	*Ricinus communis* L.	Euphorbiaceae	S
850.	*Rorippa indica* (L.) Hiem.	Brassicaceae	H
851.	*Rostellularia japonica (Thumb.) Ellis.*	Acanthaceae	H
852.	*Rotala indica* (Willd.) Koehne.	Lythraceae	H
853.	*Rotala serpyllifolia (Roth.) Bremek.*	Lythraceae	H
854.	*Rourea minor* (Gaertn.) Alston.	Connaraceae	CS
855.	*Rubia cordifolia* L.	Rubiaceae	CS
856.	*Rungia crenata* T. And.	Acanthaceae	H
857.	*Rungia pectinata* (L.) Nees.	Acanthaceae	H
858.	*Rungia repens* (L.) Nees.	Acanthaceae	H
859.	*Sacciolepis myosuroides (R.Br.) A.Camus.*	Poaceae	HG
860.	*Sageraea laurifolia (Graham.) Blatter.*	Annonaceae	T
861.	*Salacia chinensis* L.	Celastraceae	S
862.	*Salacia mcrosperma Wt.*	Celastraceae	CS
863.	*Salvadora persica* L.	Salvadoraceae	S
864.	*Salvia plebeia* R.Br.	Lamiaceae	T
865.	*Samadera indica Gaertn.*	Simaroubaceae	T
866.	*Samania saman* (Bth.) Merr.	Mimosaceae	T
867.	*Suntu/um a/bum L.*	Santalaceae	T
868.	*Sapindus emarginatus Vahl.*	Sapindaceae	T
869.	*Sapindus trifoliatus* L.	Spindaceae	T

Sl. No.	NAME OF PLANTS	FAMILY	HABIT
870.	*Sapium insigne var.malabaricum (Wt.) Hook.f.*	Euphorbiaceae	T
871.	*Saraca asoca de Willd.*	Caesalpiniaceae	T
872.	*Sarcostemma secamone (L.) Bennt.*	Asclepiadaceae	CH
873.	*Scaveola koenigii* Vahl.	Goodeniaceae	S
874.	*Schefflera venulosa* (Wt. & A.) Harms.	Araliaceae	S
875.	*Schinus molle* L.	Sapindaceae.	S
876.	*Schleichera oleosa (lour.) Oken.*	Sapindaceae	T
877.	*Schoenoplectus articulatus L.*	Cyperaceae	H
878.	*Schoenoplectus supinus L.*	Cyperaceae	H
879.	*Scilla viridis* Blatt. & Hall.	Liliaceae	H
880.	*Scutia myrtina* (Burm. f.) Kurz.	Rhamnaceae	S
881.	*Securinega virosa (Roxb.ex.Willd.) Pax.& Hoffm.*	Euphorbiacsa	S
882.	*Sehima nervosum* (Rottl.) Forsk.	Poaceae	HG
883.	*Selaginella* sp.	Selaginellaceae	H
884.	*Semecarpus anacardiumL.f.*	Anacardiaceae	T
885.	*Senecio dalzellii* Clark.	Asteraceae	H
886.	*Senecio grahami* Hook.	Asteraceae	H
887.	*Sesamum indicum* L.	Pedaliaceae	H
888.	*Sesamum laciniatum Klein.*	Pedaliaceae	H
889.	*Sesbania bispinasa (Jacq.) Fawcett.*	Fabaceae	H
890.	*Sesbania grandinora (L.) Poir.*	Fabaceae	T
891.	*Sesbania sesban* (L.) Merr.	Fabaceae	H
892.	*Setaria glauea* Beauv.	Poaceae	HG
893.	*Setaria tomentosa (Roxb.) Kunth.*	Poaceae	HG
894.	Sida *aeuta* BurmJ.	Malvaceae	H
895.	Sida *cordata* Borsum.	Malvaceae	H
896.	Sida *cordifolia* L.	Malvaceae	H
897	Sida *rhombifolia* L.	Malvaceae	H
898.	Sida *rhombifolia* var. refusa Masters.	Malvaceae	H
899.	Sida *veronieifolia* Lamk.	Malvaceae	H
900.	*Sideroxylon tomentosum Roxb.*	Sapotaceae	T
901.	*Smilax zeylanica* L.	Smilacaceae	H
902.	*Smithia bigemina* Dalz.	Fabaceae	H
903.	*Smithia conferta* Sm.	Fabaceae	H
904.	*Smithia hirsuta* Dalz.	Fabaceae	H
905.	*Smithia purpurea* Hook.	Fabaceae	H
906.	*Smithia sensitiva* Ail.	Fabaceae.	H
907.	*Solanum giganteum Jacq.*	Solanaceae	S
908.	*Solanum melongena* L.	Solanaceae	H
909.	*Solanum nigrum* L.	Solanaceae	H

Sl. No.	NAME OF PLANTS	FAMILY	HABIT
910.	*Solanum tuberosum* L.	Solanaceae	H
911.	*Solanum violaceum Ortega.*	Solanaceae	H
912.	*Solanum virginianum* L.	Solanaceae	H
913.	*Solena amplexicaulis (Lamk.) Gandhi.*	Cucurbitaceae	CS
914.	*Sonchus asper (L.) Garsault*	Asteraceae	H
915.	*Sonchus oleraeeus* L.	Asteraceae	H
916.	*Sopubia delphinifolia G.Don.*	Boraginaceae	H
917.	*Spermadictyon suaveolens Roxb.*	Rubiaceae	S
918.	*Sphaeranthus indicus* L.	Asteraceae	H
919.	*Sphenoclea zeylanica* L.	Sphenocleaceae	H
920.	*Sphenostylis bracteata (Baker.) Gillett.*	Fabaceae	S
921.	*Spilanthes acmella* Murr.	Asteraceae	H
922.	*Spilanthus clava* DC.	Asteraceae	H
923.	*Spondias pinnata (U) Kurz.*	Anacardiaceae	T
924.	*Sporobolus diander (Retz.) Beauv.*	Poaceae	HG
925.	*Stemodia serrata* (Hook.) Benth.	Scrophulariaceae	H
926.	*Stemodia viscosa* Roxb.	Scrophulariaceae	H
927.	*Sterculia guttata* Roxb.	Sterculiaceae	T
928.	*Sterculia urens* Roxb.	Sterculiaceae	T
929.	*Sterculia vil/osa* Roxb.	Sterculiaceae	T
930.	*Stereospermum personatum (Hassk.) Chaterjee*	Bignoniaceae	T
931.	*Streblus asper* Lour.	Moraceae	H
932.	*Striga asitica (L.) Kuntz.*	Scrophulariaceae	H
933.	*Striga densinora* Benth.	Scrophulariaceae	H
934.	*Striga gesneroides (Willd.) Vatke*	Scrophulariaceae	H
935.	*Striga lutea* Lour	Scrophulariaceae	H
936.	*Strychnos nux- vomica* L.	Loganiaceae	T
937.	*Stylosanthus fruticosa (Retz.) Aist.*	Fabaceae	H
938.	*Sutera glandulosa* Roth.	Scrophulariaceae	H
939.	*Symphorema involucaratum Roxb.*	Verbenaceae	S
940.	*Syzygium caryophyllifolia Lamk.*	Myrtaceae	T
941.	*Syzygium cumini* (L.) Skeels	Myrfaceae	T
942.	*Syzygium heyneanum (Duthie.) Gamble.*	Myrtaceae	T
943.	*Syzygium zeylanicum* (L.) DC.	Myrtaceae	T
944.	*Tagetes patula* L.	Asteraceae	H
945.	*Tamarindus incJlca* L.	Caesalpiniaceae	T
946.	*Tamarix ericoides* Rottl.	T amaricaceae	T
947.	*Taxillus euneatus* (Roth.) Danser	Loranthaceae	CH
948.	*Tectaria cicutaria* (L.) Copel.	Aspidiaceae	HG
949.	*Tectona grandis* L.f.	Verbenaceae	T

Sl. No.	NAME OF PLANTS	FAMILY	HABIT
950.	*Tephrosia coccinea* Wall.	Fabaceae	H
951.	*Tephrosia pumila* (Lamk.) Pers.	Fabaceae	H
952.	*Tephrosia purpurea* Pers.	Fabaceae	H
953.	*Teramnus labialis* (L.f.) Spreng.	Fabaceae	CH
954.	*Terminalia alata* Roth.	Combretaceae	T
955.	*Terminalia afjuna* (Roxb.) 'Wt. & Am.	Combretaceae	T
956.	*Terminalia bellirica (Gaertn.) Roxb.*	Combretaceae	T
957.	*Terminalia catapa* L.	Combretaceae	T
958.	*Terminalia ehebula* Retz.	Combretaceae	T
959.	*Terminalia crenulata Roth.*	Combretaceae	T
960.	*Terminafia paniculata Roth.*	Combretaceae	T
961.	*Terminalia tomentosa Wt. & Am.*	Combretaceae	T
962.	*Tertrapogon tenellus (Roxb.) Choiv.*	Poaceae	HG
963.	*Thelepaepale ixiocephala (Benth.) Sremek.*	Acanthaceae	H
964.	*Themeda quadrivalvis (L.) O. Kuntze*	Poaceae	HG
965.	*Thespesia populnea Soland.*	Malvaceae	T
966.	*Thevetia peruviana (Pers.) K. Sch.*	Apocynaceae	S
967.	*Thunbergia alata* Boj.	Acanthaceae	CS
968.	*Thunbergia grandiflora Roxb.*	Acanthaceae	CS
969.	*Tinospora cordifolia (Willd.) Miers.*	Menispermaceae	CS
970.	*Tinospora glabra (Burm.f.) Merrill.*	Menispermaceae	CS
971.	*Tinospora sinensis (Lour.) Merrill.*	Menispermaceae	CS
972.	*Toona hexandra* (Wall.ex Roxb.) Roemer	Meliaceae	S
973.	*Trachispermum stictocarpum* Link.	Apiaceae	H
974.	*Tragia involucrata* L.	Euphorbiaceae	H
975.	*Tragia muelleriana* var. unicolor (Muell.- Arg.) Pax. & Hoffm.	Euphorbiaceae	H
976.	*Trema orientalis* (L.) Blume.	Ulmaceae	T
977.	*Trewia polycarpa* Benth.	Euphorbiaceae	T
978.	*Trlbulus terrestris* L.	Zygophyllaceae	S
979.	*Trichilia connaroides (Wt. & Am.) Benth.*	Meliaceae	T
980.	*Trichodesma indicum R.Br.*	Boraginaceae	H
981.	*Trichodesma sedgwickianum Banerjee.*	Boraginaceae	H
982.	*Tricholepis indica (Willd.) Almeida*	AstefJJceae	H
983.	*Tricholepis radicans* DC.	Asteraceae	H
984.	*Trichosanthes anguina* -L.	Cucurbitaceae.	CS
985.	*Trichosanthes bracteata (Lamk.) Voigt*	Cucurbitaceae	CS
986.	*Trichosanthes cucumerina L.*	Cucurbitaceae	CS
987.	*Tridax procumbens* L.	Asteraceae	H
988.	*Triticum vulagare* Vill.	Poaceae	HG

Sl. No.	NAME OF PLANTS	FAMILY	HABIT
989.	*Triumfetta annua* L.	Tiliaceae	H
990.	*Triumfetta rhomboidea Lam.*	Tiliaceae	H
991.	*Tumera ulmifolia* var. angustifolia	Tumeraceae	H
992.	*Turraea villosa* Benn.	Meliaceae	T
993.	*Tylophora dalzellii* Hk. f.	Asclepiadaceae	CH
994.	*Typha angustata* Bory. & Chaub.	Typhaceae	H
995.	*Uraria pieta* Desv.	Fabaceae	H
996.	*Uraria rufeseens* (DC.) Schlndl.	Fabaceae	H
997.	*Urena lobata* L. var. lappago Almeida	Malvaceae	H
998.	*Urena lobata* L.	Malvaceae	H
999.	*Utricularia arcuata* Wight	Lentibulariacee	H
1000.	*Utrieularia exoleta* R. Sr.	Lentibulariaceae	H
1001.	*Utricularia stellaris* L.	Lentibulariaceae	H
1002.	*Utrieularia striatula* 5m.	Lentibulariaceae	H
1003.	*Uvaria hookeri* King	Annonaceae	CS
1004.	*Vallaris solanaeeb* (Roth.) O. Kuntze.	Apocynaceae	CS
1005.	*Vanda roxburghii* R.Br.	Orchidaceae	EH
1006.	*Vanda testacea* (Lind!.) Reichab.	Orchidaceae	EH
1007.	*Vangueria spinosa* Roxb.	Rubiaceae	S
1008.	*Ventilago maderaspatana Gaertn.*	Rhamnaceae	CS
1009.	*Verbaseum chinense Santapau*	Scrophulariaceae	S
1010.	*Vemonia cinerea* (L.) Less.	Asteraceae	S
1011.	*Vemonia divergens (Roxb.) Edg.*	Asteraceae	S
1012.	*Vicoa cemua* Dalz.	Asteraceae	H
1013.	*Vicoa indica* (Willd.) DC.	Asteraceae	H
1014.	*Vigna aconitifolia* (Jacq.) Marshall.	Fabaceae	H
1015.	*Vigna capensis* Walp.	Fabaceae	H
1016.	*Vigna khandalensis (Sant.) Raghavan & Wadhwa*	Fabaceae	H
1017.	*Vigna radiata* (L.) Wilczek.	Fabaceae	H
1018.	*Vigna trilobus* (Ait.)	Fabaceae	H
1019.	*Vigna unguiculata* (L.) Walp.	Fabaceae	H
1020.	*Viscum angulatum Heyne*	Loranthaceae	CH
1021.	*Vitex negundo* L.	Verbenaceae	S
1022.	*Vitex trifolia* L.	Verbenaceae	S
1023.	*Vitis elongata* Wall. Ex Wt. & Am.	Vitaceae	CS
1024.	*Waltheria indica* L.	Sterculiaceae	H
1025.	*Wedelia biflora* DC.	Asteraceae	CS
1026.	*Woodfordia fruiticosa* (L.) Kurz.	Lythraceae	S
1027.	*Wrightia tinctoria* R. Sr.	Apocynaceae	S
1028.	*Xanthium strumarium* L.	Asteraceae	S

Sl. No.	NAME OF PLANTS	FAMILY	HABIT
1029.	*Xantolis tomentosa (Roxb.)Raf.*	Sapotaceae	T
1030.	*Xeromphis spinosa (Thumb.) Keay*	Rubiaceae	S
1031.	*Xylia xylocarpa* (Roxb.) Jaub.	Fabaceae	T
1032.	*Zanthoxylum rhetsa (Roxb.) DC.*	Rutaceae	T
1033.	*Zea mays* L.	Poaceae	HG
1034.	*Zingiber macrostachyum Dalz.*	Zingiberaceae	H
1035.	*Zizyphus glaberrima Santapau*	Rhamnaceae	S
1036.	*Zizyphus mauritiana Lamk.*	Rhamnaceae	S
1037.	*Zizyphus oenoplia* Mill.	Rhamnaceae	S
1038.	*Zizyphus rugosa* Lamk.	Rhamnaceae	S
1039.	*Zomia diphylla (L.)Pers.*	Fabaceae	H
1040.	*Zomia gibbosa* Span.	Fabaceae	H

APPENDIX 5. SPECIES DIVERSITY HAVING MEDICINAL PROPERTIES FOUND IN SACRED GROVES OF MANIPUR (AFTER KHUMBONGMAYUM *et al.*, 2005).

Sl. No.	NAME OF PLANTS	FAMILY	HABIT
1.	Cissus *discolor* Blume	Vitaceae	Herb
2.	*Clerodendrum serratum* (L.) Moon	Verbenaceae	Shrub
3.	*Clerodendrum viscosum Vent.*	Verbenaceae	Shrub
4.	*Coix lacryma-jobi* Linn.	Poaceae	Herb
5.	*Colocasia esculenta* (L.) Scott	Araceae	Herb
6.	*Commelina benghalensis Linn.*	Commelinaceae	Herb
7.	*Cordia grandis* Roxb.	Boraginaceae	Tree
8.	*Costus speciosus* (Koenig) Sm.	Zingiberaceae	Herb
9.	*Cymbopogon flexuosus (Steud.) Wats.*	Poaceae	Herb
10.	*Cynodon dactylon* Pers.	Poaceae	Herb
11.	*Cyperus rotundus* Linn.	Cyperaceae	Herb
12.	*Dactyloctenium aegyptium Beauv.*	Poaceae	Herb
13.	*Datura suaveolens* Humb. & Bonpl.ex Willd.	Solanaceae	Shrub
14.	*Dioscorea alata* Linn.	Dioscoreaceae	Herb
15.	*Dioscorea bulbifera* Linn.	Dioscoreaceae	Herb
16.	*Drymaria cordata* Wild.	Caryophyllaceae	Herb
17.	*Duchesnea indica* Focke	Rosaceae	Herb
18.	*Duranta repens* Linn.	Verbenaceae	Shrub
19.	*Eclipta prostrata* (Linn.) Linn.	Asteraceae	Herb
20.	*Entada phaseoloides* Merill	Mimosaceae	Tree
21.	*Eucalyptus citriodora* Hook.	Myrtaceae	Tree
22.	*Eupatorium cannabinum Linn.*	Asteraceae	Herb
23.	*Ficus benghalensis* Linn.	Moraceae	Tree
24.	*Ficus benjamina* Linn.	Moraceae	Tree
25.	*Ficus glome rata* Roxb.	Moraceae	Tree
26.	*Ficus hispida* Linn. f.	Moraceae	Tree
27.	*Ficus religiosa* Linn.	Moraceae	Tree
28.	*Ficus semicordata* Buch.Ham. ex Sm.	Moraceae	Tree
29.	*Flacourtia jangomas Raeusch.*	Flacourtiaceae	Tree
30.	*Galinsoga parviflora* Cav.	Asteraceae	Herb
31.	*Gardenia campanulata Roxb.*	Rubiaceae	Tree
32.	*Glycosmis arborea* Correa	Rutaceae	Shrub

Sl. No.	NAME OF PLANTS	FAMILY	HABIT
33.	*Gmelina arborea* Roxb.	Verbenaceae	Tree
34.	*Gynura cusimbua* Moore	Asteraceae	Herb
35.	*Hemidesmus indicus* R. Br.	Asclepiadaceae	Herb
36.	*Holigarna longifolia* Roxb.	Anacardiaceae	Tree
37.	*Houttuynia cordata* Thunb.	Saurauriaceae	Herb
38.	*Hydrocotyle javanica Thunb.*	Apiaceae	Herb
39.	*Imperata cylindrica* Beauv.	Poaceae	Herb
40.	*Lannea coromandelica (Houtt.) Merill*	Anacardiaceae	Tree
41.	*Lantana camara* Linn.	Verbenaceae	Shrub
42.	*Utsea monopetala* Pers.	Uraceae	Tree
43.	*Utsea glutinosa* Robins	Lauraceae	Tree
44.	*Lygodium japonicum (Thumb) Sw.*	Schizaeaceae	Herb
45.	*Maesa indca* Wall.	Myrsinaceae	Shrub
46.	*Mallotus philippensis Muell-Arg.*	Euphorbiaceae	Tree
47.	*Mangifera indica* Linn.	Anacardiaceae	Tree
48.	*Melastoma malabathricum Linn.*	Melastomaceae	Shrub
49.	*Melia azedarach* Linn.	Meliaceae	Tree
50.	*Melothria maderaspatana (Linn.) Cogn.*	Curcubitaceae	Herb
51.	*Meyna laxiflora* Robyns	Rubiaceae	Tree
52.	*Milamia micrantha* Kunth	Asteraceae	Herb
53.	*Muscari commutalum* Guss.	Liliaceae	Herb
54.	*Oroxylum indkum* Vent	Bignoniaceae	Tree
55.	*Oxalis comkulata* Linn.	Oxalidaceae	Herb
56.	*Paederiafoetida* Linn.	Rubiaceae	Herb
57.	*Parkia roxburghii* G. Don	Mililosaceae	Tree
58.	*Peristrophe bicalyculata Nees*	Acanthaceae	Herb
59.	*Phlogacanthus thyrsifolius Nees*	Acanthaceae	Shrub
60.	*Phyllanlhus emblica* Linn.	Euphorbiaceae	Tree
61.	*Phyllanthusfratemus* Web.	Euphorbiaceae	Herb
62.	*Pinus insularis* End.	Pinaceae	Tree
63.	*Piper longum* Linn.	Piperaceae	Herb
64.	*Plantago erosa* Wall. Ex Roxb.	Plantaginaceae	Herb
65.	*Polygonum orientale* Linn.	Polygonaceae	Herb
66.	*Pteris ensiformis* Burm.f.	Pteridaceae	Herb
67.	*Ranunculus sceleratus* Linn.	Ranunculaceae	Herb
68.	*Rhus chinensis* Mill.	Anacardiaceae	Tree
69.	*Rubus moluccanus* Linn.	Rosaceae	Shrub
70.	*Rumex nepalensis* Spreng.	Polygonaceae	Herb
71.	*Schefflera hypoleuca* Harms	Araliaceae	Tree
72.	*Schima wallichii* (DC.) Korth.	Theaceae	Tree

Sl. No.	NAME OF PLANTS	FAMILY	HABIT
73.	*Scutellaria discolor* Colebr.	Lamiaceae	Herb
74.	*Sida rhombifolia* Linn.	Malvaceac	Shrub
75.	*Smilax zeylanica* Linn.	Liliaceae	Herb
76.	*Solanum torvum* Sw.	Solanaceae	Shrub
77.	*Spilanthus acmella* Murr.	Asteraceae	Herb
78.	*Spondias pinnata* (Linn.f.) Kurz	Anacardiaceae	Tree
79.	*Stephania hernandifolia Walp.*	Menisperrnaceae	Herb
80.	*Syzygium jambos* (Linn.) Alston.	Myrtaceae	Tree
81.	*Terminalia citrina* Roxb.ex Flem.	Combretaceae	Tree
82.	*Thunbergia grandiflora Roxb.*	Acanthaceae	Herb
83.	*Tournefortia montana* Lour.	Boraginaceae	Shrub
84.	*Trema orientalis* Blume	Ulmaceae	Tree
85.	*Viola pilosa* Blume	Violaceae	Herb
86.	*Vitex tri/olia* Linn.	Verbenaceae	Shrub
87.	*Wendlandia tinctoria* DC.	Rubiaceae	Tree
88.	*Xanthium strumarium* Linn.	Asteraceae	Shrub
89.	*Xylosma longifolium* Clos	Flacourtiaceae	Tree
90.	*Zanthoxylum limnonella Alston*	Rutaceae	Tree

APPENDIX 6. SPECIES DIVERSITY FOUND IN SACRED GROVES OF MEGHALAYA (AFTER TIWARI *et al.*, 1999).

T= Tree, S = Shrub, C = Climber, CS = Climbing shrub, Cl = Climber, H= Herb, E= Epiphyte, HG = Herb grass L = Liana, RET = Rare, endangered and threatened category

Sl. No.	NAME OF PLANTS	HABIT	STATUS
1.	*Antidesma acuminatum* Wall.	T	
2.	*Eugenia* Sp.	T	
3.	*Luculia pinceana* HookJ	S	
4.	23. *Eragrostiella leioptera* (Slapf.) Bor.	H	
5.	9. *Bauhinia* sp.	T	
6.	*Acrocarpus fraxinifolius* Wight	T	
7.	*Adenostemma lavenia* (L). O. Ktze	H	
8.	*Aechmanthera gossypina* Nees	S	
9.	*Aeschenanthus manii* Kurz ex CI		
10.	*Aeschynanthes parasticus* (Roxb) Wall	H	
11.	*Agapetes obovata* (Wt) Hook.f.	H	
12.	*Ageratum conyzoides*	H	
13.	*Agrimonia eupatora L.*	H	
14.	*Agrostis zenkeri* Trin	H	
15.	*Ainsliaca angustifolia* Hook.f. & Thomas	H	
16.	*Aiuga lobnta* Don.	H	
17.	*Alangium begoniaefolia* (Roxb.) Baill.	T	
18.	*Albizzia lebbek*	T	
19.	*Albizzia procera* Benth.	T	
20.	*Alpinia allughas* Roxb.	Cl	
21.	*Alseodaphne petiolaris* Hook.f.	T	
22.	Amomum sp.	Cl	
23.	*Anaphalis adnata.* Dc	H	
24.	*Anaphalis contorta* (D. Don) Hook.f.	H	
25.	*Anaphalis timmua* D. Don	H	
26.	*Anemone rivularis* Buch. Ham. Ex d.	H	
27.	*Anotis ingrata Wall*	S	
28.	*Anotis oxyphylla* HookJ.	S	
29.	*Anotis wightiana* Hook.f.	H	
30.	*Apios cornea* Benth		

Sl. No.	NAME OF PLANTS	HABIT	STATUS
31.	*Apodites dimidiata* Arn		
32.	*Aporosa roxburghii* Baill.	T	
33.	Aquilaria agallocha Roxb.	T	
34.	Ardisia crisp a (Thunb) Dc	S	
35.	*Ardisia undulata* Clarke	S	
36.	*Argyreia hookeri* CI		
37.	*Artabotrys caudautus* Wall.	Cl	
38.	Artocarpus gomezianus Wall ex		
39.	Aspidopterys elliptica A. Juss.	Cl	
40.	*Axonopus compressus* (Swartz) P. Beauv	H	
41.	*Balanophora dioica* R.Br.	H	
42.	*Baliospermum micranthum Muell-Arg*	T	
43.	*Bauhinia khasiana* (Boker). Thoth.	T	
44.	*Bauhinia nervosa* Wall.	T	
45.	*Bauhinia purpurea*	T	
46.	*Bauhinia vahlii*	T	
47.	*Bauhinia veriegata* Linn.	T	
48.	*Begonia pedunculosa* Wall	H	
49.	*Begonia picta* Sm.	H	
50.	*Begonia polmota* D. Don	H	
51.	*Beilschimiedia assamica* Meissn.	T	
52.	Beilschmiedia brandisii Hk.f.	T	
53.	*Berberis wallichiana* Dc	S	
54.	*Berchemia floribunda* (Wall) Brongn	S	
55.	*Bielschmedia brandisii* Hk.		(rare species)
56.	*Blachnum* sp.	H	
57.	*Boechmeria platyphylla* D. Don	S	
58.	*Bombax* ceiba	T	
59.	*Bombax malabarica*	T	
60.	Bombax malabaricum D.C.	T	
61.	Borreria sp.	H	
62.	*Breynia retusa* (Dennst) Aist.	T	
63.	Brucea mollis Kurz	T	
64.	*Brunella vulgaris* L.Yar. Hispida Benth.	H	
65.	Calamus erectus Roxb.	Cl	
66.	*Calcicarpa arborescens*	T	
67.	*Calliandra umbrosa* Benth.	T	
68.	*Callicarpa arborea*	T	
69.	Callicarpa arborea Roxb.	T	
70.	Callicarpa psilocalyx. CI.	T	

Sl. No.	NAME OF PLANTS	HABIT	STATUS
71.	*Camellia caduca* Brandis	S	
72.	*Camellia kissi.* Wall	T	
73.	Capparis zeylanica Linn.	T	
74.	*Cardiopteris lobata* R. Br.	Cl	
75.	*Carex vesiculosa* Booth	H	
76.	Careya *arborea* Roxb.	T	
77.	Careya arboreali	T	
78.	*Carpesium cernuum* L.	H	
79.	*Carpinus viminea.* Lind.	T	
80.	Casearia *kurzi;* C.B. Clarke	T	
81.	*Cassia occidentalis* Linn.	S	
82.	*Castanopsis armata*	T	
83.	*Castanopsis armata* Spach	T	
84.	*Castanopsis hystrix*	T	
85.	*Castanopsis indica*	T	
86.	*Castanopsis indica* A. Dc	T	
87.	Castanopsis indica A. DC.	T	
88.	*Castanopsis kurzi;* (Hance). S.N. Biswas	T	
89.	*Castanopsis kurzii*	T	
90.	*Castanopsis mystrix*	T	
91.	*Castanopsis tribuloides*	T	
92.	Castanopsis tribuloides A. DC.	T	
93.	Cayrata *pedata* (Lour) Gagnep	H	
94.	Celastrus stylosus Wall	S	
95.	Centranthera grandiflora Benth	H	
96.	*Chirita* hamosa R.Br		
97	Chonemorpha sp.	T	
98.	*Cleidion javanicum* Blume.	T	
99.	*Cinnamomum impressinervium Meissn*	T	
100.	*Cinnomomum* sp.	T	
101.	*Clematis apiculata* Hook		
102.	Clerodendron sp.	S	
103.	*Clerodendron wallichii* Merr	T	
104.	*Clerodendrum* hasatatum lindl		
105.	*Codonopsis javanica* (BI) Hk.		
106.	Crataeva magna (Laur.) DC.	T	
107.	Creteva *nurvala* Ham		
108.	*Crossocephalum crapioidis*	H	
109.	Croton sp.	T	
110.	*Cryptocarpa andersonii* King		

Sl. No.	NAME OF PLANTS	HABIT	STATUS
111.	*Cyathocalyx martabanicus* Hk		
112.	Cynometra polyandra Roxb.	T	
113.	*Cyperus flavidus* Retz	H	
114.	*Cyperus* Sp.	H	
115.	Cyperus sp.	H	
116.	Dalbergia sissoo Roxb.	T	
117.	Daphne bhalua Buch. Ham. ex.D. Don	T	
118.	*Daphne shillong* Banerji	T	
119.	*Dendrocalamus gigantea*	T	
120.	Dendrocalamus hamiltonii	T	
121.	Derris ferruginea Benth.	Cl	
122.	*Desmodium vacemosum* Thunb	S	
123.	*Diflugossa colovata* (Nees) Breni	S	
124.	*Digitalis* sp.	H	
125.	*Dillenia indica*	T	
126.	*Dillenia pentagyna*	T	
127.	*Dillenia pentagyna* Roxb.	T	
128.	*Diospyros grata* Wall.	T	
129.	*Diospyros pilosula* (Dc) Hiern		
130.	*Diospyros stricta* Roxb.	T	
131.	*Diospyros undulata* Dc		
132.	*Docynia indica* (Wall) Decsne	T	
133.	Dracaena *spicata* Roxb.	S	
134.	*Drosera peltata* Smith	H	
135.	*Dysoxylum binactariferum* Hk.f.	T	
136.	Dysoxylum kurzii BI.	T	
137.	*Echinocarpus murex* Benth.	T	
138.	Elaeagnus conferta Roxb.	S	
139.	*Elaeocarpus acuminalis*	T	
140.	*Elaeocarpus acuminatus* Wall		
141.	*Elaeocarpus floribundus*	T	
142.	Elaeocarpus floribundus BI.	T	
143.	Elaeocarpus lancifolius Roxb	T	
144.	*Elaeocarpus prunifolius*	T	
145.	Elaeocorpus wallichii Kurz.	T	
146.	*Emblica floribunda* Wall	T	
147.	Emblica officinallis	T	
148.	Engelhardtia roxburghiana Wall	T	
149.	Engelhardtia spicata BI.	T	
150.	*Engelhardtia spicata* Blume	T	

Sl. No.	NAME OF PLANTS	HABIT	STATUS
151.	Engelhardtia spicata Blume.	T	
152.	*Eragrostis* nigra Nees ex Steud	H	
153.	*Erigeron bonariensis*	H	
154.	Erycibe paniculata Roxb.	Cl	
155.	*Erythrina arborescens*	T	
156.	Erythrina indica	T	
157.	*Erythroxylum kunthianum* Kurz	S	
158.	*Eupatorium adinophorum*	S	
159.	*Eupatorium nadiflorm* Dc	H	
160.	*Eupatorium odoratum*	S	
161.	*Eupatorium odoratum* Linn.	S	
162.	*Eupatorium riparium*	S	
163.	*Eurya acuminata* Dc	T	
164.	*Eurya acuminata* Dc.	T	
165.	*Eurya japonica* Thunb	S	
166.	Eurya japonica Thunb	S	
167.	*Exbucklandia populnea* (griff) R. Br.	T	
168.	*Exbucklandia populnea* (Griff) R.W. Brown	T	
169.	Ficus glomerata Roxb.	S	
170.	*Ficus* neriifolia J.E. Sm.	T	
171.	Ficus silhetensis Miq.	T	
172.	*Fimbristylis aestivalis* (Retz) Vahl	H	
173.	Fimbristylis dicholoma (L) Vahl	H	
174.	*Fimbristylis errgrostis* (Neez) Hance	H	
175.	*Firmiana colorata* Roxb.	T	
176.	*Fissistigma rubigonosum* (ADc) Merr		
177.	*Fissistigma* verrucosum (Hook.f.& Th.) Merr		
178.	Flacourtia jangomas (Lour) Raeusach	T	
179.	*Fraxinus f/oribundus* Wall		
180.	*Galinsoga ciliata*	H	
181.	*Galinsoga parviflora*	H	
182.	*Galium rotundifolium* L	H	
183.	*Garcina lancifolia*	T	
184.	*Garcinia* cowa Roxb.	T	
185.	Garnotia stricto Brongn	H	
186.	*Gastrodia exilis* Hook J.		
187.	*Gentiana quadrifaria* BI.	H	
188.	*Gleichenia* sp.	H	
189.	*Glochidion velutinum* Wight.	T	
190.	Gnetum scandens Roxb.	Cl	

Sl. No.	NAME OF PLANTS	HABIT	STATUS
191.	*Goldfussia glomerata* Nees	S	
192.	*Goniothalamus sesquipedalis (Wall) HookJ & Thomas*	S	
193.	*Goniothalamus simonsii* HookJ.& Th		
194.	*Gonithalamus sesquipedalis Hook.f. and Th.*	S	
195.	Gymnema *tingens* Roxb Spreng		
196.	Gynura cusimbua (D. Don) S.Moore	H	
197.	*Hedera nepalensis* K. Koch	S	
198.	*Hedychium spicatum* Buch-Ham Var acuminatum	S	
199.	*Hedyotis uncinella* Hook.f & Am	S	
200.	*Helica erratica* HookJ	T	
201.	*Helicia nilagirica* Bedd.	T	
202.	*Houttuynia cordata* Thunb	H	
203.	Hymenopogen parasiticus Wall	S	
204.	*Hypericum hookerianum* W.A.	S	
205.	Hypericum japonicum Thunb	S	
206.	*Hypericum mononthemum (Hook.f. & Thomas) Dyer*	S	
207	*Hypericum patulum* Thunb	S	
208.	Ilex excelsa Wall.ex.Hook.f.	T	
209.	Ilex griffithii Hook.f.	T	
210.	*Ilex Khasiana* Purkayastha		
211.	Ilex *odorata* D.Don	T	
212.	*Ilex venulosa* Hook.f.	T	
213.	Impatiens benthamii Y. Steenis	H	
214.	*Impatiens chinensis* L.	H	
215.	*Impatiens iuripa* Hook.f. & Thomas	H	
216.	*Impatiens khasiana* Hook.f.	H	
217.	Impatiens puberula Dc	H	
218.	Impatiens radiata Hook.f.	H	
219.	Impatiens tripetala Dc	H	
220.	*Imperato cylindrica*	H	
221.	*Ixora vilosa* Roxb.	S	
222.	*Jasminum dispermum* Wall	S	
223.	Justicia khasiana C.B.CI	S	
224.	Keyea floribunda Wall.	T	
225.	Khasiana *(Dyer)* Bloemb	T	
226.	*Lagerstroemia parviflora* Roxb.	T	
227.	*Lantana* camara	S	
228.	*Lasianthus longicaudata* HookJ & Thomas	S	
229.	*Lasiobema scandens* Linn.	Cl	
230.	*Leea umbraculifera* CB. Clarke.	S	

Sl. No.	NAME OF PLANTS	HABIT	STATUS
231.	*Ligustrum lucidum* Aiton	T	
232.	Ligustrum nepalense Wall	T	
233.	Ligustrum robustum (Roxb.) BI	T	
234.	Ligustrum robustum BI.	T	
235.	*Lindera melastomacea* Berth	T	(Paracitic)
236.	*Lindera pulcherrima* Benth	T	
237.	Lindera pulcherrima Benth	T	
238.	Lindera thomsoni Allen	T	
239.	*Linostoma* sp.	T	
240.	*Lithocarpus dealbatus* (Hook.f.et. Thems.Ex.Mig.) Rehder	T	
241.	*Lithocarpus elegans* (BI.) hatus	T	
242.	*Lithocarpus fenestratus (Roxb.) Rehder*	T	
243.	*Litsaea elongata* Wall	T	
244.	*Litsaea salicifolia Roxb*	T	
245.	*Litsea mechilus*	T	
246.	*Luculia pinceana* Hook.f.	T	
247.	*Luvunga scandens Ham*		
248.	*Lygodium flexuosum*	H	
249.	*Lyonia ovalifolia* (Wall) drude *var.* elliptica (Sieb & Zucc)	S	
250.	*Macaranga denticulata*	T	
251.	*Machilus odoratissima* Nees	T	
252.	*Macropanax undulatus* (Wall.ex.G. Don) Seem	T	
253.	*Mahonia pycnophylla (Fedde) Takede*	S	
254.	*Mallotus nepalensis Muel-Arg.*	T	
255.	*Manglieta caveana* Hook.f. & Thomas	T	
256.	*Manglieta* insignis (Wall) BI	T	
257.	*Manglietia insignis* (Wall) Blume	T	
258.	*Marlea bagoniaefolia* Roxb.	T	
259.	*Medinilla erochrophylla* Lind.	T	
260.	*Melanstroma nepalensis*	S	
261.	*Melastoma normale* D.Don	S	
262.	*Melia azadirachta* Linn.	T	
263.	*Meliosma manii lace*		
264.	*Meliosma simplicifolia* Roxb.	T	
265.	Mesua ferrea Linn.	T	
266.	*Mezoneurum* sp	Cl	
267.	*Michelia lanuginosa* Wall		
268.	Michelia punduana HookJ		
269.	*Mikania micrantha*	Cl	
270.	*Miliusa roxburghiana* Hk.f. & Th.	S	

Sl. No.	NAME OF PLANTS	HABIT	STATUS
271.	Miquelia kleinii Messn		
272.	*Mohonia pycnophylla* (Fedde) Takeda	S	
273.	Morinda villosa HookJ.		
274.	Morus indica L.	T	
275.	*Mucuna impricata* D.C.	Cl	
276.	*Mussaenda frondosa* L.	S	
277.	*Mycetia longifolia* O. Ktze.	S	
278.	*Myrica esculenta* Buch Ham	T	
279.	*Myrica esculenta* Buch. Ham	T	
280.	*Myriopteron* extensum (Wt. K.Schum)		
281.	Myrsie semiserrata Wall	S	
282.	*Neillia thyrisiflora* D. Don	S	
283.	*Nepenthes khasiana* HookJ		
284.	*Olea dentala Dc.*	T	
285.	*Oroxylum indicum* (L.) Vent.	T	
286.	Osbeckia glauca Naudin	S	
287.	*Osbeckia stellato* Ham.ex.Ker Gawl Var, Crinita (Naud)	S	
288.	Oxalis corniculata L	H	
289.	*Oxalis griffithii* Edgew	H	
290.	*Panax pseudoginseng* Wall. Var angustifolius	H	
291.	Parkia roxburghii G. Don.	T	
292.	Parsonsia spiralis Wall		
293.	Paspalum dilatatum	H	
294.	*Pauzoulzia*	H	
295.	*Pentapanax subcordatus (G. Don) Seem*	T	
296.	*Phorbe lanceolata* Nees	T	
297.	*Photinia arguta* Lind!.	T	
298.	*Photinia fulgens* Wall.ex.Lehn.	T	
299.	*Photinia polycarpa* (Hook.f.) Balak	T	
300.	Picrasma *javanica* BI		
301.	*Pinus kesiya* Royle ex. Gordon	T	
302.	*Pittosporum podocarpum Gagnep*	S	
303.	*Poa annua* L	H	
304.	*Poa khasiana* Stapf	H	
305.	*Polygala arillat* Buch Ham	S	
306.	*Polygala tricolopha* Chodat		
307.	Polygonum bistoria	H	
308.	*Polygonum chinense* (L) H.Gross	S	
309.	*Polygonum nepalensis* (Meissn) H. Gross	H	
310.	*Potentilla polyphylla* Wall	H	

Sl. No.	NAME OF PLANTS	HABIT	STATUS
311.	Premna punduana Wall		
312.	Prunus phaeostida Buch Ham	T	
313.	Prunus undulata Buch Ham	T	
314.	*Psycho tria symp/ocifolia Kurz*	T	
315.	*Psychotria adnephylla* Wall.	T	
316.	*Pteris* sp.	H	
317.	*Pterospermum acerifolium* Willd.	T	
318.	Pterospermum sp.	T	
319.	*Pyrularia edulis* (Wall). A. Dc	T	
320.	Pyrus baccata L.	T	
321.	*Pyrus khasiana* HookJ.	T	
322.	*Pyrus pashia* D. Don	T	
323.	*Quercus glauca* Thunb.	T	
324.	*Quercus griffithii* HookJ and Th.	T	
325.	*Quercus griHithii* Hook.f.	T	
326.	*Quercus kamroopii.* D. Don	T	
327.	*Quercus spicata* Smith	T	
328.	*Randia griffithii*	S	
329.	*Randia spinosa* (Thunb) Poir	S	
330.	*Ranunculus diffusus* Dc	H	
331.	*RauvolFia densiflora* (Wall) Hook.f.	S	
332.	Rhodedendron arboreum. Sm.	T	
333.	*Rhododendron formosum* Wall	S	
334.	*Rhus chinensis* Miller.	T	
335.	*Rhus chinensis.* Mill	T	
336.	*Rosa Moschata* Herrm	S	
337.	*Rubus assamensis Focke*	S	
338.	Rubus calycinus Wall	H	
339.	*Rubus ellipticus* Sm	S	
340.	*Rubus paniculatus* Smith	S	
341.	*Rubus* sp.	H	
342.	Sabia parviflora Wall		
343.	Sabia purpurea HookJ & th	S	
344.	Sageraea *laurine* Dalz		
345.	Sageratia hamosa Brongn		
346.	*Sageratia oppositifolia* Brongn		
347.	Salix psilostigma Anderss	S	
348.	*Sapium baccatum* Roxb.	T	
349.	Saprosma ternatum HkJ.	S	
350.	Saraca *indica* Linn.	T	

Sl. No.	NAME OF PLANTS	HABIT	STATUS
351.	*Sarcocca saligna* (D. Don) MuellArg	S	
352.	*Saurauia punduana.* Wall	T	
353.	*Saurauja roxburghii* Wall.	T	
354.	*Schefflera hypoleuca* Kurz	T	
355.	Schefflera sp.	Cl	
356.	Schima wallichii	T	
357.	Schima wallichii (Dc) Korth	T	
358.	*Schima wallichii* (Dc.) Korth, var.	T	
359.	Schleichera trijuga Willd		
360.	*Schoepfia fragrans* Wall	T	
361.	Scutellaria discolor Benth	H	
362.	*Sizygium jumbolanum* DC.	T	
363.	*Skimmia melanocarpa* Rehd. et.Wils	T	
364.	*Smilax aspera* L.	H	
365.	*Smilax lancaefolia* Roxb.	T	
366.	*Smithia* sp.	Cl	
367.	*Smythea calpicarpa* Kurr.	Cl	
368.	*Sonerila maculata* Roxb.	H	
369.	Spatholobus roxburghii Benth	Cl	
370.	*Spiraea callosa* Thunb	S	
371.	*Spodias* sp.	T	RET
372.	*Sterculia roxburghii* Wall.	T	RET
373.	*Sterculia villosa*	T	RET
374.	*Sterculia wallichii*	T	RET
375.	*Stereospermum chelonoides* DC.	T	RET
376.	*Strobilanthes* sp.	S	RET
377.	*Strophanthus wallichii* A.Dc		RET
378.	Styrax serrulatum Roxb.	T	RET
379.	*Symplocos chinensis* (Lour) Druce	S	RET
380.	*Symplocos glomerata.* King.ex. Gamble.	T	RET
381.	*Symplocos* sp.	T	RET
382.	*Symplocos spicata* Roxb.	T	RET
383.	*Symplocos spicata* Thunb	T	RET
384.	*Symplocos theifolia* D. Don	T	RET
385.	Talauma rabaniana Hk.f. & Th.		RET
386.	*Taxus baccata* L.	T	RET
387.	*Terminalia chebula* Retz.	T	RET
388.	*Ternstroemia* sp.	T	RET
389.	Thunbergia grandiflora Roxb.	Cl	RET
390.	*Thysanolaena maxima* Nees	S	RET

Sl. No.	NAME OF PLANTS	HABIT	STATUS
391.	*Thysonolaena* maxima	S	RET
392.	*Toddalis asiatica* (L) Lamk	S	RET
393.	Trecul. sp.		RET
394.	Treutelera insignis HkJ		RET
395.	*Ulmus lanceaefolia* Roxb		RET
396.	*Urena lobata* L.	H	RET
397.	Urtica parviflora Roxb	S	RET
398.	Uvaria hamiltoni Hk.f. & Th.	Cl	RET
399.	Uvaria lurida HkJ. & Th.	Cl	RET
400.	Vaccinium griffithianum Wt.	S	RET
401.	*Vaccinium sprengelii* (G. Don) Balar	T	RET
402.	*Vaccinium vacciniaceum* (Roxb) Sleum	S	RET
403.	*Ventilago madraspatana Geertn.*	Cl	RET
404.	*Vernonia volkameriaefolia* DC.	T	RET
405.	Viburnum foetidum Wall	S	RET
406.	*Viburnum sinensis* Wall	S	RET
407.	*Viola inconspicua BI*	H	RET
408.	*Wallsura* sp.	T	RET
409.	*Walsura robusta Roxb.*	T	RET
410.	*Wendlandia* sp.	T	RET
411.	*Wendlandia wallichii* W & A	S	RET
412.	*Wikstroemia canescens* Meissn	S	RET
413.	*Zanthoxylum armatum* Dc	T	RET
414.	*Zanthoxylum ovalifolium* Wt.	T	RET
415.	*Zerompus* sp.	T	RET
416.	*Zeylanicus* jarret		RET

APPENDIX 7. SPECIES DIVERSITY FOUND IN SACRED GROVES OF TAMIL NADU (AFTER SUKUMARAN *et al.*, 2005; AMRITHALINGAM, 2005).

Sl. No.	NAME OF PLANTS	FAMILY	RET
1.	*Abrus precatorius*		
2.	*Abutilon indicum*		
3.	*Acacia farnesiana*		
4.	*Acacia leucophloea*		
5.	*Acacia nilotica*		
6.	*Acacia polyantha*		
7.	Acalypha indica		
8.	Achyranthes aspera		
9.	*Acrostichum aureum Linn.*	Pteridaceae	RET
10.	Aegle marmelos		
11.	Aerva lanata		
12.	*Agave americana*		
13.	*Ailanthus malabaricum*		
14.	*Alangium salvifolium*		
15.	*Albizia lebbeck*		
16.	*Alpinia galanga* (Linn.) Wi lid.	*Zingiberaceae*	RET
17.	*Andrographis paniculata*		
18.	*Antiaris toxic aria* (Pers.) Lesch.	Moraceae	RET
19.	*Argemone mexicana*		
20.	*Aristolochia bracteolata*		
21.	*Artocarpus heterophyllus* Lam.	Moraceae	RET
22.	*Artocarpus hirsutus* Lam.	Moraceae	RET
23.	*Artocarpus integrifolia*		
24.	*Artocarpus lacucha* Roxb. Ex Buch.-Ham	Moraceae	RET
25.	*Asparagus racemosus*		
26.	*Asteriastigma macrocarpa* Bedd.	Flacourtiaceae	RET
27.	*Atalantia malabarica*		
28.	*Atalantia monophylla,* (Linn.) Corr.	Rutaceae	RET
29.	*Atalantia racemosa*		
30.	*Averrhoa carambola*		
31.	*Azadirachta indica*		
32.	Azima tetracantha		

Sl. No.	NAME OF PLANTS	FAMILY	RET
33.	Balanites aegyptiaca		
34.	Balsamodendron caudatum		
35.	*Bambusa arundinacea* (Retz.) Roxb.	Poaceae	RET
36.	Bambusa bambos		
37.	Bauhinia purpurea		
38.	Bauhinia tomentosa		
39.	Bixa orellana		
40.	Boerhaavia diffusa		
41.	Bombax ceiba		
42.	Borassus flabellifer		
43.	Buchanania lanzan		
44.	Butea monosperma		
45.	Cadaba fruticosa		
46.	Caesalpinia coriaria		
47.	Caesalpinia pulcherrima		
48.	*Calophyllum apetalum* Willd.	Clusiaceae	RET
49.	Calophyllum polyanthum Wall.ex.Ch.	Clusiaceae	RET
50.	Calotropis procera		
51.	Capparis divaricata		
52.	Cardiospermum halicacabum		
53.	*Carissa carandas*		
54.	*Cassia angustifolia*		
55.	*Cassia fistula*		
56.	*Cassia occidentalis*		
57.	*Cassia tora*		
58.	*Catharanthus roseus*		
59.	*Ceiba pentandra*		
60.	*Centella asiatica*		
61.	*Cheilanthes thwaitesii* Mett. ex. Kuhn.	Sinopteridaceae	RET
62.	*Chenopodium album*		
63.	*Chloroxylon swietinia*		
64.	*Cissus quadrangularis*		
65.	*Clitoria ternatea*		
66.	*Coccinia grandis*		
67.	*Combretum ovalifolium*		
68.	*Commiphora wightii*		
69.	*Corchorus olitorius*		
70.	*Cordia dichotoma*		
71.	*Cretaeva religiosa*		
72.	*Crotalaria retusa*		

Sl. No.	NAME OF PLANTS	FAMILY	RET
73.	*Cuscuta reflexa*		
74.	*Cycas circinalis* Linn.	Cycadaceae	RET
75.	Dalbergia latifolia		
76.	Dalbergia sissoo		
77.	*Datura metal*		
78.	*Dillenia indica*		
79.	*Dioscorea pentaphylla*		
80.	*Diospyros buxifolia* (Blume.) Hie	Ebenaceae	RET
81.	*Diospyros candolleana* Wight	Ebenaceae	RET
82.	*Diospyros ebenum* Koen.	Ebenaceae	RET
83.	*Diospyros malabarica*		
84.	*Diospyros melanoxylon*		
85.	*Diospyros paniculata* Dalzell	Ebenaceae	RET
86.	*Diospyrosfoliolosa* Wall.	Ebenaceae	RET
87.	*Emblica officinalis*		
88.	*Erythrina variegata*		
89.	*Euphorbia antiquorum*		
90.	*Ficus benghalensis*		
91.	*Ficus dalhousiae* Miq.	Moraceae	RET
92.	*Ficus racemosa*		
93.	*Ficus religiosa*		
94.	*Ficus retusa*		
95.	*Flacourtia indica*		
96.	*Garcinia gummi-gutta* (Linn.) Robs.	Clusiaceae	RET
97.	*Garcinia mangostana*		
98.	*Gloriosa superba*		
99.	*Gloriosa superba* Linn.	Liliaceae	RET
100.	*Gmelina asiatica*		
101.	*Gnetum ula* Brongn.	Gnetaceae	RET
102.	*Hemidesmus indicus*		
103.	*Hemidesmus indicus* (Linn) Shutt.		RET
104.	*Hiptage benghalensis*		
105.	*Holarrhena antidysenterica*		
106.	*Holostemma ada-kodien* Sch.	Asclepiadaceae	RET
107.	*Holigama grahamii* (Wight) Kurz	Anacardiaceae	RET
108.	*Hopea parviflora* Bedd.	Dipterocarpaceae	RET
109.	*Hugonia mystax*		
110.	*Hydnocarpus laurifolia* (Dennst.)	Flacourtiaceae	RET
111.	*Ichnocarpus frutescens*		
112.	*Impatiens balsamina*		

Sl. No.	NAME OF PLANTS	FAMILY	RET
113.	*Imperata cylindrica*		
114.	*Indigofera tinctoria*		
115.	*Indigofera uniflora* Buch-Ham ex Roxb.	Fabaceae	RET
116.	*Ipomoea pes-caprae*		
117.	*Ipomoea pes-tigridis*		
118.	*Ipomoea quamoclit*		
119.	*Ixora nigricans*		
120.	*Jasminum arborescens*		
121.	Jatropha curcas		
122.	*JustiCia beddomei* c.B.CI.	Acanthaceae	RET
123.	*Kaempfera galanga* L.	Zingiberaceae	RET
124.	Lagerstroemia indica		
125.	Lannea coromandelica		
126.	Lawsonia inermis		
127.	*Leea indica* (Burm.f.) Merr.	Leeaceae	RET
128.	*Limonia acidissima*		
129.	*Madhuca indica*		
130.	*Mangifera indica*		
131.	*Manilkara hexandra*		
132.	*Melia azedarach*		
133.	*Memecylon umbellatum*		
134.	*Memecylon umbellatum* Burm.f.	Memecylaceae	RET
135.	*Mesuaferrea* Linn. var. *coromandelica*	Clusiaceae	RET
136.	*Michelia champaca*		
137.	*Mimosa pudica*		
138	*Mimusops elengi*		
139.	*Morinda tinctoria*		
140.	*Morinda umbellata* Linn.	Rubiaceae	RET
141.	*Mucuna pruriens*		
142.	*Myrica esculenta*		
143.	*Myristica malabarica* Lam.	Myristicaceae	RET
144.	*Myrtus communis*		
145.	*Myxopyrum serratulum* A.w. Hill	Oleaceae	RET
146.	*Naregamia alata* Wight &Arn.	Meliaceae	RET
147.	*Nerium indicum*		
148.	*Nyctanthes arbor-tristis*		
149.	*Nymphea pubescens* Willd.	Nymphaeaceae	RET
150.	*Ochlandra scriptoria* (Dennst.) Ficer	Poaceae	RET
151.	Ochna squarrosa		
152.	Ocimum sanctum		

Sl. No.	NAME OF PLANTS	FAMILY	RET
153.	Operculina turpethum		
154.	Opuntia dillenii		
155.	*Osbeckia aspera* (L.) Blume var.wightiana	Melastomataceae	RET
156.	Ougeinia oojeinensis		
157.	*Persea macrantha* (Nees.) Kosterm.	Lauraceae	RET
158.	Phoenix sylvestris		
159.	*Pinanga dicksonii* (Roxb) Blume	Arecaceae	RET
160.	Pithecellobium dulce		
161.	Plumbago zeylanica		
162.	*Polyalthia fragrans* (Dalzell) Bedd	Annonaceae	RET
163.	Polyalthia longifolia		
164.	Pongamia pinnata		
165.	Portulaca oleracea		
166.	Prosopis spicigera		
167.	*Psilotum nudum* Linn.	Psilotaceae	RET
168.	Psoralea corylifolia		
169.	*Pteris confusa* Linn.	Pteridaceae	RET
170.	*Pteris vittata* Linn.	Pteridaceae	RET
171.	Pterocarpus marsupium		
172.	Quisqualis indica		
173.	Randia malabarica		
174.	*Rauvolfia serpentina* (Linn.) Benth ex Kurz	Apocynaceae	RET
175.	*Reinvardtiodendron anamallayanum Bedd.*	Meliaceae	RET
176.	Ricinus communis		
177.	Rumex vesicarius		
178.	Salix tetrasperma		
179.	Sansevieria roxburghiana		
180.	*Saraca asoca* (Roxb). Wilde	Caesalpinaceae	RET
181.	Schleichera oleosa		
182.	Semecarpus anacardium		
183.	Sida rhombifolia		
184.	Solanum anguivi		
185.	Solanum surattense		
186.	Spinacia oleracea		
187.	Spondias pinnata		
188.	Sterculia foetida		
189.	Streblus asper		
190.	*Strychnos minor* Dennst.	Strychnaceae	RET
191.	Strychnos nux-vomica		
192.	Strychnos potatorum		

Sl. No.	NAME OF PLANTS	FAMILY	RET
193.	Swertia chirayita		
194.	Syzygium cumini		
195.	Syzygium jambos		
196.	Tamarindus indica		
197.	*Tamilnadia uliginosa* (Retz.) Trivej & Sastre	Rubiaceae	RET
198.	*Tectaria zeylanica* (Hout.), Sledge	Tectarioideae	RET
199.	Tephrosia purpurea		
200.	Terminalia arjuna		
201.	*Terminalia paniculata* Roth.	Combretaceae	RET
202.	*Tetracera akara* (BurmJ.) Merr.	Dilleniaceae	RET
203.	Thespesia populnea		
204.	Thevetia peruviana		
205.	Tinospora cordifalia		
206.	*Toddalia asiatica*		
207.	Tribulus lanuginosus		
208.	Triumfetta rhomboidea		
209.	Tylophora indica		
210.	*Vateria indica* Linn.	Dipterocarpoceae	RET
211.	Vernonia arborea		
212.	*Vitex altissima* Linn.	Verbenaceae	RET
213.	Woodfordia fruiticosa		
214.	Wrightia tinctoria		
215.	Zizyphus mauritiana		
216.	Zizyphus oenoplia		

APPENDIX 8. BIRDS FROM SACRED GROVES OF KODAGU DISTRICT, KARNATAKA (BHAGWAT *et al.*, 2005).

Sl. No.	NAME OF THE BIRD
1.	Asian Brown Flycatcher
2.	Asian Fairy Bluebird
3.	Asian Koel
4.	Alexandrine Parakeet
5.	Asian Paradise Flycatcher
6.	Banded Bay Cuckoo
7.	Black-crested Bulbul
8.	Brown-cheeked Fulvetta
9.	Black Bulbul
10.	Black Drongo
11.	Black-naped Monarch
12.	Black-rumped Flameback
13.	Black-shouldered Kite
14.	Blue-winged Leafbird
15.	Baya Weaver
16.	Chestnut-bellied Nuthatch
17.	Crimson-backed Sunbird
18.	Common Chiffchaff
19.	Crimson-fronted Barbet
20.	Chestnut-headed Bee-eater
21.	Common Flameback
22.	Common Iora
23.	Common Myna
24.	Common Woodshrike
25.	Crested Serpant Eagle
26.	Chestnut-shouldered Petronia
27.	Chestnut-tailed Starling
28.	Dark Fronted Babbler
29.	Eurasian Golden Oriole
30.	Emerald Dove
31.	Green Bee-eater
32.	Grey-headed Canary Flycatcher

Sl. No.	NAME OF THE BIRD
33.	Gold-fronted Leafbird
34.	Greater Coucal
35.	Greater Racket-tailed Drongo
36.	Greater Flameback
37.	Hill Myna
38.	House Sparrow
39.	House Crow
40.	House Swift
41.	Heart-spotted Woodpecker
42.	Indian Scimitar Babbler
43.	Jungle Myna
44.	Jungle Prinia
45.	Large-billed Crow
46.	Loten's Sunbird
47.	Malabar Grey Hornbill
48.	Mountain Imperial Pigeon
49.	Malabar Parakeet
50.	Malabar Trogon
51.	Malabar Whistling Thrush
52.	Nilgiri Flycatcher
53.	Nilgiri Wood Pigeon
54.	Oriental Magpie Robin
55.	Pale-billed flowerpecker
56.	Plum-headed Parakeet
57.	Purple-rumped Sunbird
58.	Puff-throated Babbler
59.	Purple Sunbird
60.	Red-whiskered Bulbul
61.	Scarlet Minivet
62.	Shikra
63.	Spotted Dove
64.	Tickell's Blue Flycatcher
65.	Velvet-fronted Nuthatch
66.	Vernal Hanging Parrot
67.	White-browed Fantail
68.	White-bellied Treepie
69.	White-bellied Woodpecker
70.	White-cheeked Barbet
71.	White-eyed Buzzard
72.	White-throated Kingfisher

Sl. No.	NAME OF THE BIRD
73.	White-browed Wagtail
74.	Yellow-browed Bulbul
75.	Yellow-footed Green Pigeon

APPENDIX 9. MACROFUNGAL MORPHOPHYTES FROM SACRED GROVES OF KODAGU DISTRICT, KARNATAKA (BHAGWAT *et al.*, 2005).

Sl. No.	MACROFUNGAL MORPHOPHYTES
1.	Agaricus sp. (brown)
2.	Agaricus sp.
3.	Amanita sp.
4.	Ascomycetes (yellow-colored, ball-like sporocarps)
5.	Ascomycetes (elephant dung)
6.	Ascomycetes (spoon)
7.	Ascomycetes (thread)
8.	Astraeus sp.
9.	Auricularia sp.
10.	Boletus sp.
11.	Callocybe sp.
12.	Clavaria sp. (brown)
13.	Clavaria sp.
14.	Clavaria sp. (orange)
15.	Clavaria sp. (purple)
16.	Clavaria sp. (tree)
17.	Clavaria sp. (white)
18.	Clitocybe sp.
19.	Collybia sp. (brown in colour)
20.	Collybia sp. (Hygrophorus like)
21.	Collybia sp. (unknown)
22.	Coprinus sp.
23.	Cordyceps sp. (club)
24.	Cordyceps sp. (orange)
25.	Cordyceps sp. (tree)
26.	Coriolus sp. (Foemes like)
27.	Coriolus sp. (hirsute)
28.	Coriolus sp.
29.	Cortinarius sp.
30.	Cortinarius sp. (cyboid)
31.	Cortinarius sp. (Hebeloma
32.	Cortinarius sp. (Inocybe like)

Sl. No.	MACROFUNGAL MORPHOPHYTES
33.	Cortinarius sp. (rusty)
34.	Crepidotus sp.
35.	Daedalopsis flavida
36.	Daldinia sp.
37.	Dictyophora sp.
38.	Entolomataceae
39.	Entolomataceae (pink)
40.	Entolomataceae (white)
41.	Ganoderma sp. (big fruiting body)
42.	Ganoderma sp. (black)
43.	Ganoderma sp. (brown)
44.	Ganoderma sp. (orange colored)
45.	Ganoderma sp. (velvet)
46.	Geastrum sp.
47.	Hexagonia sp.
48.	Hygrocybe sp.
49.	Hygrophorus citratus
50.	Hygrophorus sp.
51.	Hygrophorus sp. (red)
52.	Leotia bulgaria
53.	Leotia sp. (Peziza like)
54.	Leotia sp. (brown)
55.	Leotia sp. (orange)
56.	Lycoperdon sp.
57.	Marasmius sp. (bells)
58.	Marasmius sp. (black)
59.	Marasmius sp.
60.	Marasmius sp. (oyster)
61.	Marasmius sp. (small)
62.	Microporus sp. (black)
63.	Microporus sp. (brown)
64.	Microporus sp. (brick)
65.	Microporus sp.
66.	Microporus sp (pink)
67.	Microporus sp. (spoon-like)
68.	Microporus sp. (trumpet-shaped)
69.	Microporus sp. (velvet)
70.	Mycena sp. (brown)
71.	Mycena sp. (leaf)
72.	Mycena sp. (rufous)

Sl. No.	MACROFUNGAL MORPHOPHYTES
73.	Mycena sp.
74.	Myxomyceteae
75.	Nidularia sp. (Cyathus like)
76.	Otidia sp. (Marasmius like)
77.	Otidia sp. (orange)
78.	Otidia sp. (Scutellinia like)
79.	Peziza sp. (disk)
80.	Phallus sp. (Mutinus like)
81.	Phallus sp. (stalk)
82.	Phellinus sp.
83.	Physarium sp.
84.	Physarium sp. (white)
85.	Pleurotus sp. (orange)
86.	Pleurotus sp.
87.	Polyporus sp. (brown)
88.	Polyporus sp. (button)
89.	Polyporus sp. (club)
90.	Polyporus sp. (Coriolus like)
91.	Polyporus sp. (grey)
92.	Polyporus sp. (Hexagonia like)
93.	Polyporus sp. (orange)
94.	Polyporus sp. (oyster)
95.	Polyporus sp. (pink)
96.	Polyporus sp. (polyporous)
97.	Polyporus sp. (resupinate)
98.	Polyporus sp. (rusty)
99.	Polyporus sp. (scars)
100.	Polyporus sp. (sulfur)
101.	Polyporus sp. (trumpet)
102.	Polyporus sp. (tubes)
103.	Polyporus sp. (velvet)
104.	Polyporus sp. (white)
105.	Rhizopogon sp.
106.	Russula sp. (brown)
107.	Russula sp. (pink)
108.	Russula sp. (purple)
109.	Russula sp. (red)
110.	Sarcocypha sp. (orange)
111.	Sarcocypha sp.
112.	Schizophylum sp.

Sl. No.	MACROFUNGAL MORPHOPHYTES
113.	Tephrocybe sp.
114.	Termitomyces sp.
115.	Tremella sp. (jelly)
116.	Tremella sp. (orange)
117.	Tricholomataceae (Armillaria like)
118.	Tricholomataceae (black)
119.	Tricholomataceae (brown)
120.	Tricholomataceae (campanulate)
121.	Tricholomataceae (gills)
123.	Tricholomataceae (huge)
124.	Tricholomataceae (large, edible)
125.	Tricholomataceae
126.	Tricholomataceae (mucilage and brown)
127.	Tricholomataceae (orange)
128.	Tricholomataceae (Oudemansiella like)
129.	Tricholomataceae (purple)
130.	Tricholomataceae (ring)
131.	Tricholomataceae (small, edible)
132.	Tricholomataceae (silver)
133.	Tricholomataceae (trumpet)
134.	Tricholomataceae (white)
135.	Xylaria sp.
136.	Xylaria sp. (balls)
137.	Xylaria sp. (carrot)
138.	Xylaria sp. (club-shaped)
139.	Xylaria sp. (long)
140.	Xylaria sp. (monstrous)
141.	Xylaria sp. (rod-like)
142.	Xylaria sp. (short)
143.	Xylaria sp. (thin)

APPENDIX 10. OUTDOOR EXHIBITION ON SACRED GROVES

The Indira Gandhi Rashtriya Manav Sangrahalaya is a unique institution dedicated to the preservation and revitalization of life enhancing cultural elements. Sanghralaya has made, special efforts for recreating sacred groves, from different ecological zones of India, in its 200-acre museum precinct at Bhopal. Simultaneously, a core group has been formed with involvement of eminent experts from all over the country to work out an action plan for enhancing awareness about the effectiveness of this ancient Indian practice of in-situ conservation of cultural, biological and genetic diversity. Our efforts are gaining momentum in different parts of the country. Sacred groves, representing Tamil Nadu, Rajasthan, Chattisgarh, Maharashtra, north Bengal and Meghalaya, have been installed in the museum campus, with the help and support of community representatives from these regions. Details of each of the sacred groves are given below.

KOVIL-KADU (SACRED GROVES OF TAMIL NADU)

Period of establishment - July 1999
Coordinator - Dr. Jhon Britto

Nature worship is an ancient Indian tradition, existing since time immemorial. Sacred groves, representing one form of nature worship, are a component of the village landscape in Tamil Nadu. Many groves have temples within them. While the presiding deity in most of the sacred groves is the snake god, *Ayyappam*, *Murugan* and *Amman* are also worshippped in some places. On full moon days, communities offer prayers collectively. The villagers believe that the groves provide livelihood directly or indirectly and restrict natural catastrophes. Trees, shrubs and herbs, climbers and lianas like *Aegle marmelos* (bael), *Ailanthus malabarica* (gugul), *Basia latifolia* (Mahua), *Cocos nucifera* (coconut), *Erythrina indica* (parijata), *Mangifera indica* (mango), *Terminalia* (harra), *Cassia tora* (chaksu), *Ervatamiasp, Parviflorasp* (maula), are grown in Kovil-Kadus. Apart from these, patches of land treated as sacred groves, where natural vegetation has been protected; there are sacred gardens, locally created. These are called Thirundavanas. These gardens are meant exclusively for growing flowers for the deity. Such gardens are found in Srirangam, Chidambaram, Suchindram, Madurai and Srivilliputhur. Sanctum sanctorum comprising 21 stone sculptures of Tamil folk deities associated with sacred groves of Tamil Nadu has been created in IGRMS precincts, with display of various ritual objects associated with their worship.

MAWBUKHAR (SACRED GROVES OF MEGHALAYA)

Period of establishment - August 1999
Coordinator- Prof. B.K. Tewari
Implementing agency - North Eastern Hill University, Shillong.

Sacred groves have been a part of the life and culture of the people of Meghalaya. Many sacred groves are still well-protected, in spite of rapid decline in the traditional value system. The traditional religious beliefs that the gods and spirits of ancestors live in these groves. A large number of groves are located in the Cherrapunji region of the east Khasi hill district. The Mawphlang grove, close to Shillong town, and the Mawsmai grove in Cherrapunji are some of the famous groves in the north-east India. Traditionally, people around these groves believe that removal of plants or plant parts would offend the ruling deity, leading to local calamities. The sacred grove precinct of IGRMS was strengthened with the induction of Maw-Bukhar of the Khasis of Meghalaya, with the help of a priest from Mawphlang area.

DEVRAHATI (SACRED GROVES OF MAHARASHTRA)

Period of establishment - September 1999
Coordinator - Dr. A. Godbole and Dr. Swapana Prabhu
Implementing agency - Applied Environmental Research Foundation, Pune

In Ratnagiri and Sindhudurg districts of Maharashtra, each village has at least one Devrahati. With a few exceptions of privately owned Devrahati, lands of all sacred groves, belong to the Government (Revenue Department), though they are symbolically handed over to the village development bodies and village panchayat for their management and revitalization. But, traditionally, the decision-making body of the village, consisting of Mankaries and Goakars, plays an important role in the administration of Devrahaties. Apart from this, the villagers believe that the entire property within the sacred grove belongs to the deity. Extraction of timber or any NTFP (non timber forest produces) from Devrahati is prohibited for personal use. However, it has been observed that, these groves have not been preserved merely as protected areas, but more as community resource with control on use. Devrahaties harbour many important plant species, especially the medicinal plants from western Ghats, which are hardly found elsewhere or being lost, as a result of deforestation or over-exploitation. Many of these Devrahaties have giant species of *Antiaris toxicaria, Terminalia bellerica* and *Tetrameles nudiflora* as well as Lianas like *Entada*. Population of the species like *Antiaris toxicaria, Sageraea laurifolia, Holigarna arnottiana, Anamirta cocculus, Butea parivtlora* and many species of *Amorphophyllus*, etc. are now restricted only to the groves. Besides their role as repositories of the natural wealth, Devrahaties play an important role in the socio-cultural life of the villagers. These provide a place for village gatherings during festivals as well as at the time of decision making with respect to community concerns, such as, beginning of agricultural or developmental activities. In many villages, a forest patch is specially preserved as cremation or burial ground. The trees in these groves are well-preserved and sometimes brought in use for the purpose of cremation. Many of these sacred groves have perennial sources of water. Devrahaties have helped in recharging the wells in their vicinity and have proved to be the vital source of retaining water during water scarcity in dry seasons.

ORAN (SACRED GROVES OF RAJASTHAN)

Period of establishment - September 1999
Coordinator - Dr. Sudipto Chatterjee
Implementing agency - WWF India, New Delhi

Orans are sacred forests, attached to the Sathris (temples) of the Bishnoi community of Rajasthan. Possibly, the word "oran" is derived from the Sathris word "uparanya", which means a small forest. It is mandatory for every Sathris to have an oran, from where cutting of any tree is strictly prohibited, as per Bishnoi principles. Oran serves as refuge to many birds and is frequented by many animal species like Blackbucks and Chinkara, which are receiving protection under the Wildlife Protection Act (1972). In the IGRMS campus, the Gran precinct has been created with the plantation of about 100 rare and endangered species, collected from western Rajasthan. Major plant species in this precinct comprises *Prosopis cineraria* (Khejari), *Tecomella undulata* (Rohlda), *Capparis dedidua* (Khair), and *Calligonum polygonides* (Phog). The process for erecting a traditional Sathri of western Rajasthan is nearing completion.

SARNA (SACRED GROVES OF JHARKHAND/CHHATTISGARH)

Period of establishment - July 1999
Coordinator - Dr. Amitab Pandey, Dr. S. Patnaik and Shri J.A.C.S Rao
Implementing agency – Indian Institute of Forest Management, Bhopal and Forest Deptt. Bilaspur

Sarna is the term used to refer to a sacred grove in the Chotanagpur plateau (Jharkhand) and Chhattisgarh. Sarna is religious centre of the community within the village ecosystem, where the village deity resides. The Munda, Oraon and Korwa, etc. are communities having belief in the Sarna religion. Mahadani Sarna is a type of Sarna found in many villages. Its deity is Mahadani (a male god), who is trusted to be, protecting the village and its property from various natural calamities and diseases. The villagers would regularly conduct rituals in the Sarna. Sacrificial offerings of buffaloes are also made at an interval of every three years. Women and children are prohibited to enter into the grove. The prominent trees found in Sarnas are *Sohrea robusta* (Sal), *Ficus religiosa* (Peepal), *Terminalia billerica* (Bahera), *Ficus benghalensis* (Bargad), etc. The most prominent ritual associated with the Sarna is known as *Sarhul*. It is celebrated in the new local calendar year (March-April), at the time of flowering of Sal tree. Other festivals like Kadleta (worship of oxen), Hariyali (crop-growth festival) and Nawakhani (crop-harvest festival) are also associated with Sarna. The religious representative of the village, known as Baiga, takes care of the vegetation in and around the Sarna, and also carries out the rituals associated with the grove. About 100 plant saplings, representing Sarna of eastern Madhya Pradesh now in Chhattisgarh, have been planted in the IGRMS campus. Creation of a suitable sanctum-sanctorum with ritual icons of Sarna are in progress.

PAVITHRA VANAM I KAVU (SACRED GROVES OF KERALA)

Period of establishment - September 1999
Coordinator – Dr. N. Viswanathan Nair
Implementing agency - KIRTADS, Kozhikode

Kavu are numerous in the length and breadth of Kerala. These sacred groves perform a unique role of biodiversity management system in Kerala. There are over 2000 well-preserved sacred groves, managed by private individuals and Devaswam Trusts in Kerala (Rajendra Prasad). There are many myths, legends and faiths, associated with the sacred groves of Kerala.

Ayyappa Kavu, the sacred groves dedicated to Lord Ayyappa, used to be the most common in Kerala in the past. The sacred groves in north Kerala are mostly associated with goddesses or ancestral spirits (*Amma, Ayalakshi, Ayiravalli, Bhagavati, Durga, Mahishasur Mardini, Vana Durga, Vanadevatha, Marutha, Madan, Yakshi, Gandharvan, Yogeeswaran,*

Muthappan, etc.), while in south Kerala, these are generally associated with snake worship (*Nagam, Nagaraja, Nagini, Sarpam*). The rites and rituals, performed in the sacred groves vary with the regional caste and patron deity of the sacred grove. A ritualistic recitation called Sarpam Pattu is performed in central and south Kerala, once in every 10 or 12 years, to propitiate the snake gods. In the sacred groves, associated with goddesses in north Kerala, a ritual dance is performed in Kavu called *theyyam* or *theyyattam*. About 200 plants sapling associated with sacred groves of Kerala have been planted. A prototype of a Naga thara (sanctum-sanctorum related to worship of snake gods) has been installed in IGRMS precinct.

APPENDIX 11. INVENTORY OF PLANT SPECIES PLANTED IN SACRED GROVES

1. MAWBUKHAR, SACRED GROVES OF MEGHALAYA
Area 840 Sq. Mt. (00.84 ha.)

Sl. No.	BOTANICAL NAME	LOCAL NAME	FAMILY
1.	*Elaeocarpus spp.*		Elaeocarpaceae
2.	*Mesua ferra*	Nagkesar	Clusiaceae
3.	*Parkia roxburghii*	Khorial	Mimosaceae
4.	*Garcinia cowa*	Kaphal	Sapindaceae
5.	*Sterculia urens*	Kulu	Sterculiaceae
6.	*Syzygium spp.*	Jamun	Myrtaceae
7.	*Ficus religiosa*	Peepal	Moracace
8.	*Ficus racemosa*	Gular	Moracace
9.	*Ixora Spp.*		Rubiaceae
10.	*Lagerstroemia speciosa*	Ajar	Lythraceae
11.	*Albizia lebbek*	Siris	Mimosaceae
12.	*Bauhinia Purpurea*	Kachnar	Caesalpiniaceae

2. RAJ BANSHI, SACRED GROVES OF NORTH BENGAL
Area 225 Sq. Mt. (0.25 ha.)

Sl. No.	BOTANICAL NAME	NAME	FAMILY
1.	*Bambusa vulgaris Var. Striata*	Yellow Bamboo	Poaceae

3. SARNA, SACRED GROVES OF JHARKHAND/CHHATTISGARH
Area 3915 Sq. Mt. Or 00.3915 ha.

Sl. No.	BOTANICAL NAME	NAME	FAMILY
1.	*Shorea robusta*	Sal	Dipterocarpaceae
2.	*Chloroxylon swietenia*	Behra	Rutaceae
3.	*Syzygium cuminii*	Jamun	Myrtaceae
4.	*Mangifera indica*	Aam	Anacardiaceae
5.	*Bambusa spp*	Bamboo	Poaceae

Sl. No.	BOTANICAL NAME	NAME	FAMILY
6.	*Ficus religiosa*	Peepal	Moraceae
7.	*Michelia champca*	Champa	Magnoliaceae
8.	*Madhuca longifolia*	Mahua	Sapotaceae
9.	*Buchanania lanzan*	Chironji	Anacardiaceae
10.	*Albizia lebbek*	Siris	Mimosaceae
11.	*Ziziphus nummularia*		Rhamnaceae
12.	*Terminalia arjuna*	Arjuna	Myrtaceae
13.	*Asparagus racemosus*	Satawar	Liliaceae
14.	*Butea monosperma*	Palas	Papilionaceae
15.	*Dalbergia sissoo*	Sissoo	Papilionaceae
16.	*Bombax ceiba*		Bambusaceae
17.	*Rauvolfia serpentina*	Sarpgandha	Apocyanaceae

4. ORAN, SACRED GROVES OF RAJASTHAN
Area 10560 Sq. Mt. Or 1.056 ha.

Sl. No.	BOTANICAL NAME	NAME	FAMILY
1	Prosopis cineraria		Mimosaceae
2	Tecomella undulata		Bignoniaceae
3	Capparis decidua		Capparaceae
4	Ziziphus nummularia		Rhamnaceae
5	Leptadaenia reticulata		Asclepiadaceae
6	Acacia nilotica		Mimosaceae

5. DEVRAHATI, SACRED GROVES OF MAHARASHTRA
Area 6750 Sq. Mt. Or 0.675 ha.

Sl. No.	BOTANICAL NAME	NAME	FAMILY
1.	Acacia catechu	Khair	Mimosaceae
2.	Acacia concinna	Shikekai	Mimosaceae
3.	Adhatoda vasica	Adusa	Acanthaceae
4.	Aegle marmelose	Bael	Rutaceae
5.	Albizia lebbek	Siris	Mimosaceae
6.	Alstonia scholaris	Saptaparani	Apocyanaceae
7.	Anacardium occidentale	Kaju	Anacardiaceae
8.	Anogeissus latifolia	Dhavada	Combretaceae
10.	Azadirachta indica	Neem	Meliaceae
11.	Bambusa spp		Bambusaceae

Sl. No.	BOTANICAL NAME	NAME	FAMILY
12.	Bombax ceiba		Bambusaceae
13.	Buchanania lanzen	Achar	Anacardiaceae
14.	Butea monosperma	Palas	Papilionaceae
15.	Calatropis gigentea	Aak	Asclepiadaceae
16.	Carrisa carandas	Caronda	Apocyanaceae
17.	Cassia fistula	Aamaltas	Caesalpiniaceae
18.	Dalbergia sissoo	Sissoo	Papilionaceae
19.	Pongamia pinnata	Karanja	Papilionaceae
20.	Emblica officinalis	Amala	Euphorbiaceae
21.	Ficus benghalensis	Bargad	Moracace
22.	Ficus religosa	Peepal	Moracace
23.	Ficus racemosa	Gular	Moracace
24.	Flacourtia indica		Flacoutiaceae
25.	Ailanthous excelsa	Mahaneem	Simarobuaceae
26.	Helicteres isora	Marorphali	Sterculiaceae
27.	Jatropha curcus	Safed arand	Euphorbiaceae
28.	Lagerstroemia indica	Phurush	Lythraceae
29.	Mimusops elengi	Maulsari	Sapotaceae
30.	Madhuca indica	Mahua	Sapotaceae
31.	Mangifera indica	Aam	Anacardiaceae
32.	Michelia champaka	Sonchampa	Magnoliaceae
33.	Mitragyna parviflora	Kaddam	Rubiaceae
34.	Moringa pterigosperma	Sahinjna	Moringaceae
35.	Pterocarpus marsupium	Bijasal	Papilionaceae
36.	Rauvalfia serpentina	Sarpgandha	Apocyanaceae
37.	Ricinus communis	Erand	Euphorbiaceae
38.	Sapindus emerginatus	Ritha	Sapinadaceae
39.	Saraca asoca	Sitaashoka	Caesalpiniaceae
40.	Semecarpus anacardium	Bivla	Anacardiaceae
41.	Strychnos nu x-vomica	Kuchla	Strychnaceae
42.	Syzygium cumini	Jamun	Myrtaceae
43.	Tamarindus indica	imli	Caesalpiniaceae
44.	Terminalia arjuna	Arjuna	Combretaceae
45.	Terminalia bellerica	Baheda	Combretaceae
46.	Terminalia chebula	Harra	Combretaceae
47.	Tinospora cordifolia	Gulancha	Menispermaceae
48.	Wrightia tinctoria	Dudhi	Apocyanaceae

Sl. No.	BOTANICAL NAME	NAME	FAMILY
49.	Zizyphus mauritiana	Ber	Rhamnaceae
50.	Zizphus oenopila	Makai	Rhamnaceae
51.	Tectona grandis	Sagwan	Verbenaceae
52.	Randia dumetorum	Mainphal	Rubiaceae
53.	Rubia cordifolia	Manjistha	Rubiaceae
54.	Murraya koenigii	Mitha neem	Rutaceae
55.	Nerium odorum	Kaner	Apocyanaceae
56.	Nyctanthus arbor-tristis	Parijat	Nyctanthaceae
57.	Plumeria alba	Champa	Apocyanaceae
58.	Ocimum sanctum	Tulsi	Labiatae

6. KOVIL-KADU, SACRED GROVES OF TAMIL NADU

Area 8165 Sq. Mt. Or 0.8165 ha

Sl. No.	BOTANICAL NAME	NAME	FAMILY
1.	Tinospora cordifolia		Menispermaceae
2.	Flacourtia indica		Flacourtiaceae
3.	Abutilon indicum		Malvaceae
4.	*Rauvolfia serpentina*	Sarpgandha	Apocyanaceae
5.	Chloroxylon swietenia		Rutaceae
6.	Limonia acidissima		Rutaceae
7.	Azadirachta indica	Neem	Meliaceae
8.	Jasminum grandiflorum		Oleaceae
9.	Ziziphus mauritiana		Rhamnaceae
10.	Ziziphus oenoplia		Rhamnaceae
11.	Cissus quadrangularis		Vitaceae
12.	Sapindus mukorossi	Ritha	Spindaceae
13.	Lannea coromandelica		Anacardiaceae
14.	Mangifera indica		Anacardiaceae
15.	Abrus precatorius		Papilionaceae
16.	Dalbergia lanceolaria		Papilionaceae
17.	Dalbergia sissoo		Papilionaceae
18.	Indigofera barberi		Papilionaceae
19.	Pongamia pinnata		Papilionaceae
20.	Delonix elata		Caesalpiniaceae
21.	Bauhinia racemosa		Caesalpiniaceae

Sl. No.	BOTANICAL NAME	NAME	FAMILY
22.	Cassia auriculata		Caesalpiniaceae
23.	Cassia fistula	Amolths	Caesalpiniaceae
24.	Tamarindus indica		Caesalpiniaceae
25.	Prosopis juliflora		Mimosaceae
26.	Abizia amara		Mimosaceae
27.	Albizia lebbeck		Mimosaceae
28.	Eugenia jambolana		Myrtaceae
29.	Syzygium cumini		Myrtaceae
30.	Coccinia grandis		Cucurbitaceae
31.	Alangium salvifolium		Alangiaceae
32.	Randia malabarica		Rubiaceae
33.	Ixora pavetta		Rubiaceae
34.	Carissa carandas		Apocyanaceae
35.	Wrightia tinctoria		Apocyanaceae
36.	Hemidesmus indicus		Asclepiadaceae
37.	Tylophora tenuis		Asclepiadaceae
38.	Calotropis gigantean		Asclepiadaceae
39.	Mimusops elengi		Sapotaceae
40.	Bassia longifilia		Sapotaceae
41.	Strychnos nu x-vomica		Loganiaceae
42.	Solanum surrattence		Solanaceae
43.	Premna latifolia		Verbenaceae
44.	Achyranthes aspera		Amaranthaceae
45.	Aervea lanata		Amaranthaceae
46.	Aristolochia indica		Aristolochiaceae
47.	Jatropha gossipifolia		Euphorbiaceae
48.	Bombax ceiba		Bambusaceae
49.	Parkia biglandulosa		Mimosaceae
50.	Terminalia arjuna	Arjuna	Combretaceae
51.	Punica granatum	Anar	Punicaceae
52.	Tectona grandis	Sagwan	Verbenaceae
53.	Madhuca indica	Mahua	Sapotaceae
54.	Helicteres isora	Marorphali	Sterculiaceae
55.	Santalum album	Chandan	Santalaceae
56.	Murraya koenigii	Mitha neem	Rutaceae
57.	Terminalia bellerica	Baheda	Combretaceae

7. PAVITHRA VANAM KAVU, SACRED GROVES OF KERALA
Area 2400 Sq. Mt Or 0.24 ha.

Sl. No.	BOTANICAL NAME	NAME	FAMILY	MALYALAM NAME
1.	Helicteres isora	Marorphali	Sterculiaceae	Edampiri valampiri
2.	Cassia fistula	Amaltas	Caesalpiniaceae	Kanikonna
3.	Embilica officinalis	Aonla	Euphorbiaceae	Neli
4.	Rauvolfia serpentina	Sarpgandha	Apocyanaceae	Sarpagandhi
5.	Ficus racemosa	Gular	Moracace	Athi
6.	Terminalia bellirica	Bahera	Combertaceae	Thanni
7.	Ipomea digita	Bilaikand	Convolvulaceae	Palmuthukku
8.	Albizia procera	Safed Siris	Mimosaceae	Nenmenivaka
9.	Cinnamomum comphora	Kapur	Lauraceae	Karappa
10.	Ixora coccinea	Rukmani	Rubiaceae	Kattuchethi
11.	Mimusops elengi	Molshree	Sapotaceae	Elengi
12.	Mussaendra frondosa	Bedina	Rubiaceae	Vellila
13.	Pongamia pinnata	Karanj	Papilionaceae	Ungu
14.	Syzygium cumini	Jamun	Myrstaceae	Njaval
15.	Tylophora asthamatica	Antamul	Asclepiadaceae	Vallippala
16.	Mangifera indica	Aam	Anacardiaceae	Mavu
17.	Alstonia scholaris	-	Apocyanaceae	Ezhilampala
18.	Holarrhena antidysenterica	Kurachi	Apocyanaceae	Kudagappala
19.	Bombax ceiba	Semal	Bombacaceae	Poola
20.	Garuga pinnata	Kharpat	Burseraceae	Annakkara
21.	Galopuyllum polyanthum		Guttiferae	Kattupunna
22.	Garcinia combogia		Guttiferae	Kodappuli
23.	Terminatia arjuna	Arjun	Combertaceae	Kulamaruthu
24.	Terminalia paniculata		Combertaceae	Maruthu
25.	Dalbergia lanceolaria	Takoli	Papilionaceae	Velleeti
26.	Erytrina stricta		Papilionaceae	Mullumurukku
27.	Pterocarpus marsupium	Bijasal	Papilionaceae	Venga
28.	Persea macrantha	Pear	Lauraceae	Ooravu
29.	Strychnos nux-vomica	Kuchla	Loganiaceae	Kanjiram
30.	Lagerstroemia lanceolata		Lytheraceae	Vanthukku
31.	Lagerstroemia reginae	Jarul	Lytheraceae	Manimaruthu
32.	Albizzia lebbek	Siris	Mimosaceae	Vakka
33.	Artocarpus heterophyllus	Kathal	Moracace	Plavu
34.	Artocarpus hirsutus		Moracace	Anjili
35.	Ficus tinctoria		Moracace	Itthi
36.	Clerodendrum viscosum		Verbenaceae	Vattaparuvalam

Sl. No.	BOTANICAL NAME	NAME	FAMILY	MALYALAM NAME
37.	Tectona grandis	Sagon	Verbenaceae	Thekku
38.	Xanthoxylum retza			Mullilam
39.	Tinospora cordifolia	Amrita	Menispermaceae	Amrithu
40.	Adhatoda Vasica	Adusa	Acanthaceae	Adalodakam
41.	Azadirachta indica	Neem	Meliaceae	Aryaveppu
42.	Piper longum	Pippli	Piperaceae	Thippalli
43.	Ocimum sanctum	Tulsi	Labitae	Thulasi
44.	Symplocos racemosa	Lodh	Symplocaceae	Pachotti
45.	Curcuma longa	Haldi	Zingiberaceae	Manjal
46.	Asparagus racemosus	Satawar	Liliaceae	Sathavari
47.	Curculigo orchioides	Musli	Amaryllidaceae	Nilappana
48.	Biophylum sensitivum		Oxalidaceae	Mukutti
49.	Gloriosa superba	Karihari	Liliaceae	Menthonni
50.	Sapindus tryfoliantus	Reetha	Sapindaceae	Uruvanchi
51.	Desmodium ganjettikam	Sarivan	Papilionaceae	Orila
52.	Jatropha carcass	Safedarand	Euphorbiaceae	Avanakkukattu
53.	Caryota urens	Mari	Palmae	Choondapana
54.	Bambusa spp	Bans	Gramineae	Mula
55.	Bridelia crenulata		Euphrbiaceae	Mulluvenga
56.	Calophyllum apetalum		Guttifereae	Cherupunna
57.	Vitex altissima		Verbenaceae	Myla
58.	Lannea coromandelica	Jhigan	Anacardiaceae	Uthi
59.	Ficus obtusifolia		Moraceae	Eruma nakku
60.	Chukrasia tabularis		Meliaceae	Karadi
61.	Buchanania lanceslata		Anacardiaceae	Nattumavu
62.	Areca catechu	Supari	Arecaceae	Adakka

BIBLIOGRAPHY

Achar, K.P. and V. Naik. 2006. *Dakshina Kannada Devarakaadugalu (Sacred Groves of Dakshin Kannada)*, Nagarika Seva Trust, Guruvayanakere.

Amrithalingam, M. 1998a. "Sthala Vrikshas of Tamil Nadu" in N. Krishna and J. Prabhakaran (eds.), *The Ecological Traditions of Tamil Nadu*, C.P.R. Environment Education Centre, Chennai.

——. 1998b. *Sacred Groves of Tamilnadu – A Survey*, C.P.R. Environment Education Centre, Chennai.

——. 2005. "Conservation Strategy for Sacred Groves of Tamilnadu" in C. Kunhikannan and B.G. Singh (eds.), *Strategy for Conservation of Sacred Groves*, Institute of Forest Genetics and Tree Breeding, pp. 189-199.

Bachmann, V.K. 1992. *Mythen. Geo. Wissen.*, Hamburg.

Basha, S. Chand. 1998. "Conservation and Management of Sacred Groves in Kerala" in P.S. Ramakrishnan, K.G. Saxena and U.M. Chandrashekara (eds.), *Conserving the Sacred for Biodiversity Management*, Oxford and IBH Publishing Co., New Delhi, pp. 337-347.

Bhagwat, S., C. Kushalappa, P. Williams, N. Brown. 2005. "The Role of Informal Protected Areas in Maintaining Biodiversity in the Western Ghats of India", *Ecology and Society*, 10(1): 8.

Brandis, D. 1897. "Indigenous Indian Forestry: Sacred Groves" in *Indian Forestry*, Working Oriental Institure, pp. 12-13.

——. 1897. *Indian Forestry*, Working Oriental Institute.

Buchanan, F. 1870. *Journey through the Northern Part of Kanara* (1801-2), Vol. 2, Higginbothams, Madras.

Budge, E.A.W. 1911. *Osiris and the Egyptian Resurrection*, 2 Vols., The Medici Society, London.

Chandran, M.D.S. 1995. "Peasant Perception of Bhutas, Uttar Kannada" in B. Saraswati (ed.), *Integral Vision: Primal Element of Oral Tradition*, D.K. Publishers, New Delhi.

Chandran, M.D.S. and M. Gadgil. 1993. "Sacred Groves and Sacred Trees of Uttara Kannada (A Pilot Study)", *Mimeograph*, Centre for Ecological Sciences, Indian Institute of Science, Bangalore.

Chandran, M.D.S., M. Gadgil and J.D. Hughes. 1998. "Sacred Groves of the Western Ghats" in P.S. Ramakrishnan, K.G. Saxena and U.M. Chandrasekhara (eds.), *Conserving the Sacred for Biodiversity Management*, Oxford and IBH Publishing Co., New Delhi, pp. 211-32.

Chandrashekara, U.M. and S. Sankar. 1998. "Structure and Function of Sacred Groves: Case Studies in Kerala" in P.S. Ramakrishnan, K.G. Saxena and U.M. Chandrashekara (eds.), *Conserving the Sacred for Biodiversity Management*, Oxford and IBH Publishing Co., New Delhi, pp. 323-36.

Chatterjee, S., A.R.K. Sastry, B.N. Roy and R. Lahon. 2000. "Sacred Groves of Sikkim and Arunachal Pradesh" abstract *National Workshop on Community Strategies on the Management of Natural Resources*, Bhopal.

Chhatre, A., T. Lothiyal and V. Sharma. 1998. "Nature in Retreat: Development and Conservation in Himachal Pradesh", *Mimeograph*, WWF-India, New Delhi.

Cohen, M.P. 1984. *The Pathless Way: John Muir and American Wilderness*, University of Wisconsin Press, Madison, Wisconsin.

Das, I. and S.K. Chanda. 1997. "*Philautus Sanctisilvaticus* (Anura: Rhacophoridae), A New Frog from the Sacred Groves of Amarkantak, Central India", *Hamdryad*, 22: 21-27.

Das, K. and K.C. Malhotra. 1998. "Sacred Groves among the Tribes of India: A Literature Survey of Ethnographic Monographs", *Mimeograph*, IRDWSI, Semiliguda.

Deb, D. 2003. "Culture and Biodiversity" in K.C. Malhotra (2003), *Mimeograph.*

Deb, D., K. Deuti and K.C. Malhotra. 1997. "Sacred Grove Relics as Bird Refugia", *Current Science*, 73: 815-817.

Deb, D. and K.C. Malhotra. 1997. "Interface between Biodiversity and Tribal Cultural Heritage: An Exploratory Study", *J. Human Ecology*, 8: 157-63.

——. 2001. "Conservation Ethos in Local Traditions: The West Bengal Heritage", *Society and Natural Resource*, 114: 711-724.

Deb, D., R. Mahato, N. Mandai and D. Bhattacharya. *Sacred Groves of Southwestern Districts* of West Bengal (In press).

Deepak, K., C.K. Punuoose, F. Wasil and S. Malhotra 2006. *Candid Environmental Education*, Evergreen Publication (India) Ltd., Jalandhar.

Deshmukh, S. 1999. *Conservation and Development of Sacred Groves of Maharashtra*, BNHS, Bombay.

Deshmukh, S., M.G. Gogate and A.K. Gupta. 1998. "Sacred Groves and Biological Diversity: Providing New Dimensions to Conservation Issue" in P.S. Ramakrishnan, K.G. Saxena and U.M. Chandrashekara (eds.), *Conserving the Sacred for Biodiversity Management*, Oxford and IBH Publishing Co., New Delhi, pp. 397 414.

D.N. 1990. "Women and Forests", *Economic and Political Weekly*, April 14.

Devi, S. 2000. "Sacred Groves of Manipur" abstract *National Workshop on Community Strategies on the Management of Natural Resources*, Bhopal.

Dewing, H.B. 1961. *Buildings of Procopius* (6th Century A.D.), Loeb Classical library, Harvard Heinemann, Cambridge.

Dorm-Adzobou, Clement, Okyeame Ampadu-Agyei and Peter G. Veit. 1991. *Religious Beliefs and Environmental Protection: The Malshegu Sacred Grove in Northern Ghana*. From the Ground up Case Study No. 4. Centre for International Development and Environment, World Resources Institute, USA, Nairobi and New York.

Erman, A. 1894. *Life in Ancient Egypt*, Macmillan, London.

Fernandes, W. 1993. "Forest and Tribals, Informal Economy: Dependence and Management Decision" in Miri (ed.), *Community and Change in Tribal Society*, Indian Institute of Advanced Study, Shimla.

Frazer, J.G. 1935. *The Golden Bough, Part I: The Magic Art and the Evolution of Kings*, 2 Vols., Macmillan, New York.

Gadgil, M. and V.D. Vartak. 1976. "Sacred Groves in Western Ghats in India", *Economic Botany*, 30:152-60.

——. 1981. "Sacred Groves in Maharashtra – An inventory" in S.K. Jain (ed.), *Glimpses of Indian Ethnobotany*, Oxford and IBH Publishing Co., New Delhi, pp. 279-294.

Gadgil, M., N.S. Hemam and B.M. Reddy. 1998. "People, Refugia and Resilience" in F. Berkes, C. Folke and J. Colding (eds.), *Linking Social and Ecologiail Systems: Management Practices and Social Mechanisms for Building Resilience*, Cambridge University Press, pp. 30-47.

Gandhi, K. 1994. "Kesar Chirkav – Traditional System of Forest Protection", *Sevamandir* Newsletter.

Godbole, A., A. Watve, S. Prabhu and J. Sarnaik. 1998. "Role of Sacred Groves in Biodiversity Conservation with Local People's Participation: A Case Study from Ratnagiri District, Maharashtra" in P.S. Ramakrishnan, K.G. Saxena and U.M. Chandrashekara (eds.), *Conserving the Sacred for Biodiversity Management*, Oxford and IBH Publishing Co., New Delhi, pp. 233-46.

Gokhale, Y. 2000. "Sacred Conservation Tradition in India: An Overview" abstract *National Workshop on Community Strategies on the Management of Natural Resources*, Bhopal.

——. 2002. *Studies on the Role of Sacred Grove Institution in Conservation of Plants*, Ph.D. Thesis, Bombay Natural History Society, Mumbai University.

——. 2005. "Use of Plants as Indicator of Management of Sacred Groves in the Western Ghats of Karnataka" in C. Kunhikannan and B.G. Singh (eds.), *Strategy for Conservation of Sacred Groves*, Institute of Forest Genetics and Tree Breeding, pp. 82-92.

Gokhale, Y., R. Velankar, M.D. Subhash Chandran and M. Gadgil. 1998. "Sacred Woods, Grasslands and Waterbodies as Self-organized Systems of Conservation in P.S. Ramakrishnan, K.G. Saxena and U.M. Chandrashekara (eds.), *Conserving the Sacred for Biodiversity Management*, Oxford and IBH Publishing Co., New Delhi, pp. 365-98.

Gomez-Pompa, Arturo, Jose Salvador Flores and Mario Aliphat Fernandez. 1990. "The Sacred Cacao Groves of the Maya", *Latin American Antiquity*, 1: 247-257

Guha, K., A. Gupta and B.K. Dutta. 1999. "Indigenous Conservation Initiatives in Barak Valley, Assam" in B. Kharbuli, D. Syiem and H. Kayang, (eds.), *Biodiversity: North East India Perspectives*, pp. 42-46. North Eastern Biodiversity Research Cell, North Eastern Hill University, Shillong, Meghalaya.

Gupta, A. 2003. "Culture and Biodiversity" in K.C. Malhotra (2003), *Mimeograph.*

Gupta, A. and K. Guha. 2002. "Tradition and Conservation in Northeastern India: An Ethical Analysis", *Eubios*, Journal of Asian and International Bioethics, 12: 15-18.

Gupta, A.K. 1998. "Policy and Institutional Aspects of Sacred Groves: Tending the Spirit, Sustaining and Sacred" in P.S. Ramakrishnan, K.G. Saxena and U.M. Chandrashekara (eds.), *Conserving the Sacred for Biodiversity Management*, Oxford and IBH Publishing Co., New Delhi, pp. 397-414.

Gupta, A., S. Shukla, D. Koradiya, P. Bhavsar, Ramji Anil, P. Patel and R. Taviyad. 2000. "A Cultural and Ecological Study of Sacred Groves in Balaram-Ambaji and Jessore

Sanctuary in Banaskantha District of Gujarat" abstract *National Workshop on Community Strategies on the Management of Natural Resources*, Bhopal.

Haridasan, K. and P.R. Rao. 1985. *Forest Flora of Meghalaya*, Vol. 1, Bishen Singh, Dehradun.

Hemam, S.N., K.C. Malhotra and S. Stanley. 1997. *The Bamboo Sacred Grove, Kantabaushini, Thakurma of Sindipad village, Koraput district, Orissa (unpublished).*

Hembram, P.C. 1983. "Return to the Sacred Groves" in K.S. Singh (ed.), *Tribal Movements in India*, Manohar Publications, New Delhi, Vol. 2, pp. 87-91.

Hughes, J.D. 1984. "Sacred Groves: The Gods, Forest Protection, and Sustained Yield in the Ancient World" in Harold K. Steen (ed.), *History of Sustained-Yield Forestry: A Symposium*, Forest History Society, Durham, North Carolina, pp. 331-343.

——. 1996. *North American Indian Ecology*, Texas Western Press, EI Paso.

——. 1994. *Pan's Travail Environmental Problems of the Ancient Greeks and Romans*, Johns Hopkins University Press, Baltimore, Maryland.

Hughes, J.D. and M.D. Subhash Chandran. 1998. "Sacred Groves around the Earth: An Overview" in P.S. Ramakrishnan, K.G. Saxena and U.M. Chandrashekara (eds.), *Conserving the Sacred for Biodiversity Management*, Oxford and IBH Publishing Co., New Delhi, pp. 69-86.

Hughes, J.D. and J. Swan. 1986. "How Much of the Earth is Sacred Space?", *Environmental Review*, 10 (4): 247-260.

IGRMS. 2002. "A Field Report on Documentation of 33 Sacred Groves in Manipur", *Memeograph.*

Induchoodan, N.C. 1996. *Ecological Studies of the Sacred Groves of Kerala*, Ph.D. Thesis submitted to the Central University of Pondicherry.

Jha, M., H. Vardhan, S. Chatterjee, K. Kumar and A.R.K. Sastry. 1998. "Status and Role of Orans (Sacred Groves) in Peepasar village (district Naguar) and Khejarli in (district Jodhpur), Rajasthan" in P.S. Ramakrishnan, K.G. Saxena and U.M. Chndrashekara (eds.), *Conserving the Sacred for Biodiversity Management*, Oxford and IBH Publishing Co., New Delhi, pp. 263-276.

Kalam, M.A. 1996. *Sacred Groves in Kodagu District of Karnataka (South India): A Socio-Historical Study*, Institute Francais de Pondichery, Pondichery.

Khiewtam, R.S. and P.S. Ramakrishnan. 1989. "Socio-cultural Studies of the Sacred Groves at Charrapunji and Adjoining Areas in North-Eastern India", *Man in India*, 69:64-71.

Khumbongmayum, A.D., M.L. Khan and R.S. Tripathi. 2005. "Ethnomedicinal Plants in the Sacred Groves of Manipur", *Indian Journal of Traditional Knowledge*, 4(1): 21-32.

Kim, H. 1994. *Maul sup: Han'guk chont'ong purak ui tangsup kwa sugu magi- (Maul sup: the Korean village grove)*, Yorhwadang, Seoul.

Kosambi, D.D. 1962. *Myth and Reality: Studies in the Formation of Indian Culture*, Popular Press, Bombay.

Krishna, N. 1997. "The Terracotta Tradition of the Sacred Groves" in Krishna, N. and Prabhakaran, J. (eds.), *The Ecological Traditions of Tamil Nadu*, C.P.R. Environment Education Centre, Chennai.

Kunhikannan, C. and B.G. Singh (eds.). 2005. *Strategy for Conservation of Sacred Groves*, Institute of Forest Genetics and Tree Breeding (ICFRE), Coimbatore.

Kushalappa, C.G. and Kushalappa. 1996. "Preliminary Report: Impact Assessment of Working in the Western Ghats Forest", College of Forestry, Poonampet.

Lebbie, A.R. and R.P. Guries. 1995. "Ethnobotanical Value and Conservation of Sacred Groves of the Kpaa Mende in Sierra Leone", *Economic Botany*, 49: 297-308.

Logan, W. 1951. *Manual of Malabar District,* Madras Government Press.

Malai, D. 2006. "Nongtluh Sacred Grove and its Associated Megaliths", *Memeograph.*

Malhotra, K.C. 1984. "Population Structure among the Dhangar Caste Cluster of Maharashtra, India" in J.R. Lukas (eds.), *The People of South Asia,* Plenum Press, New York, pp. 295-324.

——. 1990. "Supply and Safety Forests in Mizoram" abstract *Vth International Conference of Ecological Sciences,* Yokohama.

——. 1998. "Anthropological Dimensions of Sacred Groves in India: An Overview" in P.S. Ramakrishnan, K.G. Saxena and U.M. Chandrashekara (eds.), *Conserving the Sacred for Biodiversity Management,* Oxford and IBH Publishing Co., New Delhi, pp. 423-38.

——. 2002. "Sacred Groves as Common Property Resources: An Exploratory Study" in D.K. Marothia (ed.), *Institutionalizing Common Pool Resources,* Concept Publishing Company, New Delhi, pp. 511-532.

——. 2003. *Culture and Biodiversity,* National Biodiversity and Action Plan, Ministry of Environment and Forests, GoI. Mimeo.

Malhotra, K.C. and K. Das. 1997. "Interface between Faunal Biodiversity and Cultural Heritage in South-West Bengal, in India" in N. Fujiki and R.J. Macer (eds.), *Bioethics in Asia, Eubois Ethics Institute,* Japan, pp. 346-51.

Malhotra, K.C., S. Stanley, N.S. Hemam and K. Das. 1997. "Biodiversity Conservation and Ethics: Sacred Groves and Pools" in N. Fujiki and R.J. Macer (eds.), *Bioethics in Asia, Eubois Ethics Institute,* Japan, pp. 338-45.

Malhotra, K.C., N.S. Hemam, S. Stanley and K. Das. 1998. "Cultural and Ecological Value of Natural Sacred Biodiversity Sites in Orissa, India: Threats and Opportunities", *Proceedings Volume of International Symposium on Natural Sacred Sites Cultural Diversity and Biological Diversity,* UNESCO, Paris, 1998.

Malhotra, K.C., Y. Gokhale, S. Chatterjee and S. Shrivastava. 2000a. *Sacred Groves in India: An Overview,* Indira Gandhi Rashtriya Manav Sangrahalaya, Bhopal.

Malhotra, K.C., K.K. Chakravarty, B.V. Bhanu, S. Chatterjee, D. Deb, Y. Gokhale and S. Shrivastava. 2000b. *Sacred Groves of India: A Travelling Exhibition,* Indira Gandhi Rashtriya Manav Sangrahalaya, Bhopal.

Malhotra, K.C., Y. Gokhale and K. Das. 2001a. *Sacred Groves of India: An Annotated Bibliography,* Indian National Science Academy and Development Alliance, New Delhi.

Malhotra, K.C., Y. Gokhale, S. Chatterjee and S. Shrivastava. 2001b. *Cultural and Ecological Dimensions of Sacred Groves in India,* Indian National Science Academy and Indira Gandhi Rashtriya Manav Sangrahalaya, Bhopal.

Manniche, L. 1989. *An Ancient Egyptian Herbal,* University of Texas Press, Austin.

Matunga, H. 1994. "Waahi Tapu: Maori Sacred Sites" in D.L. Carmichael, J. Hubert, B. Reeves, and A. Schanche (eds.), *Sacred Sires, Sacred Places,* Routledge, London, pp. 217-226.

Michaloud, G. and Dury, S. 1998. "Sacred Trees, Groves, Landscapes, and Related Cultural Situations may Contribute to Conservation and Management in Africa" in P.S. Ramakrishnan, K.G. Saxena and U.M. Chandrashekara (eds.), *Conserving the Sacred for Biodiversity Management,* Oxford and IBH Publishing Co., New Delhi, pp. 129-143.

Mikesell, M.W. 1969. "The Deforestation of Mt. Lebanon", *Geographical Review,* 59: 1-28.

Mitra, A. and S. Pal. 1994. "The Spirit of the Sanctuary", *Down to Earth,* January 31.

Mohanan, C.N. and N.C. Nair. 1981. "*Kunstleria Prain* - A New Genus Record for India and a New Species in the Genus", *Proc. Ind. Acad. Sci.,* B 90:207-210.

Molyneaux, B.L. 1995. *The Sacred Earth*, Little, Brown and Company, Boston.

NAEB, 1995. *Sacred Groves of Kurukshetra, Haryana*, National Afforestation and Eco-development Board, Ministry of Environment and Forests, Govt. of India, New Delhi.

Nagarika Seva Trust (NST). 2003. *Devarakaadugalu (Naagabanagalu Mutthu Bhoothasthanagalu) A Study Report on the Sacred Grove of Belthanagady Taluk (in Dakshina Kannada District)*, Nagarika Seva Trust, Guruvayanakere.

Nair, N.C. and C.N. Mohanan. 1995. "On the Rediscovery of four Threatened Species from the Sacred Groves of Kerala", *J. Econ. Taxon. Bot.*, 2: 233-235.

Nath, Y.V.S. 1960. *Bhils of Ratanmal*, Maharaja Sayajirao University, Baroda.

Oakerson, R.J. 1986. "A Model for the Analysis of Common Property Problems" in *Proceedings of the Conference on Common Property Resource Management*, Washington DC: Natural Academy Press, pp. 13-30.

Oldfather, C.H. 1933. *Bibliotheke of Diodorus of Sicily* (1st Century BC), Loeb Classical Library, Harvard-Heinemann, Cambridge Mass., and London.

Ono, S. 1962. *Shinto: The Kami Way*, Bridge way Press, Tokyo.

Ostrom, E. 1986. "Issues of Definition and Theory: Some Conclusions and Hypothesis" in *Proceedings of the Conference on Common Property Resource Management*, Washington DC: Natural Academy Press, pp. 13-30.

——. 1990. *Governing the Commons: The Evolution of Institutions for Collective Action*, New York: Cambridge University Press.

——. 1992. *Crafting Institutions for Self-governing Irrigation Systems*, San Francisco, California: Institute for Contemporary Studies.

Ovsyannikov, O.V. and N.M. Terebikhin. 1994. "Sacred Groves in the Culture of the Arctic Regions" in D.L. Carmichael, J.H.B. Reeves, and A. Schanche (eds.), *Sacred Sites, Sacred Places*. Routledge, London, pp. 44-81.

Pandey, Arun. 2000. "From Sarana (Sacred Groves) to Sustainable Natural Resources Management" abstract *National Workshops on Community Strategies on the Management of Natural Resources*, Bhopal.

Pandey, D.N. 1998. *Ethnoforestry: Local Knowledge for Sustainable Forestry and Livelihood Security*, Himanshu Publications, Udaipur.

Patnaik, S. and A. Pandey. 1998. "A Study of Indigenous Community based Forest Management System: Sarna (Sacred Groves)" in P.S. Ramakrishnan, K.G. Saxena and U.M. Chandrasekhara (eds.), *Conserving the Sacred for Biodiversity Management*, Oxford and IBH, New York, pp. 315-322.

Paulraj, S. 1996. "Conservation of Sthala Vriksha: A Biodiversity Approach", Paper presented at Seminar on *Sacred Groves of India, their Biodiversity and Conservation*, Hyderabad.

Pranjipye, V. 1989. "Deorai (Sacred Groves): An Indian Concept of Common Property Resources" in N.D. Jayal (ed.), *Deforestation and Drought*, INTACH, New Delhi.

Prasad, G.A. and C.N. Mohanan. 1995. "The Sacred Groves of Kerala and Biodiversity Conservation" in P.K. Iyenger (ed.), *Proceedings of the 7th Kerala Science Congress*, State Committee on Science, Technology and Environment, Kerala, pp. 125-126.

Pushpangadan, P., M. Rajendraprasad and P.N. Krishnan. 1998. "Sacred Groves of Kerala A Synthesis on the State of – Art - of Knowledge" in P.S. Ramakrishnan, K.G. Saxena and U.M. Chandrashekara (eds.), *Conserving the Sacred for Biodiversity Management*, Oxford and IBH Publishing Co., New Delhi, pp. 193-210.

Rajendraprasad, M. 1995. *The Floristic, Structural and Functional Analysis of Sacred Groves of Kerala*, Ph.D. Thesis, University of Kerala, Thiruvananthapuram.

Ramakrishnan, P.S. 1996. "Conserving the Sacred: From Species to Landscapes", *Nature and Resources*, 32: 11-19.

——. 1998. "Conserving the Sacred for Biodiversity: The Conceptual Framework" in P.S. Ramakrishnan, K.G. Saxena and U.M. Chandrashekara (eds.), *Conserving the Sacred for Biodiversity Management*, Oxford and IBH Publishing Co., New Delhi.

Ramakrishnan, P.S., K.G. Saxena and U.M. Chandrashekara (eds.). 1998. *Conserving the Sacred for Biodiversity Management*, Oxford and IBH Publishing Co., New Delhi.

Rodgers, W.A. 1994. "The Sacred Grove of Meghalaya", *Man in India*, 74 (4): 339-348.

Roy, S.C. 1912. *Munda and their Country*, City Book, Soc. Calcutta.

Roy Burman, J.J. 1992. "The Institution of Sacred Groves", *Journal of Indian Anthropological Society*, 27: 219-38.

——. 1995. "The Dynamics of Sacred Groves", *J. Human Ecology*, 6: 245-254.

——. 1996. "A Comparison of Sacred Groves among the Mahadeo Kolis and Kunbis of Maharashtra", *Indian Anthropologist*, 26: 37-46.

Sandars, N.K. 1960. *The Epic of Gilgamesh* (translated), Penguin Books, Harmondsworth.

Sashikumar, C. 2005. "Avifauna of Sacred Groves of North Kerala" in C. Kunhikannan and B.G. Singh (eds.), *Strategy for Conservation of Sacred Groves*, Institute of Forest Genetics and Tree Breeding, pp. 97-107.

Sawant,V. 1990. "Phondaghat: Udhwai Parisar", *Maharashtra Times*, 22 December.

Sharma, B.R. 2000. "Sacred Groves and their Role in Social life in Himachal Himalayas" abstract *National Workshops on Community Strategies on the Management of Natural Resources*, Bhopal.

Singh, G.S. and K.G. Saxena. 1998. "Sacred Groves in the Rural Landscape: A Case Study of the Shekhala Village in Jodhpur District of Desert Rajasthan" in P.S. Ramakrishnan, K.G. Saxena and U.M. Chandrashekara (eds.), *Conserving the Sacred for Biodiversity Management*, Oxford and IBH Publishing Co., New Delhi, pp. 277-88.

Singh, G.S., K.S. Rao and K.G. Saxena. 1998. "Eco-cultural Analysis of Sacred Species and Ecosystems in Chhakinal Watershed, Himachal Pradesh" in P.S. Ramakrishnan, K.G. Saxena and U.M. Chandrashekara (eds.), *Conserving the Sacred for Biodiversity Management*, Oxford and IBH Publishing Co., New Delhi, pp. 301-314.

Singh, K. 1994. *Managing Common Pool Resources: Principles and Case Studies*, Oxford University Press, Delhi.

Sinha, A.P. 1989. *Religious Life of Tribal India*, Classical Publishers, New Delhi.

Sinha, B. and R.K. Maikhuri. 1998. "Conservation through Socio-Cultural-Religious Practices in Garhwal Himalayas: A Case Study of Hariyali Sacred Forest" in P.S. Ramakrishnani, K.G. Saxena and U.M. Chandrashekara (eds.), *Conserving the Sacred for Biodiversity Management*, Oxford and IBH Publishing Co., New Delhi, pp. 289-300.

Sisodia, V. and K.C. Malhotra. 1963. "Terracotta Motifs among the Warlis of Dharampur", *East and West*, 14: 97-105.

Sontheimer. 1989. "The Dynamics of Sacred Groves" in J.J. Roy Burman (1995), *J. Human Ecology*, 6: 245-254.

Spindel, C. 1989. *In the Shadow of the Sacred Grove*, Vintage Books, New York.

Subramanian, K., K.R. Sasidharan and N. Venkatsubramanian. 2005. "Floristic Diversity of Iringole Kavu, Ernakulam District, Kerala" in C. Kunhikannan and B.G. Singh (eds.), *Strategy for Conservation of Sacred Groves*, Institute of Forest Genetics and Tree Breeding, pp. 59-64.

Sukumaran, S., A.D.S. Raj and P. Daniel. 2005. "Sacred Groves as Sanctuaries for Residual (RET) Plants: A Case Study" in C. Kunhikannan and B.G. Singh (eds.), *Strategy for*

Conservation of Sacred Groves, Institute of Forest Genetics and Tree Breeding, pp. 206-215.

Swamy, P.S., S.M. Sundarapandian and S. Chandrasekaran. 1998. "Structure and Function of Sacred Groves: Case Studies in Tamil Nadu" in P.S. Ramakrishnan, K.G. Saxena and U.M. Chandrashekara (eds.), *Conserving the Sacred for Biodiversity Management*, Oxford and IBH Publishing Co., New Delhi, pp. 275-64.

Tiwari, B.K., S.K. Barik and R.S. Tripathi. 1998. "Sacred Groves of Meghalaya" in P.S. Ramakrishnan, K.G. Saxena and U.M. Chandrashekara (eds.), *Conserving the Sacred for Biodiversity Management*, Oxford and IBH Publishing Co., New Delhi, pp. 253-62.

——. 1999. *Sacred Forests of Meghalaya: Biodiversity and Cultural Diversity*, Regional Centre for National Afforestation and Ecodevelopment Board, NEHU, Shillong.

Tozzer, AM. (ed. and trans.) 1941. *Diego de Landa. Re"ci-n de las cosas de Yucatn. Manuscrito en la Real Academia de la Historia, Madrid. Papers of the Peabody Museum of Archaeology and Ethnology*, Vol. 18, Harvard University, Cambridge, Massachusetts.

Troisi, J. 1978. *Tribal Religion: Religion and Practice among the Santhals*, Manohar Publishers, New Delhi.

Unnikrishnan, E. 1990. *Part Played by the Sacred Groves in Local Environments*, Centre for Science and Environment, New Delhi.

Unnikrishnan, V. 1995. *Sacred Groves of North Kerala: An Ecofolklore Study (in Malayalam), Jeevarekha,* Thrissur.

Untawala, A.G., S. Wafar and M. Wafer. 1998. "Sacred Mangroves in India" in P.S. Ramakrishnan, K.G. Saxena and U.M. Chandrashekara (eds.), *Conserving the Sacred for Biodiversity Management*, Oxford and IBH Publishing Co., New Delhi, pp. 247-252.

Vellupillai, T.K. 1940. *The Travancore State Manual*, 4 Vols., Government of Travancore.

Vest, J.H.C. 1985. "Will-of-the-Land: Wilderness among Primal Indo-Europeans", *Environmental Review*, 9: 323-329.

Vidyarthi, L.P. 1963. *Maler: A Study in Nature-Man-Spirit Complex of a Hill Tribe of Bihar*, Bookland Pvt. Ltd., Calcutta.

Vidyarthi, L.P and B.K. Rai 1977. *Tribal Culture of India*, Concept Publisher, Delhi.

Viji, C. 1995. "The Sacred Groves", *The Hindu*, 5 September.

WWF- Andhra Pradesh. 1996. *Sacred Groves of Andhra Pradesh*, Andhra Pradesh State Office, Hyderabad.

Wachtel, P.S. 1993. "Asia's Sacred Groves", *International Wildlife*, 23: 24-27.

Ward and Conner. 1827. *Memoirs of the Survey of Travancore and Cochin State*, cited in Pushpangadan *et al.*, 1998.

——. 1894. *Memoir of the Survey of the Travancore and Cochin States*, Government of Kerala.

Weiss, P. 1995. *Kandinsky and Old Russia: The Artist as Ethnographer and Shaman*, Yale University Press, New Haven.

Yin, S. 1991. *Yige chongman zhengyi de wenhua shengtai tixi: Yunnan daogeng huozhong yanjiu (A Highly Controversial Culturo-Ecological System: Slash-and-Burn Cultivation in Yunnan.)*, Yunnan Renmin Chubanshe, Kunming.

——. 1994. *Senlin yunyu de nonggeng wenhua: Yunnan daogeng huozhong zhi (A. Farming Culture Formed by Forest: Slash-and Burn Cultivation in Yunnan.)*, Yunnan Renmin Chubanshe, Kunming.